HOW TO FORM A CORPORATION IN NEW YORK

with forms

Brette McWhorter Sember
Mark Warda
Attorneys at Law

Sphinx® Publishing
A Division of Sourcebooks, Inc.
Naperville, IL • Clearwater, FL

Copyright © 1988, 1991, 1994, 1998, 1999 by Brette McWhorter Sember and Mark Warda
Cover design © 1999 by Sourcebooks, Inc.®

All rights reserved. No part of this book may be reproduced in any form or by any electronic or mechanical means including information storage and retrieval systems—except in the case of brief quotations embodied in critical articles or reviews, or in the case of the exercises in this book solely for the personal use of the purchaser—without permission in writing from its publisher, Sourcebooks, Inc.

First Edition, 1999

Published by: **Sourcebooks, Inc.**®

Naperville Office
P.O. Box 372
Naperville, Illinois 60566
630-961-3900
Fax: 630-961-2168

Clearwater Office
P.O. Box 25
Clearwater, Florida 33757
727-587-0999
Fax: 727-586-5088

Interior Design and Production: Amy S. Hall, Sourcebooks, Inc.

This publication is designed to provide accurate and authoritative information in regard to the subject matter covered. It is sold with the understanding that the publisher is not engaged in rendering legal, accounting, or other professional service. If legal advice or other expert assistance is required, the services of a competent professional person should be sought.
From a Declaration of Principles Jointly Adopted by a Committee of the American Bar Association and a Committee of Publishers and Associations

Library of Congress Cataloging-in-Publication Data

Sember, Brette McWhorter.
    How to form a corporation in New York : with forms / Brette McWhorter Sember.
Mark Warda. -- 1st ed.
       p.   cm.
    Includes index.
    ISBN 1-57248-105-6 (pbk.)
      1. Corporation law--New York (State) Popular works.
      2. Corporation law--New York (State) Forms. I. Sember, Brette
    McWhorter.   II. Title.
KFN5345.Z9W37   1999
346.747'066--dc21   99-33980
                                                                                                    CIP

Printed and bound in the United States of America.

Paperback — 10 9 8 7 6 5 4 3 2 1

How to Form a Corporation in New York

CONTENTS

USING SELF-HELP LAW BOOKS 1

INTRODUCTION 3

CHAPTER 1: WHAT IS A CORPORATION? 5

CHAPTER 2: SHOULD YOU INCORPORATE? 9
    Advantages
    Disadvantages

CHAPTER 3: WHAT TYPE OF CORPORATION IS BEST? 15
    New York Corporation or Foreign Corporation
    S Corporation or C Corporation
    Inc. or P.C.
    Not-for-Profit Corporations

CHAPTER 4: START-UP PROCEDURES 21
    Name Check
    Certificate of Incorporation
    Shareholder Agreement
    Organizational Paperwork
    Tax Forms
    Corporate Supplies
    Organizational Meeting
    Minute Book
    Bank Accounts
    Licenses

CHAPTER 5: SELLING CORPORATE STOCK 41
    Securities Laws
    Federal Exemptions from Securities Laws
    New York Securities Laws
    Internet Stock Sales
    Payment for Shares
    New York's Securities Registration

CHAPTER 6: RUNNING A CORPORATION 49
    Day to Day Activities
    Corporate Records
    Shareholder Meetings
    Board of Directors
    Bi-Annual Reports

CHAPTER 7: AMENDING A CORPORATION 57
    Certificate of Incorporation
    Bylaws

CHAPTER 8: DISSOLVING A CORPORATION 59
    Voluntary Dissolution
    Involuntary Dissolution
    Post-Dissolution
    Restoration of a Dissolved Corporation
    Bankruptcy

APPENDIX A: CHECKLIST 63

APPENDIX B: SELECTED NEW YORK CORPORATION STATUTES 65

APPENDIX C: FORMS 123

INDEX 211

For Ruth and Harry and Olive and Ray

Using Self-Help Law Books

Whenever you shop for a product or service, you are faced with various levels of quality and price. In deciding what product or service to buy, you make a cost/value analysis on the basis of your willingness to pay and the quality you desire.

When buying a car, you decide whether you want transportation, comfort, status, or sex appeal. Accordingly, you decide among such choices as a Neon, a Lincoln, a Rolls Royce, or a Porsche. Before making a decision, you usually weigh the merits of each option against the cost.

When you get a headache, you can take a pain reliever (such as aspirin) or visit a medical specialist for a neurological examination. Given this choice, most people, of course, take a pain reliever, since it costs only pennies; whereas a medical examination costs hundreds of dollars and takes a lot of time. This is often the most logical choice: it's rare to need anything more than a pain reliever for a headache. But in some cases, a headache may indicate a brain tumor, and failing to see a specialist right away can result in complications. Should everyone with a headache go to a specialist? Of course not, but people treating their own illnesses must realize that they are betting on the basis of their cost/value analysis of the situation; they are taking the most logical option.

The same cost/value analysis must be made in deciding to do one's own legal work. Many legal situations are very straight forward, requiring a simple form and no complicated analysis. Anyone with a little intelligence and a book of instructions can handle the matter without outside help.

But there is always the chance that complications are involved that only an attorney would notice. To simplify the law into a book like this, several legal cases often must be condensed into a single sentence or paragraph. Otherwise, the book would be several hundred pages long and too complicated for most people. However, this simplification necessarily leaves out many details and nuances that would apply to special or unusual situations. Also, there are many ways to interpret most legal questions. Your case may come before a judge who disagrees with the analysis of our authors.

Therefore, in deciding to use a self-help law book and to do your own legal work, you must realize that you are making a cost/value analysis. You have decided that the money you will save in doing it yourself outweighs the chance your case will not turn out to your satisfaction. Most people handling their own simple legal matters never have a problem, but occasionally people find that it ended up costing them more to have an attorney straighten out the situation than it would have if they had hired an attorney in the beginning. Keep this in mind while handling your case, and be sure to consult an attorney if you feel you might need further guidance.

Introduction

Each year hundreds of thousands of corporations are registered in this country, tens of thousands in New York alone. The corporation is the preferred way of doing business for most people because it offers many advantages over partnerships and sole proprietorships. It is not a coincidence that the largest businesses in the world are corporations.

The main reason people incorporate is to avoid personal liability. While sole proprietors and partners have all of their personal assets at risk, corporate shareholders risk only what they paid for their stock. With so many people ready to sue for any reason or for no reason, the corporation is one of the few inexpensive protections left.

Creating a simple corporation is very easy and it is the purpose of this book to explain, in simple language, how you can do it yourself. A simple corporation as used in this book is one in which there are five or fewer shareholders and all of them are active in the business. If you plan to sell stock to someone who is not active in the business or to have six or more shareholders, you should seek the advice of an attorney. However, some guidance is provided throughout this book as to what some of the concerns will be in these circumstances.

If your situation is in any way complicated or involves factors not mentioned in this book, you should seek the advice of an attorney practicing corporate law. The cost of a short consultation can be a lot cheaper than the consequences of violating the law.

If you plan to sell stock to outside investors, you should consult with a lawyer who specializes in securities laws. Selling a few thousand shares of stock to friends and neighbors may sound like an easy way to raise capital for your business, but it is not! Since the stock market crash of the 1930s there have been federal laws regulating the sale of securities. There are harsh criminal penalties for violators and the laws don't have many loopholes. The basic rules are explained in chapter 5.

This book also explains the basics of corporate taxation, but you should discuss your own particular situation with your accountant before deciding what is best for you. He or she can also set you up with an efficient system of bookkeeping which can save both time and money.

Good luck with your new business!

What Is a Corporation?

A *corporation* is a legal "person" which can be created under state law. As a person, a corporation has certain rights and obligations such as the right to do business and the obligation to pay taxes. Sometimes, one hears of a law referring to "natural persons." That is to differentiate them from corporations which are persons, but not natural persons.

Business corporations were invented hundreds of years ago to promote risky ventures. Prior to the use of corporations, persons engaged in business faced the possibility of unlimited liability. By using a corporation, many people could put up a fixed sum of money for a new venture such as a voyage to explore the new world. If the venture made money, they shared the profits. If the venture went into debt, the most they could lose was their initial investment.

The reasons for having a corporation are the same today as they were hundreds of years ago: they allow investors to put up money for new ventures without risk of further liability. While our legal system is making more and more people liable for more and more things, the corporation remains one of the few innovations which has not yet been abandoned. New York's laws governing corporations are contained in the New York Business Corporation Law (NYBCL), Chapter 855 of the New York Consolidated Laws.

Before forming a corporation, you should be familiar with these common corporate terms which will be used in the text:

SHAREHOLDERS
A *shareholder* is a person who owns stock in a corporation. In most small corporations, the shareholders are the same as the officers and directors, but in large corporations, most shareholders are not officers or directors. Sometimes small corporations have shareholders who are not officers, such as when the stock is in one spouse's name and the other spouse runs the business. Specific laws regarding issuance of shares and shareholders' rights are in NYBCL § 601 through § 603 in appendix A of this book.

OFFICERS
Officers are usually the president, secretary, treasurer, and vice president. These persons run the day-to-day affairs of the business. They are elected each year by a vote of the board of directors. In New York, one person can hold all of the offices of a corporation.

BOARD OF DIRECTORS
The *board of directors* is the controlling body of a corporation that makes major corporate decisions and elects the officers. It usually meets just once a year. A corporation can have one director (who can also hold all offices and own all the stock). The board members in a small corporation are often officers as well.

REGISTERED AGENT
The *registered agent* is the person designated by the corporation to receive legal papers that must be served on the corporation. In New York, the secretary of state must be the registered agent and is designated in the certificate of incorporation. The secretary of state forwards any correspondence to the corporation. An additional registered agent may also be designated by the corporation. The additional registered agent should be regularly available at the registered office of the corporation, but may be any New York resident or person with a New York business address. The registered office is the address for the registered agent(s).

A person accepting the position as registered agent must sign a statement that he or she understands the duties and responsibilities of the position. These are spelled out in NYBCL § 304 and § 305 which are included in appendix A of this book.

CERTIFICATE OF INCORPORATION

Certificate of Incorporation is the name of the document that is filed with the secretary of state to start the corporation. In most cases, it legally needs to contain only seven basic statements. Some corporations have a lengthy certificate of incorporation, but this just makes it harder to make changes in the corporate structure. It is usually better to keep the certificate short and put the details in the bylaws.

BYLAWS

Bylaws are the rules governing the structure and operation of the corporation. Typically, the bylaws will set out rules for the board of directors, officers, shareholders, and corporate formalities.

New York Business Corporation Laws 20-203 contain most of New York's laws regarding general corporate activities. For example, it lists all of the powers of corporations so they do not have to be recited again in the articles or bylaws.

Legal definitions of other corporate terms are included in NYBCL § 101 through § 112 contained in appendix A.

Should You Incorporate? 2

Before forming a corporation, the business owner or prospective business owner should become familiar with the advantages and disadvantages of incorporating.

Advantages

The following are some of the advantages that a corporation has over other forms of businesses such as sole proprietorships and partnerships.

LIMITED LIABILITY

The main reason for forming a corporation is to limit the liability of the owners. In a sole proprietorship or partnership, the owners are personally liable for the debts and liabilities of the business, and creditors can go after all of their assets to collect. If a corporation is formed and operated properly, the owners can be protected from all such liability.

EXAMPLES

☛ If several people are in partnership and one of them makes many large extravagant purchases in the name of the partnership, the other partners can be held liable for the full amount of all such purchases. The creditors can take the bank accounts, cars, real estate, and other property of any partner to pay the debts of the partnership. If only one partner has money, he or she may have to pay all of the debts accumulated by all the other partners. When doing business in the corporate form, the corporation may go bankrupt and the shareholders may lose their initial investment, but the creditors cannot touch the assets of the owners.

- If a person runs a taxi business and one of the drivers causes a terrible accident, the owner can be held liable for the full amount of the damages. If the taxi driver was on drugs and killed several people and the damages amount to millions of dollars more than the insurance coverage, the owner may lose everything he owns. With a corporation, only the corporation would be liable and if there was not enough money, the owner still couldn't be touched. One true example is a business owner who owned hundreds of taxis. He put one or two in each of hundreds of different corporations which he owned. Each corporation only had minimum insurance and when one taxi was involved in an accident, the owner only lost the assets of that corporation.

WARNING

Note: If a corporate officer or shareholder does something negligent himself, or signs a debt personally, or guarantees a corporate debt, the corporation will not protect him from the consequences of his own act or from the debt. Also, if a corporation does not follow the proper corporate formalities, it may be ignored by a court and the owners or officers may be held personally liable. The formalities include having separate bank accounts, holding meetings, and keeping minutes. When a court ignores a corporate structure and holds the owners or officers liable, it is called *piercing the corporate veil.* The corporate veil may also be pierced if the owners dominate the corporation and this is used to commit fraud. There is a long line of cases that discuss this. The current law in New York is described in *Morris v. New York State Department of Taxation and Finance,* 82 N.Y.2d 135, 603 N.Y.S.2d 807 (1993).

CONTINUOUS EXISTENCE

A corporation may have a perpetual existence. When a sole proprietor or partner dies, the assets of their business may go to their heirs but the business does not exist any longer. If the surviving spouse or other heirs of a business owner want to continue the business in their own names, they will be considered a new business even if they are using the assets of the old business. With a partnership, the death of one partner may cause a dissolution of the business.

EXAMPLES
- ☞ If a person dies owning a sole proprietorship, his or her spouse may want to continue the business. That person may inherit all of the assets but will have to start a new business. This means getting new licenses and tax numbers, registering the name and establishing credit from scratch. With a corporation, the business continues with all of the same licenses, bank accounts, etc.

- ☞ If one partner dies, the partnership may be forced out of business. The heirs of the deceased partner can force the sale of their share of the assets of the partnership even if the surviving partner needs them to continue the business. If he does not have the money to buy the heirs out, the business may have to be dissolved. With a corporation, the heirs would only inherit stock. With properly drawn documents the business could continue.

EASE OF TRANSFERABILITY
A corporation and all of its assets and accounts may be transferred by the simple assignment of a stock certificate. With a sole proprietorship or partnership, each of the individual assets must be transferred and the accounts, licenses, and permits must be individually transferred.

EXAMPLE
- ☞ If a sole proprietorship is sold, the new owner will have to get a new occupational license, set up his own bank account and apply for a new taxpayer identification number. The title to any vehicles and real estate will have to be put in his name and all open accounts will have to be changed to his name. He will probably have to submit new credit applications. With a corporation, all of these items remain in the same corporate name. As the new shareholder, he would elect himself director and as director he would elect himself president, treasurer, and any other offices he wanted to hold.

Note: In some cases, the new owners will have to submit personal applications for such things as credit lines or liquor licenses.

TRANSFER OF OWNERSHIP
By distributing stock, the owner of a business can share the profits of a business without giving up control. This is done by keeping a majority

of stock or by issuing different classes of stock some with voting rights and others without voting rights.

EXAMPLE
☛ If a person wants to give his children some of the profits of his business, he can give them stock and pay dividends to them without giving them any control over the management. This would not be practical with a partnership or sole proprietorship.

EASE OF RAISING CAPITAL
A corporation may raise capital by selling stock or borrowing money. A corporation does not pay taxes on money it raises by the sale of stock.

EXAMPLE
☛ If a corporation wants to expand, the owners can sell off ten, fifty, or ninety percent of the stock and still remain in control of the business. The people putting up the money may be more willing to invest if they know they will have a piece of the action than if they were making a loan with a limited return. They may not want to become partners in a partnership.

Note: There are strict rules about the sale of stock with criminal penalties and triple damages for violators. See chapter 5.

SEPARATE RECORD KEEPING
A corporation has all its own bank accounts and records. A partner or sole proprietor may have trouble differentiating which of his expenses were for business and which were for personal items.

TAX ADVANTAGES
There are some tax advantages that are available only to corporations. Some of these are:

☛ Medical insurance for your family may be fully deductible.
☛ A tax deferred trust can be set up for a retirement plan.
☛ Losses are fully deductible for a corporation whereas an individual must prove there was a profit motive before deducting losses.

EASE OF ESTATE PLANNING
With a corporation, shares of a company can be distributed more easily than with a partnership. Different heirs can be given different percentages and control can be limited to those who are most capable.

PRESTIGE
The name of a corporation sounds more prestigious than the name of a sole proprietor to some people. John Smith d/b/a Acme Builders sounds

like one lone guy. Acme Builders, Incorporated, sounds like it might be a large operation. No one needs to know that it is run out of a garage. One female writer on the subject has suggested that a woman who is president of a corporation looks more successful than one doing business in her own name. This probably applies to everyone.

SEPARATE
CREDIT RATING

A corporation has its own credit rating, which can be better or worse than the owner's credit rating. A corporate business can go bankrupt while the owner's credit remains unaffected, or an owner's credit may be bad, but the corporation may maintain a good rating.

DISADVANTAGES

EXTRA
TAX RETURN

A corporation is required to file its own tax return. This is a bit longer and more complicated than the form required by a sole proprietorship and may entail additional expenses if the services of an accountant are required. A partnership must also file its own tax return so there is no advantage or disadvantage over a partnership as far as tax returns are concerned.

ANNUAL REPORT

A corporation must file a bi-annual report with the state (which lists names and addresses of officers and directors) for which there is a $9 fee.

SEPARATE
RECORDS

The owners of a corporation must be careful to keep their personal business separate from the business of the corporation. The corporation must have its own records and have minutes of meetings. Money must be kept separate. Records should be separate in every business, so the corporate structure might make it easier to do so.

EXTRA
EXPENSES

There are, of course, expenses in operating a corporation compared to not operating one. People who employ an attorney to form their corporation pay a lot more than people who use this book. A corporation owner will have to pay unemployment compensation for himself which he wouldn't have to pay as a sole proprietor. The state unemployment rate starts at 3.7% of the first $8500 and then varies depending on the unemployment experienced.

CHECKING ACCOUNTS
Checks made out to a corporation cannot be cashed; they must be deposited into a corporate account. Some banks have higher fees just for businesses which are incorporated. See page 37 for tips on avoiding high bank fees.

What Type of Corporation Is Best?

New York Corporation or Foreign Corporation

A person wishing to form a corporation must decide whether the corporation will be a New York corporation or a *foreign* corporation. A foreign corporation is one incorporated in another state but which does business in New York.

Delaware Corporations
In the past, there was some advantage to incorporating in Delaware, since that state had very liberal laws regarding corporations, and many national corporations are incorporated there. However, in recent years most states have liberalized their corporation laws—so today there is no advantage to incorporating in Delaware for most people.

Nevada Corporations
Nevada has liberalized its corporation laws recently to attract businesses. It allows bearer stock and has other rules that allow more privacy to corporate participants. It also does not share information with the Internal Revenue Service and does not have a state income tax.

Today, New York has very favorable corporate laws so out-of-state laws are not an advantage. If you form a corporation in a state other than New York, you will probably have to have an agent or an office in that state and will have to register as a foreign corporation doing business in

New York. This is more expensive and more complicated than just registering as a New York corporation. Also, if you are sued by someone who is not in your state, they can sue you in the state in which you are incorporated which would probably be more expensive for you than a suit filed in your local court. In some states, your corporation may be required to pay state income tax.

S Corporation or C Corporation

A corporation has a choice of how it wants to be taxed. It can make the election at the beginning of its existence or at the beginning of a new tax year. The choices are as follows:

S CORPORATION

Formerly called a *Subchapter S corporation*, an *S corporation* pays no income tax and may only be used for small businesses. All of the income or losses of the corporation for the year are passed through to the shareholders who report them on their individual returns. At the end of each year, the corporation files an *information return* listing all of its income, expenses, depreciation, etc. It also sends to each shareholder a notice of his or her share as determined by percentage of stock ownership.

Advantages. Using this method avoids double taxation and allows pass-through of losses and depreciation. The business is treated like a partnership. Since many businesses have tax losses during the first years due to start-up costs, many businesses elect S status and switch over to C corporation status in later years. Once a corporation terminates its S status, there is a five year waiting period before it can switch back. S corporations receive a reduction in the New York corporate tax rate. The rate is the difference between the corporate rate and the personal income tax rate with a set minimum.

Disadvantages. If stockholders are in high income brackets, their share of the profits will be taxed at those rates. Shareholders who do not "materially participate" in the business cannot deduct losses. Some fringe benefits such as health and life insurance may not be tax deductible in an S corporation.

Requirements. To qualify for S corporation status, the corporation must:

- have no more than seventy-five shareholders, none of whom are non-resident aliens or corporations, all of whom consent to the election (shares owned by a husband and wife jointly are considered owned by one shareholder);
- have only one class of stock;
- not be a member of an "affiliated group;"
- generate at least twenty percent of its income in this country and have no more than twenty percent of its income from "passive" sources (interest, rents, dividends, royalties, securities transactions);
- file Form 2553 before the end of the 15th day of the third month of the tax year for which it is to be effective and have it approved by the IRS; and
- if federal election is approved, file New York form CT-6.

Multiple Corporations. The IRS has approved the use of two or more S corporations in partnership to increase the number of allowable investors in a venture. It may also be possible for an S corporation to form a partnership with a C corporation.

C CORPORATION

A C *corporation* pays taxes on its net earnings at corporate tax rates. Salaries of officers, directors, and employees are deducted from income so are not taxed to the corporation, but money paid out in dividends is taxed twice. It is taxed at the corporation's rate as part of its profit, and then the stockholders must include the amounts they receive as dividends in their income.

Advantages. If taxpayers are in a higher tax bracket than the corporation and the money will be left in the company for expansion, taxes are saved. Fringe benefits such as health, accident, and life insurance are deductible expenses.

Disadvantages. Double taxation of dividends by the federal government is the biggest problem with a C corporation. This tax does not apply to money taken out as salaries, and many small business owners take all profits out as salaries to avoid double taxation. But there are rules requiring that salaries be reasonable and if a stockholder's salary is deemed to be too high, relative to his or her job, the salary may be considered dividends and subject to the double taxation.

Requirements. None. All corporations are C corporations unless they specifically elect to become S corporations.

Inc. or P.C.

Certain types of services can only be rendered by a corporation if it is a *Professional Corporation*. These are such businesses as attorneys, physicians, certified public accountants, veterinarians, architects, life insurance agents, chiropractors, and similarly licensed professionals. A professional corporation comes under nearly all of the rules regarding corporations in general, unless they conflict with the rules which specifically govern professional service corporations. The major differences between the two are:

Purpose — A professional corporation must have one specific purpose spelled out in the certificate of incorporation and that purpose must be to practice one of the professions. It may not engage in any other business, but it may invest its funds in real estate, stocks, bonds, mortgages, or other types of investments. A professional corporation may change its purpose to another legal purpose, but it will then no longer be a professional service corporation (NYBCL § 1506).

Name — The name of a professional corporation must end with the words "Professional Corporation" or the abbreviation "P.C." A professional service corporation may not use any words not permissible for a partnership practicing that profession to use. It may contain the name of some or all of the shareholders and may contain the names of deceased or retired shareholders (NYBCL § 1512).

Only persons licensed to practice the profession may be shareholders of a professional corporation. A shareholder who loses his or her right to practice must immediately sever all employment with and financial interests in such corporation. If such a shareholder does not, the corporation may be dissolved by the state. No shareholder may enter into a voting trust or other similar arrangement with anyone (NYBCL § 1507).

MERGER   A professional corporation may not merge with any other corporation except a New York professional corporation which is licensed to perform the same type of services (NYBCL §1513).

NOT-FOR-PROFIT CORPORATIONS

Not-for-profit corporations are usually used for social clubs, churches, and charities, and are beyond the scope of this book. While they are similar to for-profit corporations in many aspects, such as limited liability and the required formalities, there are additional state and federal requirements which must be met.

In some cases, a business can be formed as a not-for-profit corporation. It would not be allowed to distribute profits to its founders but it could pay substantial salaries and enjoy numerous tax advantages. For information on not-for-profit corporations, see *How to Form a Nonprofit Corporation* by Mark Warda available from Sphinx Publishing.

Start-Up Procedures 4

Name Check

The very first thing to do before starting a corporation is to thoroughly check out the name you wish to use to be sure it is available. Many business have been forced to stop using their name after spending thousands of dollars promoting it.

Local Records
To check for other corporations using the name you want, you should write to:

> New York State Department of State
> Miscellaneous Records Unit
> 41 State Street
> Albany, NY 12231

They will give you pre-clearance of the name for a $5 fee. If your name is too similar to another corporate name, you will not be allowed to register it.

Business Listings
Since some businesses neglect to properly register their name (yet still may have superior rights to the name) you should also check phone books and business directories. Many libraries have phone books from around the country as well as directories of trade names.

Yellow Page Listings
If you have internet access, you can search every yellow pages listing for free. Just search for "yellow pages" with any web search engine (i.e.,

Yahoo, WebCrawler, Lycos, etc.). You can select a state, enter your business name, and it will tell you if any other companies are listed with that name. One site that allows you to search all states at once is:

http://www.switchboard.com

Since the sites may not be 100% accurate, you should check a few different ones to be sure your search is thorough. If you do not have access to a computer, you may be able to use one at your public library or have the search done for you at the library for a small fee.

TRADEMARK SEARCH

To be sure that your use of the name does not violate someone else's trademark rights, you should have a trademark search done of the mark in the United States Patent and Trademark Office. In the past, this required a visit to their offices or the hiring of a search firm for over a hundred dollars. But in 1999 the USPTO put its trademark records online and you can now search them at:

http://www.uspto.gov/tmdb/index.html

If you do not have access to the internet, you might be able to do it at a public library or, for a small fee, have one of their employees order an online search for you. You can have the search done through a firm if this is not available to you. Some firms that do searches are:

Government Liaison Services, Inc.
3030 Clarendon Blvd., Suite 209
P. O. Box 10648
Arlington, VA 22210
800-642-6564; 703-524-8200

Thomson & Thomson
500 Victory Road
North Quincy, MA 02171-1545
800-692-8833

XL Corporate Service
62 White Street
New York, NY 10013
800-221-2972

NAME
RESERVATION

It is possible to reserve a name for a corporation for a period of sixty days for a fee of $20. However, this is usually pointless because it is just as easy to file the certificate of incorporation as it is to reserve the name. One possible reason for reserving a name would be to hold it while waiting for a trademark name search to arrive.

SIMILAR
NAMES

Sometimes it seems like every good name is taken. But a name can often be modified slightly or used on a different type of goods. If there is a "TriCounty Painting, Inc." in Albany, it may be possible to use something like "TriCounty Painting of Buffalo, Inc." if you are in a different part of the state. Try different variations if your favorite is taken.

FORBIDDEN
NAMES

A corporation may not use certain words in its name if there would be a likelihood of confusion. There are state and federal laws which control the use of these words. In most cases, your application will be rejected if you use a forbidden word. Some of the words that may not be used without special licenses or registration are:

Assurance	Insurance
Bank	Investment
Banker	Labor
Blind	Lawyer
Doctor	Trust
Finance	Union

You can look in the Business Corporation Act for more help in packing a name. Some of the articles listed in this act can be found in appendix B.

TRADEMARKS

The name of a business can not be registered as a trademark, but if the name is used in connection with goods or services, it may be registered and such registration will grant the holder exclusive rights to use that name except in areas where someone else has already used the name. A trademark may be registered either in New York or in the entire country.

Each trademark is registered for a certain "class" of goods. If you want to sell "Zapata" chewing gum, it doesn't matter that someone has registered the name "Zapata" for use on shoes. If you want to register the mark for several types of goods or services, you must register it for each different class into which the goods or services fall, and pay a separate fee for each category.

For protection within the state of New York the mark may be registered with the New York Department of State. The cost begins at $50. Application forms and instructions are contained in the book *How to Start a Business in New York*, published by Sourcebooks, or they can be obtained from:

> NYS Department of State
> Miscellaneous Records Unit
> 41 State Street
> Albany, NY 12231-0001

For protection across the entire United States, the mark can be registered with the United States Patent and Trademark Office and the cost is about $245. The procedure for federal registration is more complicated than state registration and is explained in the book *How to Register Your Own Trademark* available from Sourcebooks.

CERTIFICATE OF INCORPORATION

The act which creates the corporation is the filing of the certificate of incorporation with the secretary of state in Albany. Some corporations have long, elaborate certificate that spell out numerous powers and functions, but most of this is unnecessary. The powers of corporations are spelled out in New York law (See NYBCL § 202 in appendix B) and do not have to be repeated. (In fact the statute says that the powers do not have to be repeated in the certificate, but they often are. Attorneys can charge a lot more for certificates of incorporation that are long and look complicated.) The main reason to keep the certificate of incorporation short is to avoid having to amend it later. By putting all but the basics in the bylaws of the corporation, you can make changes in the

start-up procedures

corporate structure much more easily. The certificate included in this book (forms 2 and 3) are as simple as possible for this purpose.

REQUIREMENTS

New York law requires that only six things be included in the certificate of incorporation. Some things, such as regulations for the operation of the corporation, and a par value of the stock may be spelled out in the certificate of incorporation, but this is not advisable since any changes would require the complicated process of amending the certificate. It is better to spell these things out in the bylaws. The five matters required to be contained in the certificate and a few of the optional provisions are:

Name of the corporation. The corporation name must include one of the following three words or their abbreviation:

- Incorporated (Inc.)
- Corporation (Corp.)
- Limited (Ltd.)

The reason is that persons dealing with the business will be on notice that it is a corporation. This is important in protecting the shareholders from liability. The last choice, "Limited" is not as good as the others because they are not clear notice that the business is incorporated.

Address of the corporation. The address of the principal office and the mailing address of the corporation must be provided. The name of the county must be provided as well.

The number of shares of stock the corporation is authorized to issue. This is usually an even number such as 100, 1000 or 1,000,000. Some people authorize 1,000,000 shares (with a par value of $0.01 or 0.001) because it sounds impressive. However, in New York it is more expensive to form a corporation with more than 200 shares, so most corporations in New York are formed with 200 no par shares.

In some cases, it may be advantageous to issue different classes of stock such as common and preferred, or voting and non-voting, but such matters should be discussed with an attorney or accountant.

If there are different classes of stock, the certificate of incorporation must contain a designation of the classes; the number of shares in each class; the par value of the stock and a statement of the preferences; limitations; and relative rights of each class. In addition, if there are to be any preferred or special shares issued in series, the articles must explain the relative rights and preferences and/or any authority of the board of directors to establish preferences. Any preemptive rights must also be noted in detail.

This book will explain how to form a corporation with one class of stock. It is usually advisable to authorize double or quadruple the amount of stock which will be initially issued. The unissued stock can be issued later if more capital is contributed by a shareholder or by a new member of the business.

One important point to keep in mind when issuing stock is that the full par value must be paid for the shares. If this is not done, the shareholder can later be held liable for the full par value. For more important information about issuing stock see chapter 5.

A statement naming the secretary of state as agent of the corporation upon whom process (court papers) may be served, and a post office address to which the secretary of state may forward copies of any process which have been accepted for the corporation. The corporation may also have a registered agent upon whom process can also be served and the agent's name and address can be included on the certificate.

Statement of Addresses and Directors. A statement must be filed giving the names and business addresses of the chairpersons of the board of the corporation and the address to which the secretary of state should mail papers. This statement must be filed within two years of the date of incorporation and then every two years following initial filing.

Duration. The duration of the corporation need not be mentioned if it is to be perpetual. If not, the duration must be in the certificate.

PROFESSIONAL
CORPORATIONS
There are several additional requirements for corporations which will be professional corporations (see page 18). These are:

- The purpose of the corporation must be stated and must be limited to the practice of one profession.
- The name must end with the designation "Professional Corporation" or "P.C."
- The certificate of incorporation must contain the names and addresses of all shareholders, directors and officers.
- A certificate of authorization must be attached for each professional holding shares. This is obtained from the licensing authority for that profession (the Regents of the State of New York, the state education department or the Appellate Division).
- A certified copy of the certificate of incorporation must be filed with the appropriate licensing authority within thirty days of its filing.

Effective date. A specific effective date may be in the certificate but is not required. It is effective upon filing. If an effective date is specified, it may not be more than five days prior to, or more than ninety days after, filing.

EXECUTION
The certificate of incorporation must be signed by the incorporator and dated. There is no longer a need to have it notarized. Anyone can be the incorporator, and there is no need to have more than one person sign. Rights of other parties can be spelled out at the incorporation meeting.

FORMS
Certificates of incorporation need not be on any certain form. They can be typed on blank paper or can be on a fill-in-the-blank form. In the back of this book are forms of certificates of incorporation for both a regular corporation (form 2) and a Professional Corporation (form 3).

FILING The articles of incorporation must be filed with the New York Department of State by sending them to:

> NYS Department of State
> Division of Corporations
> State Records and Uniform Commercial Code
> 41 State Street
> Albany, NY 12231

You should mail them along with a transmittal letter (form 1) and the filing fees. The fees (as of 1999) are $125, plus the minimum of $10 for issuing shares. (See "Corporate Supplies" in this chapter for more information about this). If you wish to receive a certified copy of the certificate, the cost is $10. This is an unnecessary expense since such certified copy is rarely, if ever, needed. The better alternative is to enclose a photocopy along with the certificate and ask that it be "stamped with the filing date" and returned.

The return time for the certificate is usually one to four weeks. If there is a need to have it back quickly, "Expedited Handling" must be written on the envelope and an additional $25 fee must be enclosed. The certificate will be processed within twenty-four hours of receipt if this method is used.

SHAREHOLDER AGREEMENT

Whenever there are two or more shareholders in a corporation they should consider drawing up a *shareholder agreement*. This document spells out what is to happen in the event of a disagreement between the parties. In closely held corporations the minority shareholders have a risk of being locked into a long term enterprise with little or no way to withdraw their capital. A shareholder agreement is a fairly complicated document and you should consider having it drawn up by an attorney. This may be costly but the expense should be weighed against the costs of lengthy litigation should the parties split. A less expensive alternative

start-up procedures

is to obtain a few sample agreements from a law library and tailor one to fit your needs. Some of the things which may be addressed in such an agreement are as follows:

- Veto by minority shareholder
- Greater than majority voting requirement
- Cumulative voting
- Deadlocks
- Arbitration
- Dissolution
- Compulsory buy-out
- Preemptive rights
- Restrictions on transfers of shares
- Refusal of a party to participate

New York has specific rules on shareholder agreements contained in NYBCL § 616, 620, 709, and 715.

ORGANIZATIONAL PAPERWORK

BYLAWS
Every corporation must have bylaws and must maintain a set of minutes of its meetings. The bylaws must be adopted at the first organizational meeting and the first minutes of the corporation will be of the organizational meeting.

The bylaws are the rules for organization and operation of the corporation. NYBCL § 202 and § 601 govern bylaws. Two sets of bylaws are included with this book. Form 8 is for simple corporations and form 9 is for professional corporations. To complete them you should fill in the name of the corporation, the city of the main office of the corporation, the proposed date of the annual meeting (this can be varied each year as needed), and the number of directors to be on the board.

WAIVER OF NOTICE   Before a meeting of the incorporators, the board of directors, or the shareholders can be held to transact lawful business, formal notice must be given to the parties ahead of time. Since small corporations often need to have meetings on short notice and do not want to be bothered with formal notices, it is customary to have all parties sign written waivers of notice. New York law allows the waiver to be signed at any time, even after the meeting has taken place, for both shareholders (NYBCL § 606) and for directors (NYBCL § 711). Waivers of notice are included in this book for the organizational meeting (form 6) and for the annual and special meetings (forms 16, 18, 20, and 22).

MINUTES   As part of the formal requirements of operating a corporation, minutes must be kept of the meetings of shareholders and the board of directors. Usually only one meeting of each is required per year (the annual meeting) unless there is some special need for a meeting in the interim (such as the resignation of an officer). The first minutes that will be needed are the minutes of the organizational meeting of the corporation. At this meeting, the officers and directors are elected; the bylaws, corporate seal and stock certificates are adopted; and other organizational decisions made. Most of the forms should be self-explanatory, but sample filled-in forms are in appendix C of this book. Every shareholder has the right to examine the minutes.

LEDGER   A ledger must be kept containing the names, addresses of shareholders, the number of shares held, and the date of acquisition.

RESOLUTIONS   When the board of directors or shareholders make major decisions, it is usually done in the form of a resolution. The important resolutions at the organizational meeting are those choosing a bank (form 10) and adopting S corporation status (form 15).

WAIVER OF MEETING   New York law (NYBCL § 708) allows corporate officers to execute incorporation papers without a meeting if there is unanimous consent but it is better to have a formal meeting to prove to possible future creditors that you conducted the corporation in a formal manner. Any papers executed in this way must be included in the minute book.

Tax Forms

Form SS-4 (Employer Identification Number)

Prior to opening a bank account, the corporation must obtain a "taxpayer identification number," which is the corporate equivalent of a social security number. This is done by filing Form SS-4, included in this book as form 5. This usually takes two or three weeks, so it should be filed early. Send the form to:

> Internal Revenue Service Center
> Atlanta, GA 39901

If you need the number quickly, you may be able to obtain the number by phone by calling the IRS at 404-455-2360 before 2:30 P.M. Be sure to have your SS-4 form complete and in front of you before calling.

When you apply for this number, you will probably be put on the mailing list for other corporate tax forms. If you do not receive these, you should call your local IRS forms number and request the forms for new businesses. These include Circular E explaining the taxes due, the W-4 forms for each employee, the tax deposit coupons and the Form 941 quarterly return for withholding.

Form 2553 (S Corporation)

If your corporation is to be taxed as an S corporation, you must file Form 2553 with the IRS within seventy-five days of incorporation. As a practical matter, you should sign and file this at your incorporation meeting; otherwise, you may forget. Form 2553 is included in this book as form 14 and a filled-in sample is shown in appendix D. To make the S corporation status "official," you should also adopt a corporate resolution electing to be taxed as an S corporation and keep it in your minute book.

Form DTS-17 (Application for Registration as a Sales Tax Vendor)

If you will be selling or renting goods or services at retail, you must collect New York Sales and Use Tax. Some services such as doctors' and lawyers' fees and newspaper advertising are not taxed, but most others are. If you have any doubt, check with the New York Department of Taxation. First, you must obtain a tax number and fill out a form. To obtain this form you can call the Department of Taxation (You can find your local office in the government pages of your phone book under New York State Government Offices/Taxation, Dept. of) call the Albany office at 1-800-225-5829. A form is also included in our book *How to Start a Business in New York*. After you obtain your tax number, you will be required to collect sales tax on all purchases. Tax returns must be filed quarterly or annually.

Corporate Supplies

Corporate Kits

A corporation needs to keep a permanent record of its legal affairs. This includes the original charter; minutes of all meetings; records of the stock issued, transferred and cancelled and any other legal matters. The records are usually kept in a ring binder. Any ring binder will do, but it is possible to purchase a specially prepared *corporate kit* that has the name of the corporation printed on it and usually contains forms such as minutes, stock certificates, etc. Most of these items are included with this book so purchasing such a kit is unnecessary unless you want to have a fancy leather binder or specially printed stock certificates.

Some sources for corporate kits are:

> Ace Industries, Inc.
> 54 NW 11th Street
> Miami, FL 33136-9978
> 305-358-2571
> 800-433-2571

> Corpex
> 480 Canal Street
> New York, NY 10013
> 800-221-8181

start-up procedures

Midstate Legal Supply Co., Inc.
P. O. Box 2122
Orlando, FL 32802
407-299-8220

CORPORATE SEAL

One thing that is not included with this book is a *corporate seal.* New York does not require a corporation seal, but you may wish to have one. They are specially made for each corporation. Most corporations use a metal seal like a notary's seal to emboss the paper. These can be ordered from many office supply companies. In recent years, many have been using rubber stamps for corporate seals. These are cheaper, lighter, and easier to read. Rubber stamp seals can also be ordered from office supply stores, printers, and specialized rubber stamp companies. The corporate seal should contain the full, exact name of the corporation, the word "SEAL" and the year of incorporation. It is usually round or rectangular.

STOCK CERTIFICATES AND OFFERS TO PURCHASE STOCK

New York corporations are no longer required to issue stock certificates to represent shares of ownership. However, as a practical matter it is a good idea to do so. This shows some formality and gives each person tangible evidence of ownership. If you do issue shares, the face of each certificate must show the corporate name; that the corporation was organized under New York law; the name of the shareholder(s); and the number, class, and series of the stock. The certificate must be signed by one or more officers designated by the bylaws or the board of directors.

If there are two or more classes or series of stock, the front or back of the certificate must disclose that upon request and without charge the corporation will provide to the shareholder the preferences, limitations, and relative rights of each class or series; the preferences of any preferred stock; and the board of directors' authority to determine rights for any subsequent classes or series. If there are any restrictions they must be stated on the certificate, or a statement must be included that they are available without charge.

The stock certificates can be fancy, with engraved eagles, or they can be typed or even handwritten. Stock certificate forms are included at the end of this book. They should be completed like the sample on the next page. For professional corporations, the following statement should be typed on the certificate: "The transfer of the shares represented by this certificate is restricted by the bylaws of the corporation."

Before any stock is issued, the purchaser should submit an "Offer to Purchase Stock" (form 11). The offer states that it is made pursuant to IRS Code § 1244. The advantage of this section is that in the event the business fails or the value of the stock drops, the shareholder can write off up to $50,000 ($100,000 for married couples) as ordinary income, rather than as a long term capital lose which would be limited to $3,000 a year.

Some thought should be given to the way in which the ownership of the stock will be held. Stock owned in one person's name alone is subject to probate upon death. Making two persons joint owners of the stock (joint tenants with full rights of survivorship) would avoid probate upon the death of one of them. However, taking a joint owner's name off in the event of a disagreement (such as divorce) could be troublesome. Where a couple jointly operates a business, joint ownership would be best. But where one person is the sole party involved in the business, the desire to avoid probate should be weighed against the risk of losing half the business in a divorce. Another way to avoid probate is to put ownership of the stock in a living trust.

Tax on Shares

When you file your certificate of incorporation, you must also pay tax on the stock you are authorized to issue. If you issue 200 or fewer shares of no par value stock or if the total par value of all the stock is $20,000 or less, the tax is $10. Over these amounts, the tax rate is 5¢ per share of no par value stock and .05% of par value shares.

ORGANIZATIONAL MEETING

The real birth of the corporation takes place at the initial meeting of the incorporators and the initial board of directors. At this meeting, the stock is issued and the officers and board of directors are elected. Other business may also take place, such as opting for S corporation status or adopting employee benefit plans.

Usually minutes, stock certificates, and tax and other forms are prepared before the organizational meeting and used as a script for the meeting. They are signed at the end of the meeting. Otherwise, they may be forgotten until it is too late.

The agenda for the initial meeting is usually as follows:

1. Signing the waiver of notice of the meeting (form 6).
2. Noting persons present.
3. Presentation and acceptance of certificate of incorporation (the copy returned by the secretary of state).
4. Election of Directors.
5. Adoption of bylaws (form 8 or form 9).
6. Election of officers.
7. Presentation and acceptance of corporate seal (if one is used).
8. Presentation and acceptance of stock certificate (form 30).
9. Designation of bank (form 10).
10. Acceptance of stock offers (form 11). (Use form 13, Bill of Sale, if property is traded for stock.)
11. Resolution to pay expenses.
12. Adoption of special resolutions such as S corporation status (forms 14 and 15).
13. Adjournment.

The stock certificates are usually issued at the end of the meeting, but in some cases, such as when a prospective shareholder does not yet have money to pay for them, they are issued when payment in complete.

To issue the stock, the certificates at the end of this book should be completed by adding the name of the corporation, a statement that the corporation is organized under the laws of New York, the number of shares the certificate represents and the person to whom the certificate is issued. Each certificate should be numbered in order to keep track of them. A record of the stock issuance should be made on the stock transfer ledger (form 28) and on the "stubs" (form 29). The stubs should be cut apart on the dotted lines, punched and inserted in the ring binder.

Minute Book

After the organizational meeting you should set up your minute book. As noted on page 32, this can be a fancy leather book or a simple ring binder. The minute book usually contains the following:

1. A title page ("Corporate Records of _____")
2. A table of contents
3. The letter from the secretary of state acknowledging receipt and filing of the certificate of incorporation
4. Copy of the certificate of incorporation
5. Copy of any trademark registration
6. Waiver of Notice of Organizational Meeting
7. Minutes of Organizational Meeting
8. Bylaws
9. Sample stock certificate
10. Offer to purchase stock

11. Tax forms:

    Form SS-4 and Employer Identification Number certificate

    Form 2553 and acceptance (for S corporations)

    Form DTS-17 and state tax number certificate

12. Stock ledger
13. Stock stubs

BANK ACCOUNTS

A corporation must have a bank account. Checks payable to a corporation cannot be cashed; they must be deposited into an account.

FEES
Unfortunately, many banks charge ridiculous rates to corporations for the right to put their money in the bank. You can tell how much extra a corporation is being charged when you compare a corporate account to a personal account with similar activity.

EXAMPLE
For similar balance and activity, an individual might earn $6.00 interest for the month while a corporation pays $40.00 in bank fees. Surely the bank is not losing money on every personal account. Therefore, the corporate account is simply generating $46.00 more in profit for the bank. This money will probably be used to buy more art objects or corporate jets for the bank's officers.

Usually, there is a complicated scheme of fees with charges for each transaction. Many banks today are even bold enough to charge companies for the right to make a deposit! (Twenty-five cents for the deposit plus 10¢ for each check that is deposited. Deposit thirty checks and this will cost you $3.25!) Often the customer is granted an interest credit on the balance in the account, but it is usually small and if the credit is larger than the charges, you lose the excess. The officers in some banks cannot even tell you how the fees are figured because the system is so complicated.

Fortunately, some banks have set up reasonable fees for small corporations such as charging no fees if a balance of $1,000 or $2,500 is maintained. Because the fees can easily amount to hundreds of dollars a year, it pays to shop around. Even if the bank is relatively far from the business, using bank-by-mail can make the distance meaningless. But don't be surprised if a bank with low fees raises them. The authors know of one company that changed banks four times in one year as each one raised its fees or was bought out by a bank with higher fees.

As the banking industry got deeper into trouble, fewer and fewer banks were offering reasonable fees for corporate checking accounts. Even with their balance sheets improving, they are not eager to give up this new source of wealth. But you can usually find loopholes if you use your imagination. One trick is to open a checking account and a money market account. (Money market accounts pay higher interest and do not charge for making deposits. You can only write three checks a month but you can usually make unlimited withdrawals.) Then make all of your deposits into the money market account and just pay bills out of the regular checking account, transferring funds as needed. But banks are catching on to this and starting to charge for deposits into money market accounts. So start one at a brokerage firm.

Another way to save money in bank charges is to order checks from a private source rather than through the bank. These are usually much cheaper than those the bank offers because the bank makes a profit on the check printing. If the bank officer doesn't like the idea when you are opening the account, just wait until your first batch runs out and switch over without telling the bank. They probably won't even notice, as long as you get the checks printed correctly. While most "business checks" are large (and expensive), there is no reason you cannot use small "personal size" checks for your business. They are easier to carry around and work just as well unless you want to impress people with the size of your check. One source is the Current Company at 1-800-204-2244 or www.currentchecks.com.

PAPERWORK   All you should need to open a corporate bank account is a copy of your certificate of incorporation and your federal tax identification number. Some banks, however, want more, and they sometimes don't even know what it is they want. After opening numerous corporate accounts with only the two items listed above, one of the authors encountered a bank employee who wanted "something certified so we know who your officers are. Your attorney will know what to draw up." He explained that he was his own attorney and was the president, secretary, and treasurer of the corporation and he would write out and sign and seal whatever they wanted. No, it had to be a nice certificate signed by the secretary of the corporation and sealed. So, he typed out a statement in legalese, put a gold foil seal on it, and the bank opened the account. If you have trouble opening the account, you can use the Banking Resolution (form 10) included with this book, or you can make up a similar form.

LICENSES

Counties and municipalities are authorized to levy a license tax on the "privilege" of doing business. (Some would argue that earning a living is a basic human right and not a privilege, but this is not a philosophy book.) Before opening your business, you should obtain a county occupational license, and if you will be working within a city, a city occupational license. Businesses that perform work in several cities, such as builders, must obtain a license from each city in which they work. This does not have to be done until you actually begin a job in a particular city.

County occupational licenses can be obtained from the tax collector in the county courthouse. City licenses are usually available at city hall. Be sure to find out if zoning allows your type of business before buying or leasing property because the licensing departments will check the zoning before issuing your license.

Home Businesses

Problems occasionally arise when persons attempt to start a business in their home. Small new businesses cannot afford to pay rent for commercial space and cities often try to forbid business in residential areas. Getting a county occupational license often gives notice to the city that a business is being conducted in a residential area.

Some people avoid the problem by starting their businesses without occupational licenses, figuring that the penalties are nowhere near the cost of office space. Others get the county license and ignore the city rules. If a person has commercial trucks and equipment parked on his property, there will probably be complaints by neighbors and the city will most likely take legal action. But if a person's business consists merely of making phone calls out of the home and keeping supplies inside the house, the problem may never arise.

If the problem does occur regarding a home business that does not disturb the neighbors, a good argument can be made that the zoning law that prohibits the business is unconstitutional. When zoning laws were first instituted they were not meant to stop people from doing things in a residence that had historically been part of the life in a residence. Consider a painter. Should a zoning law prohibit a person from sitting in his home and painting pictures? If he sells them for a living is there a difference? Can the government force him to rent commercial space?

Similar arguments can be made for many home businesses. (The authors ares waiting for their city fathers to tell them to stop writing books in their home offices.) But court battles with a city are expensive and probably not worth the effort for a small business. The best course of action is to keep a low profile. Using a post office box is sometimes helpful in diverting attention away from the residence. However, the secretary of state and the occupational license administrator will want a street address. There should be no problem using a residential address and explaining to the city that it is merely the corporate address and that no business is conducted on the premises.

SELLING CORPORATE STOCK 5

SECURITIES LAWS

The issuance of securities is subject to both federal and state securities laws. A *security* is stock in the company (common and preferred) and debt (notes, bonds, etc.). The laws covering securities are so broad that any instrument that represents an investment in an enterprise where the investor is relying on the efforts of others for profit is considered a security. Even a promissory note has been held to be a security. Once an investment is determined to involve a security, strict rules apply. There can be criminal penalties, and civil damages can also be awarded to purchasers, if the rules are not followed.

The rules are designed to protect people who put up money as an investment in a business. In the stock market crash in the 1930s, many people lost their life savings in swindles, and the government wants to be sure that it won't happen again. Unfortunately, the laws can also make it difficult to raise capital for many honest businesses.

The goal of the laws covering sales of securities is that investors be given full disclosure of the risks involved in an investment. To accomplish this, the law usually requires that the securities must either be registered with the federal Securities and Exchange Commission and/or a similar state regulatory body, and that lengthy disclosure statements be compiled and distributed.

The law is complicated and strict compliance is required. The penalties are so harsh that most lawyers won't handle securities matters. You most likely would not be able to get through the registration process on your own. But, like your decision to incorporate without a lawyer, you may wish to consider some alternatives when attempting to raise capital without a lawyer:

- Borrow the money as a personal loan from friends or relatives. The disadvantage is that you will have to pay them back personally if the business fails. However, you may have to do that anyway if they are close relatives or if you don't follow the securities laws.

- Tailor your stock issuance to fall within the exemptions in the securities laws. There are some exemptions in the securities laws for small businesses that may apply to your transaction. (The anti-fraud provisions always apply, even if the transaction is exempt from registration.) Some exemptions are explained below, but you should make at least one appointment with a securities lawyer to be sure you have covered everything and that there have not been any changes in the law. You can often pay for an hour or so of a securities lawyer's time for $100 or $200 and just ask questions about your plans. He or she can tell you what not to do and what your options are. Then, you can make an informed decision.

For an explanation of New York securities law, a good reference source is *New York Securities Law,* published by the New York State Bar Association. Contact the New York State Bar Association at 1-518-463-3200 for ordering information (at the time of publication, the cost was $32). For technical laws and regulations of all fifty states, see the "Blue Sky Reporter" also available at most law libraries.

Federal Exemptions from Securities Laws

In most situations where one person, a husband and wife or a few partners run a business, and all parties are active in the enterprise, securities laws do not apply to their issuance of stock to themselves. These are the simple corporations that are the subject of this book. As a practical matter, if your father or aunt wants to put up some money for some stock in your business, you probably won't get in trouble. They probably won't seek triple damages and criminal penalties if your business fails. (This can't be said of your father-in-law in the event he becomes your ex-father-in-law some day!)

However, you may wish to obtain money from additional investors to enable your business to grow. This can be done in many circumstances as long as you follow the rules carefully. You do not have to file anything with the SEC in some cases but in others you must file some sort of notice.

Federal Private Placement Exemption

If you sell your stock to a small group of people without any advertising, you can fall into the private offering exemption:

- All persons to whom offers are made are financially astute, are participants in the business or have a substantial net worth.
- No advertising or general solicitation is used to promote the stock.
- The number of persons to whom the offers are made is limited.
- The shares are purchased for investment and not for immediate resale.
- The persons to whom the stock is offered are given all relevant information (including financial information) regarding the issuance and the corporation. Again, there are numerous court cases explaining each aspect of these rules, including such questions as what is a "financially astute" person.
- A filing claiming the exemption is made upon the United States Securities and Exchange Commission.

FEDERAL INTRASTATE OFFERING EXEMPTION

If you only offer your securities to residents of one state, you may be exempt from federal securities laws. This is because federal laws usually only apply to interstate commerce. Intrastate offerings are covered by SEC Rule 147 and if it is followed carefully, your sale will be exempt from federal registration.

FEDERAL SMALL OFFERINGS EXEMPTIONS

In recent years, the SEC has liberalized the rules in order to make it easier for businesses to grow. Under Regulation D, adopted by the Securities and Exchange Commission, there are three types of exemptions under rules 504, 505, and 506.

Offering of securities of up to $1,000,000 in a twelve month period can be exempt under SEC Rule 504. Offers can be made to any number of persons, no specific information must be provided and investors do not have to be sophisticated.

Under Rule 505, offering of up to $5,000,000 can be made in a twelve month period but no public advertising may be used and only thirty-five non-accredited investors may purchase stock. Any number of accredited investors may purchase stock.

Accredited investors are sophisticated individuals with high net worth or high income, large trusts or investment companies, or persons involved in the business.

Rule 506 has no limit on the amount of money that may be raised but, like Rule 505, does not allow advertising and limits the number of non-accredited investors to thirty-five.

NEW YORK SECURITIES LAWS

Unfortunately, the simplification of federal requirements has not been accompanied by similar changes at the state level. New York and most states still have much stricter requirements for the issuance of securities. There is a movement to change the laws, but for now the only way to avoid the New York registration procedures is to qualify for the New York exemption.

REGISTRATION EXEMPTION

The New York Attorney General can grant an exemption to registration requirements for certain corporation that have been in existence less than ten years and for limited offerings of stock to forty or fewer purchases. There are other more complicated exemptions available as well.

These rules may sound simple on the surface but there are many more rules, regulations, and court cases explaining each one in more detail. For example, what does "forty persons" mean? Sounds simple, but it can mean more than forty persons. Spouses, persons whose net worth exceeds a million dollars, and founders of the corporation may not be counted in some circumstances. Each state has its own "blue sky" requirements and exemptions. If you are going to raise money from investors, check with a qualified securities lawyer.

As you can see, the exemption doesn't give you much latitude in raising money. Therefore, you will have to register for most issuances

INTERNET STOCK SALES

With the advent of the internet, promoters of stock have a new way of reaching large numbers of people, most of whom are financially able to afford investments in securities. However, all securities laws apply to the internet and they are being enforced. Recently, state attorneys general have issued cease and desist orders to promoters not registered in their states.

Under current law, you must be registered in a state in order to sell stock to its residents. If you are not registered in a state, you must turn down any residents from that state that want to buy your stock.

You may wonder how the famous Spring Street Brewing raised $1.6 million for its Wit Beer on the internet. The main reason they were successful was perhaps because their president is a lawyer and could prepare his own prospectus to file with the SEC and the states.

PAYMENT FOR SHARES

When issuing stock, it is important that full payment be made by the purchasers. If the shares have a par value and the payment is in cash, the cash must not be less than the par value. In most states, promissory notes cannot be used in payment for shares. The shares must not be issued until the payment has been received by the corporation.

TRADING PROPERTY FOR SHARES

In many cases, organizers of a corporation have property they want to contribute for use in starting up the business. This is often the case where an on-going business is incorporated. To avoid future problems, the property should be traded at a fair value for the shares. The directors need to pass a resolution stating that they agree with the value of the property. When the stock certificate is issued in exchange for the property, a bill of sale should be executed by the owner of the property detailing everything that is being exchanged for the stock.

TAXABLE TRANSACTIONS

In cases where property is exchanged for something of value, such as stock, there is often income tax due as if there had been a sale of the property. Fortunately, § 351 of the IRS Code allows tax-free exchange of property for stock if the persons receiving the stock for the property or for cash *end up owning* at least eighty percent of the voting and other stock in the corporation. If more than twenty percent of the stock is issued in exchange for services instead of property and cash, the transfers of property will be taxable and treated as a sale for cash.

TRADING SERVICES FOR SHARES

In some cases, the founders of a corporation wish to issue stock to one or more persons in exchange for their services to the corporation. It has always been possible to issue shares for services that have previously been performed. Some states make it unlawful to issue shares for promises to perform services in the future. Check your corporation's statutes with regard to this.

NEW YORK SECURITIES REGISTRATION

For answers to specific questions on New York securities registration you can contact:

> New York State Attorney General
> Department of Law
> 120 Broadway
> New York, NY 10271-0332
> 1-800-771-7755

Running a Corporation 6

Day to Day Activities

There are not many differences between running a corporation and any other type of business. The most important point to remember is to keep the corporation separate from your personal affairs. Don't be continuously making loans to yourself from corporate funds and don't commingle funds.

Another important point to remember is to always refer to the corporation as a corporation. Always use the designation "Inc." or "Corp." on everything. Always sign corporate documents with your corporate title. If you don't, you may lose your protection from liability. There have been many cases where a person forgot to put the word "pres." after his name and was held personally liable for a corporate debt!

Corporate Records

MINUTES
NYBCL § 624 (a) requires that a corporation keep a permanent record of "minutes of the proceedings of its shareholders and board of directors, a record of all actions taken by the shareholders, board and executive committee, if any. The records must be easily converted to

writing. Books and records must be kept in a correct and complete manner.

RECORD OF SHAREHOLDERS

The corporation must also keep a record of its shareholders including the names and addresses, the number, class, and series of shares owned, as well as the date of acquisition [NYBCL § 624 (a)]. This record can be kept at the registered office, principal place of business, or office of its stock transfer agent (if any). The transfer ledger contained in this book as form 28 can be used for this purpose.

CORPORATE DOCUMENTS

The corporation must maintain copies of its certificate of incorporation and all amendments, bylaws and all amendments, resolutions regarding stock rights, minutes of shareholders' meetings, and records of actions taken without a meeting for the last three years, written communications to all shareholders for the last three years, financial statements furnished to shareholders for the last three years, names and addresses of all current directors and officers, and the most recent annual report.

FORM OF RECORDS

The minutes may be in writing or in any other form capable of being converted into written form within a reasonable time. This would mean that they could be kept in a computer or possibly on a videotape. However, it is always best to keep at least one written copy. Accidents can easily erase magnetic media.

EXAMINATION OF RECORDS

Any shareholder of a corporation has the right to examine the corporation's books and records after giving written notice at least five days before the date on which he wishes to inspect. An affidavit can be requested by the corporation that the inspection is not for the purpose of some other business and that the shareholder has not attempted to sell shareholder lists in the past five years. Shareholders may also request an annual balance sheet and profit and loss statement as well as any interim reports (NYBCBL § 624).

The shareholder may have his attorney or agent examine the records and may receive photocopies of the records (NYBCL § 624). The corporation may charge a reasonable fee for making photocopies. If the records are not in written form, the corporation must convert them to written form. The corporation must bear the cost of converting the certificate of incorporation and any amendments, bylaws and any amendments, resolutions by the board of directors creating different rights in the stock, minutes of all shareholders' meetings and records of any action taken by the shareholders without a meeting for the past three years, written communications to all shareholders generally or of any class, names and addresses of all officers and directors, and the most recent annual report filed with the secretary of state. The shareholder must pay for converting any other records.

If the corporation refuses to allow a shareholder to examine the records, the shareholder may get an order from the Supreme Court and in such case the corporation would have to pay the shareholder' costs and attorney fees [NYBCL § 624 (d)].

Shareholder Meetings

Each year the corporation must hold an annual meeting of the shareholders. These meetings may be formal and held in a restaurant or they may be informal and held in the swimming pool. A sole officer and director can hold them in his mind without reciting all the verbiage or taking a formal vote. But the important thing is that the meetings are held and that minutes are kept. Regular minutes and meetings are evidence that the corporation is legitimate if the issue ever comes up in court. Minute forms for the annual meetings are included with this book. You can use them as master copies to photocopy each year. All that needs to be changed is the date, unless you actually change officers or directors or need to take some other corporate action.

SPECIAL MEETINGS
When important decisions must be made by the board of shareholders between the annual meetings, the corporation can hold special meetings.

ACTION WITHOUT A MEETING

Under the procedures of NYBCL § 615(a), action may be taken by the shareholders without a formal meeting. However, for a small corporation it is best to use formal meetings in case someone later tries to pierce the corporate veil.

NOTICE OF MEETINGS

Under New York law, [NYBCL § 605(a)] shareholders with voting rights must be notified of the date, time, and place of annual and special meetings at least ten but not more than sixty days prior. No description of the purpose of an annual meeting need be given, but the purpose for a special meeting must be stated in the notice.

A shareholder may waive notice either before or after the meeting if done in writing and included in the minutes. Unless a shareholder objects, attendance at a meeting waives objection to the notice or lack thereof.

VOTING

The following rules apply to voting at the shareholders' meeting:

- Unless otherwise provided in the certificate of incorporation or bylaws, a quorum consists of a majority of the shares entitled to vote [NYBCL § 608(a), § 608(b)].

- Once a share is represented at a meeting for any purpose it is deemed present for quorum purposes for the rest of the meeting (NYBCL § 608).

- Holders of a majority of the shares represented may adjourn the meeting.

- The certificate of incorporation may authorize a quorum of less than a majority but it may not be less than one-third. The certificate may also require more than a majority for a quorum [NYBCL § 608(a), § 608(b)].

VOTING FOR DIRECTORS

Unless otherwise provided in the certificate of incorporation, directors are elected by a plurality of votes. Shareholders do not have a right to cumulative voting unless provided in the articles.

PROXIES

A proxy may be signed by a shareholder authorizing someone else to vote his or her shares. Proxies must be in writing. Proxies may authorize the other person to vote the shares once or forever. Proxies can be revoked orally, in writing or by conduct.

BOARD OF DIRECTORS

DIRECTORS There may be as few as one director on the board. Directors are elected by shareholders at the annual meeting and may also be removed by shareholders.

OFFICERS Officers are elected by the board and may include a president, vice president(s), secretary, treasurer and others. The bylaws may give shareholders the right to elect officers.

ANNUAL MEETINGS Each year the corporation must hold an annual meeting of the directors. These meetings also may be formal and held in a restaurant or they may be informal and held in the swimming pool. A sole officer and director can hold them in his mind without reciting all the verbiage or taking a formal vote. But the important thing is that the meetings are held and that minutes are kept. Regular minutes and meetings are evidence that the corporation is legitimate if the issue ever comes up in court. Minute forms for the annual meetings are included with this book. You can use them as master copies to photocopy each year. All that needs to be changed is the date, unless you actually change officers or directors or need to take some other corporate action.

SPECIAL MEETINGS When important decisions must be made by the board of directors between the annual meetings, the corporation can hold special meetings.

ACTION WITHOUT A MEETING Under the procedures of NYBCL § 708(b), action may be taken by the directors without a formal meeting. However, for a small corporation it is best to use formal meetings in case someone later tries to pierce the corporate veil.

NOTICE OF
MEETINGS
Under New York law [NYBCL §711(a)] regular meetings of the board of directors may be held without notice unless the certificate of incorporation or bylaws provide otherwise. Special meetings must be preceded by at least two days notice of the time, date, and place unless the certificate or bylaws provide for a longer or shorter period. This notice may be waived.

VOTING
The following rules apply to voting at the directors' meeting:

☞ Unless otherwise provided in the certificate of incorporation or bylaws, a quorum consists of a majority of the number of directors prescribed in the certificate or bylaws.

☞ The certificate of incorporation may authorize a quorum of less than a majority but it may not be less than one-third.

☞ If a quorum is present for a vote, a vote by a majority of those present constitutes an act of the board of directors unless otherwise provided in the certificate or bylaws.

☞ A director present at a meeting of the board or a committee is deemed to have assented to an action taken unless he or she objects at the beginning of the meeting or the vote to the meeting or the business, or votes against or abstains from voting.

COMMITTEES
If provided for by the bylaws, the board of directors may designate a committee of its members that can exercise all authority of the board except that it may not:

☞ approve or recommend actions which by law must be approved by the shareholders;

☞ fill vacancies on the board or committees thereof;

☞ adopt, repeal, or amend the bylaws;

☞ establish compensation for directors;

☞ amend or repeal any board resolution that is specifically not amendable or repealable by a committee.

Also, meeting rules of committees must comply with the rules for the board itself. Each committee must have at least two members and

LIABILITY   alternate members may be designated. Setting up a committee does not relieve a member of his duty to act in good faith in the best interests of the corporation.

Directors have a responsibility under NYBCL § 717 to perform their job with good faith and by using the degree of care that an ordinary prudent person in a similar position would use under similar circumstances. A corporation may indemnify the directors, officers and employees by simply stating so in the certificate of incorporation. A corporation may also purchase insurance to indemnify them.

BI-ANNUAL REPORTS

Every New York corporation must file a report every two years. Fortunately, this is a simple one-page form which is sent to the corporation by the Department of State and usually merely has to be signed. It contains such information as the federal tax identification number, officers' and directors' names and addresses, the registered agent's name and the address of the registered office. The fee at the time of publication is $9.

AMENDING A CORPORATION   7

CERTIFICATE OF INCORPORATION

Because the certificate of incorporation included in this book is so basic, it will rarely have to be amended. The certificate of incorporation may be amended for many reasons, including to change any of the following:

- the corporation's name
- the corporation's purpose
- the address
- the county the office is located in
- the name or address of the additional registered agent
- the number or class of shares or their par value.

Changes may also be made adding or deleting any provision authorized under the NYBCL.

To amend the certificate of incorporation, there must be a vote by the board and a vote by the shareholders authorizing the amendment. No shareholder vote is necessary to change the address or location or the additional registered agent. If there are no shareholders or directors, the incorporator may make amendments.

A Certificate of Amendment (form 25) must be filed with the Department of State for changes authorized by the board and the shareholders (NYBCL § 805). A Certificate of Change (NYBCL § 805-A) must be filed for changes authorized only by the board. The certificates must state old and new names (if there has been a change), the date of incorporation, each provision that is being changed, any new provisions that are being added or are replacing old provisions, as well as how the changes were authorized. Another option is to restate the certificate of incorporation and completely redo it with the new information. All the old information that is unchanged must be included. The authorization for the changes must be given. For more information, refer to NYBCL § 801-807.

Bylaws

The shareholders may always amend the bylaws. The board of directors may amend the bylaws if the certificate of incorporation permits them to do so. Share holders may amend or repeal any bylaw adopted by the board (NYBCL § 602).

The certificate of incorporation may allow a bylaw that requires a greater quorum or voting requirement for shareholders but such a requirement may not be adopted, amended, or repealed by the board of directors(NYBCL § 608).

A bylaw that fixes a greater quorum or voting requirement for the board of directors that was adopted by the shareholders may be amended or repealed only by the shareholders, but if it was adopted by the board, it may be amended or repealed by the board (NYBCL § 707).

DISSOLVING A CORPORATION 8

VOLUNTARY DISSOLUTION

A corporation may be dissolved by a majority vote of the shareholders. The certificate of incorporation may require more than a majority for dissolution. If there are no shareholders, people who have subscribed for shares must agree by written consent to dissolve the corporation. If there are no subscribers, the corporation may be dissolved upon written consent of a majority of the incorporators.

The certificate of incorporation may also permit dissolution by as few as one shareholder upon the happening of a trigger event (such as voting deadlock).

To dissolve a corporation, a Certificate of Dissolution (included in this book as Form 24) must be filed with the Department of State and must include:

- ☛ the current and any past names of the corporation
- ☛ the date of incorporation
- ☛ names and addresses of officers and directors
- ☛ a statement that the corporation chooses to be dissolved
- ☛ how the dissolution was authorized

A tax clearance certificate must be obtained form the State Tax Commission and attached to the Certificate of Dissolution. It may take up to three months to obtain the tax clearance.

Involuntary Dissolution

The secretary of state can dissolve a corporation for failure to pay taxes. The Attorney General may petition a court to dissolve a corporation for the following reasons:

- fraud in its formation
- exceeding its authority
- transacting business illegally or fraudulently
- untrue advertising
- unlawful selling

The shareholders or directors can petition a court for dissolution if the corporation cannot pay its creditors. A majority of shareholders may petition for dissolution for reasons such as voting deadlock.

Post-Dissolution

After a corporation has been dissolved, it must wind up its affairs by paying its creditors, collecting its debts and selling its assets. Profits must be distributed to shareholders. No new business may be conducted. Directors and officers continue to act until all business is finished.

The corporation must give notice by publication to its creditors of the dissolution and give a date by which claims must be presented. All known creditors must also be mailed the notice.

Restoration of a Dissolved Corporation

If a corporation has been dissolved by the secretary of state for failure to pay taxes, it can be reinstated by obtaining a certificate of consent from the Commissioner of Taxation and Finance with the Department of State.

A New York Supreme Court can annul any dissolution that has occurred or is pending.

If dissolution is occurring based on a trigger event in the certificate of incorporation, the certificate can simply be amended to remove the trigger.

Except for the above situations, once a corporation has been dissolved it can only be reinstated by following the incorporation process again.

Bankruptcy

If your corporation is in debt beyond its means, it can file for bankruptcy. Chapter 7 bankruptcy is for liquidation and Chapter 11 for reorganization of debts.

If the debts are small and there is little chance the creditors will pursue collection, bankruptcy is unnecessary. You can allow the state to dissolve the corporation for failure to file the annual report. However, if the debts are large and you fear the creditors will attempt to collect the debt from the officers or directors, you should go through formal bankruptcy and/or dissolution. Such a scenario is beyond the scope of this book and you should consult an attorney or bankruptcy text for further guidance.

Appendix A
Checklist

The following checklist includes all steps necessary to form a simple for-profit corporation in New York.

Checklist for Forming a New York For-Profit Corporation

✔ Decide on corporate name

✔ Prepare and file Certificate of Incorporation; pay fees including tax on shares

✔ Send for Federal Employer Identification Number (IRS Form SS-4) and New York State Sales Tax Vendor (NY form DTS 17)

✔ Prepare Shareholders' Agreement, if necessary

✔ Meet with accountant to discuss capitalization and tax planning

✔ If necessary, meet with securities lawyer regarding stock sales

✔ If desired, obtain corporate seal and ring binder for minutes

✔ Hold organizational meeting

    ✔ Complete Bylaws, Waiver, Minutes, Offers to Purchase Stock

    ✔ Sign all documents and place in minute book

✔ Issue stock certificates

    ✔ Be sure consideration is paid

    ✔ Complete Bill of Sale if property is traded for stock

    ✔ Fill in Transfer ledger

✔ Get city or county licenses, if needed

✔ Open Bank account

✔ For S corporation status, file Form 2553

Appendix B
Selected New York Corporation Statutes

Included in this appendix are the New York corporation statutes that will be most useful in organizing your corporation. There are other statutes that cover such things as mergers, buyback of shares, share dividends, proxies, voting trusts and other matters which might come up at a future time. You can obtain a full copy of the statutes from the Department of State. or you can find them on the internet at: http://www.findlaw.com/11stategov/ny/nyul.html

This appendix includes the following articles from the Business Corporation Act:

ARTICLE 1
SHORT TITLE; DEFINITIONS; APPLICATIONS; CERTIFICATES, MISCELLANEOUS
101. Short title.
102. Definitions.
103. Application.
104. Certificates; requirements, signing, filing, effectiveness.
104-A. Fees.
105. Certificates; corrections.
106. Certificates as evidence.
107. Corporate seal as evidence.
108. When notice or lapse of time unnecessary; notices dispensed with when delivery is prohibited.
109. Actions or special proceedings by attorney-general.
110. Reservation of power.
111. Effect of invalidity of part of chapter; severability.
112. References.

ARTICLE 2
CORPORATE PURPOSES AND POWERS
201. Purposes.
202. General powers.
203. Defense of ultra vires.

ARTICLE 3
CORPORATE NAME AND SERVICE OF PROCESS
301. Corporate name; general.
302. Corporate name; exceptions.
303. Reservation of name.
304. Statutory designation of secretary of state as agent for service of process.
305. Registered agent for service of process.
306. Service of process.
306-a. Resignation for receipt of process.
307. Service of process on unauthorized foreign corporation.
308. Records and certificates of department of state.

ARTICLE 4
FORMATION OF CORPORATIONS
401. Incorporators.
402. Certificate of incorporation; contents.
403. Certificate of incorporation; effect.
404. Organization meeting.
405. Day care center for children; approval of certificate.
405-a. Institution for children; approval of certificate.
406. Filing of a certificate of incorporation; facility for alcoholism or alcohol abuse.
407. Substance abuse program; consent to certificate.

408. Biennial statement; filing.
409. Penalty for failure to file; cure.

ARTICLE 5
CORPORATE FINANCE

501. Authorized shares.
502. Issue of any class of preferred shares in series.
503. Subscription for shares; time of payment, forfeiture for default.
504. Consideration and payment for shares.
505. Rights and options to purchase shares; issue of rights and options to directors, officers and employees.
506. Determination of stated capital.
507. Compensation for formation, reorganization and financing.
508. Certificates representing shares.
509. Fractions of a share or scrip authorized.
510. Dividends or other distributions in cash or property.
511. Share distributions and changes.
512. Redeemable shares.
513. Purchase, redemption and certain other transactions by a corporation with respect to its own shares.
514. Agreements for purchase by a corporation of its own shares.
515. Reacquired shares.
516. Reduction of stated capital in certain cases.
518. Corporate bonds.
519. Convertible or exchangeable shares and bonds.
520. Liability for failure to disclose required information.

ARTICLE 6
SHAREHOLDERS

601. By-laws.
602. Meetings of shareholders.
603. Special meeting for election of directors.
604. Fixing record date.
605. Notice of meetings of shareholders.
606. Waivers of notice.
607. List of shareholders at meetings.
608. Quorum of shareholders.
609. Proxies.
610. Selection of inspectors at shareholders' meetings.
611. Duties of inspectors at shareholders' meetings.
612. Qualification of voters.
613. Limitations on right to vote.
614. Vote of shareholders.
615. Written consent of shareholders, subscribers or incorporators without a meeting.
616. Greater requirement as to quorum and vote of shareholders.
617. Voting by class or classes of shares.
618. Cumulative voting.
619. Powers of supreme court respecting elections.
620. Agreements as to voting; provision in certificate of incorporation as to control of directors.
621. Voting trust agreements.
622. Preemptive rights.
623. Procedure to enforce shareholder's right to receive payment for shares.
624. Books and records; right of inspection, prima facie evidence.
625. Infant shareholders and bondholders.
626. Shareholders' derivative action brought in the right of the corporation to procure a judgment in its favor.
627. Security for expenses in shareholders' derivative action brought in the right of the corporation to procure a judgment in its favor.
628. Liability of subscribers and shareholders.
629. Certain transfers or assignments by shareholders or subscribers; effect.
630. Liability of shareholders for wages due to laborers, servants or employees.

ARTICLE 7
DIRECTORS AND OFFICERS

701. Board of directors.
702. Number of directors.
703. Election and term of directors.
704. Classification of directors.
705. Newly created directorships and vacancies.
706. Removal of directors.
707. Quorum of directors.
708. Action by the board.
709. Greater requirement as to quorum and vote of directors.
710. Place and time of meetings of the board.
711. Notice of meetings of the board.
712. Executive committee and other committees.
713. Interested directors.
714. Loans to directors.
715. Officers.
716. Removal of officers.
717. Duty of directors.
718. List of directors and officers.
719. Liability of directors in certain cases.
720. Action against directors and officers for misconduct.
721. Exclusivity of statutory provisions for indemnification of directors and officers.
722. Authorization for indemnification of directors and officers in actions or proceedings other than by or in the right of a corporation to procure a judgment in its favor.
723. Payment of indemnification other than by court award.
724. Indemnification of directors and officers by a court.
725. Other provisions affecting indemnification of directors and officers.
726. Insurance for indemnification of directors and officers.

ARTICLE 15
PROFESSIONAL SERVICE CORPORATIONS

1501. Definitions.
1502. Corporations organized under other provisions of law
1503. Organization.
1504. Rendering of professional service.
1505. Professional relationships and liabilities.

1506. Purposes of incorporation.
1507. Issuance of shares.
1508. Directors and officers.
1509. Disqualification of shareholders, directors, officers and employees.
1510. Death or disqualification of shareholders.
1511. Transfer of shares.
1512. Corporate name.
1513. Business corporation law applicable.
1514. Triennial statement.
1515. Regulation of professions.
1516. Corporate mergers, consolidations and other reorganizations.

ARTICLE 1
SHORT TITLE; DEFINITIONS; APPLICATIONS; CERTIFICATES, MISCELLANEOUS

S 101. Short title.

This chapter shall be known as the "Business Corporation Law."

S 102. Definitions.

(a) As used in this chapter, unless the context otherwise requires, the term:

(1) "Authorized person" means a person, whether or not a shareholder, officer or director, who is authorized to act on behalf of a corporation or foreign corporation.

(2) "Bonds" includes secured and unsecured bonds, debentures, and notes.

(3) "Certificate of incorporation" includes (A) the original certificate of incorporation or any other instrument filed or issued under any statute to form a domestic or foreign corporation, as amended, supplemented or restated by certificates of amendment, merger or consolidation or other certificates or instruments filed or issued under any statute; or (B) a special act or charter creating a domestic or foreign corporation, as amended, supplemented or restated.

(4) "Corporation" or "domestic corporation" means a corporation for profit formed under this chapter, or existing on its effective date and theretofore formed under any other general statute or by any special act of this state for a purpose or purposes for which a corporation may be formed under this chapter, other than a corporation which may be formed under the cooperative corporations law.

(5) "Director" means any member of the governing board of a corporation, whether designated as director, trustee, manager, governor, or by any other title. The term "board" means "board of directors."

(7) "Foreign corporation" means a corporation for profit formed under laws other than the statutes of this state, which has as its purpose or among its purposes a purpose for which a corporation may be formed under this chapter, other than a corporation which, if it were to be formed currently under the laws of this state, could not be formed under this chapter. "Authorized," when used with respect to a foreign corporation, means having authority under article 13 (Foreign corporations) to do business in this state.

(7-a) "Infant" means a person who has not attained the age of eighteen years.

(8) "Insolvent" means being unable to pay debts as they become due in the usual course of the debtor's business.

(9) "Net assets" means the amount by which the total assets exceed the total liabilities. Stated capital and surplus are not liabilities.

(10) "Office of a corporation" means the office the location of which is stated in the certificate of incorporation of a domestic corporation, or in the application for authority of a foreign corporation or an amendment thereof. Such office need not be a place where business activities are conducted by such corporation.

(11) "Process" means judicial process and all orders, demands, notices or other papers required or permitted by law to be personally served on a domestic or foreign corporation, for the purpose of acquiring jurisdiction of such corporation in any action or proceeding, civil or criminal, whether judicial, administrative, arbitrative or otherwise, in this state or in the federal courts sitting in or for this state.

(12) "Stated capital" means the sum of (A) the par value of all shares with par value that have been issued, (B) the amount of the consideration received for all shares without par value that have been issued, except such part of the consideration therefor as may have been allocated to surplus in a manner permitted by law, and (C) such amounts not included in clauses (A) and (B) as have been transferred to stated capital, whether upon the distribution of shares or otherwise, minus all reductions from such sums as have been effected in a manner permitted by law.

(13) "Surplus" means the excess of net assets over stated capital.

(14) "Treasury shares" means shares which have been issued, have been subsequently acquired, and are retained uncancelled by the corporation. Treasury shares are issued shares, but not outstanding shares, and are not assets

S 103. Application.

(a) This chapter applies to every domestic corporation and to every foreign corporation which is authorized or does business in this state. This chapter also applies to any other domestic corporation or foreign corporation of any type or kind to the extent, if any, provided under this chapter or any law governing such corporation and, if no such provision for application is made, to the extent, if any, that the stock corporation law applied to such corporation immediately prior to the effective date of this chapter. This chapter also applies to a corporation of any type or kind, formed for profit under any other chapter of the laws of this state except a chapter of the consolidated laws, to the extent that provisions of this chapter do not conflict with the provisions of such unconsolidated law. If an applicable provision of such unconsolidated law relates to a matter embraced in this chapter but is not in conflict therewith, both provisions shall apply. Any corporation to which this chapter is made applicable by this paragraph shall be treated as a "corporation" or "domestic corporation" as such terms are used in this chapter, except that the purposes of any such corporation formed or formable under such unconsolidated law shall not thereby be extended. For the purpose of this paragraph, the effective date of this chapter as to corporations to which this chapter is made applicable by this paragraph shall be June one, nineteen hundred seventy-three. This chapter shall not apply to a domestic corporation of any type or kind heretofore or hereafter formed under the banking law, insurance law, railroad law, transportation corporations law or cooperative corporations law, or under any other statute or special act for a purpose or purposes for which a corporation may be formed under any of such laws except to the extent, if any, provided under such law. It shall not apply, except to the extent, if any, provided under the banking law, insurance law, railroad law, transportation corporations law or cooperative corporations law, to a foreign corporation of any type or kind heretofore or hereafter formed which (1) has as its purpose or among its purposes a purpose for which a corporation may be formed only under the insurance law, banking law, railroad law, transportation corporations law or cooperative corporations law, and (2) is either an authorized insurer as defined in the insurance law or does in this state only the kind of business which can be done lawfully by a corporation formed under the banking law, railroad law, transportation corporations law or cooperative corporations law, as the case may be. After the effective date of this chapter the stock corporation law shall not apply to any corporation of any type or kind. The general corporation law shall not apply to a corporation of any type or kind to which this chapter applies. A reference in any statute of this state, which makes a provision of the stock corporation law applicable to a corporation of any type or kind, shall be deemed and construed to refer to and make applicable the corresponding provision, if any, of this chapter.

(b) This chapter applies to commerce with foreign nations and among the several states, and to corporations formed by or under any act of congress, only to the extent permitted under the constitution and laws of the United States.

(c) The enactment of this chapter shall not affect the duration of a corporation which is existing on the effective date of this chapter. Any such existing corporation, its shareholders, directors and officers shall have the same rights and be subject to the same limitations, restrictions, liabilities and penalties as a corporation formed under this chapter, its shareholders, directors and officers.

(d) This chapter shall not affect any cause of action, liability, penalty or action or special proceeding, which on the effective date of this chapter, is accrued, existing, incurred or pending but the same may be asserted, enforced, prosecuted or defended as if this chapter had not been enacted.

(e) After the effective date of this chapter no corporation shall be formed under the stock corporation law

S 104. Certificates; requirements, signing, filing, effectiveness.

(a) Every certificate or other instrument relating to a domestic or foreign corporation which is delivered to the department of state for filing under this chapter, other than a certificate of existence under section 1304 (Application for authority; contents), shall be in the English language, except that the corporate name may be in another language if written in English letters or characters.

(b) Whenever such instrument is required to set forth an address, it shall include the street and number, or other particular description instead of a street and number. This requirement does not apply where a post office address is specified to be set forth.

(c) Whenever such instrument is required to set forth the date when a certificate of incorporation was filed by the department of state, the original certificate of incorporation is meant. This requirement shall be satisfied, in the case of a corporation created by special act, by setting forth the chapter number and year of passage of such act.

(d) Every such certificate required under this chapter to be signed and delivered to the department of state shall, except as otherwise specified in the section providing for such certificate, be signed either an officer, director, attorney-in-fact or duly authorized person and include the name and the capacity in which such person signs such certificate.

  (4) if also there are no directors, by the holders, or such of them as are designated by the holders, of record of a majority of the votes of all outstanding shares entitled to vote thereon, or

  (5) if also there is no shareholder of record, by a subscriber for shares whose subscription has been accepted or his successor in interest or

  (6) if also no subscription for shares has been accepted, by an incorporator or anyone acting in his stead under paragraph (c) of section 615 (Written consent of shareholders, subscribers or incorporators without a meeting). His name and the capacity in which any person signs such certificate shall be stated beneath or opposite his signature. The person signing such certificate or, if more than one person signs it, one of such persons shall verify or acknowledge the certificate if required by the section providing for such certificate. In lieu of being signed and verified or acknowledged, the certificate may be subscribed by such person and affirmed by him as true under the penalties of perjury.

(e) If an instrument which is delivered to the department of state for filing complies as to form with the requirements of law and there has been attached to it the consent or approval of the state official, department, board, agency or other body, if any, whose consent to or approval of such instrument or the filing thereof is required by any statute of this state and the filing fee and tax, if any, required by any statute of this state in connection therewith have been paid, the instrument shall be filed and indexed by the department of state. No certificate of authentication or conformity or other proof shall be required with respect to any verification, oath or acknowledgment of any instrument delivered to the department of state under this chapter, if such verification, oath or acknowledgment purports to have been made before a notary public, or person performing the equivalent function, of one of the states, or any subdivision thereof, of the United States or the District of Columbia. Without limiting the effect of section four hundred three of this chapter, filing and indexing by the department of state shall not be deemed a finding that a certificate conforms to law, nor shall it be deemed to constitute an approval by the department of state of the name of the corporation or the contents of the certificate, nor shall it be deemed to prevent any person with appropriate standing from contesting the legality thereof in an appropriate forum.

(f) Except as otherwise provided in this chapter, such instrument shall become effective upon the filing thereof by the department of state.

(g) The department shall make, certify and transmit a copy of each such instrument to the clerk of the county in which the office of the domestic or foreign corporation is or is to be located. The county clerk shall file and index such copy.

S 104-A. Fees.

Except as otherwise provided, the department of state shall collect the following fees pursuant to this chapter:

(a) For the reservation of a corporate name pursuant to section three hundred three of this chapter, twenty dollars.

(b) For the resignation of a registered agent for service of process pursuant to section three hundred five of this chapter, and for the resignation for receipt for process pursuant to section three hundred six-A of this chapter, sixty dollars.

(c) For service of process on the secretary of state pursuant to section three hundred six, paragraph (e) of section three hundred six-A, or three hundred seven of this chapter, forty dollars. No fee shall be collected for process served on behalf of a county, city, town or village or other political subdivision of the state.

(d) For filing a certificate of incorporation pursuant to section four hundred two of this chapter, one hundred twenty-five dollars plus the tax on shares prescribed by section one hundred eighty of the tax law.

(e) For filing a certificate of amendment pursuant to section eight hundred five of this chapter, sixty dollars plus the tax on shares prescribed by section one hundred eighty of the tax law if such certificate shows a change of shares.

(f) For filing a certificate of change pursuant to paragraph (a) of section eight hundred five-A of this chapter, thirty dollars, and for filing a certificate of change pursuant to paragraph (b) of section eight hundred five-A of this chapter, five dollars.

(g) For filing a restated certificate of incorporation pursuant to section eight hundred seven of this chapter, sixty dollars plus the tax on shares prescribed by section one hundred eighty of the tax law if such certificate shows a change of shares.

(h) For filing a certificate of merger or consolidation pursuant to section nine hundred four of this chapter, or a certificate of exchange pursuant to section nine hundred thirteen (other than paragraph (g) of section nine hundred thirteen) of this chapter, sixty dollars plus the tax on shares prescribed by section one hundred eighty of the tax law if such certificate shows a change of shares.

(i) For filing a certificate of merger of a subsidiary corporation pursuant to section nine hundred five of this chapter, or a certificate of exchange pursuant to paragraph (g) of section nine hundred thirteen of this chapter, sixty dollars.

(j) For filing a certificate of merger or consolidation pursuant to section nine hundred four-a of this chapter, or a certificate of merger or consolidation of domestic and foreign corporations pursuant to section nine hundred seven of this chapter, sixty dollars.

(k) For filing a certificate of dissolution pursuant to section one thousand three of this chapter, sixty dollars.

(l) For filing an application by a foreign corporation for authority to do business in New York state pursuant to section thirteen hundred four of this chapter, two hundred twenty-five dollars.

(m) For filing a certificate of amendment of an application for authority by a foreign corporation pursuant to section thirteen hundred nine of this chapter, sixty dollars.

(n) For filing a certificate of change of application for authority by a foreign corporation pursuant to section thirteen hundred nine-A of this chapter, thirty dollars.

(o) For filing a certificate of surrender of authority pursuant to section thirteen hundred ten of this chapter, sixty dollars.

(p) For filing a statement of the termination of existence of a foreign corporation pursuant to section thirteen hundred eleven of this chapter, sixty dollars. There shall be no fee for the filing by an authorized officer of the jurisdiction of incorporation of a foreign corporation of a certificate that the foreign corporation has been dissolved or its authority or existence has

(q) For filing a certificate of incorporation by a professional service corporation pursuant to section fifteen hundred three of this chapter, one hundred twenty-five dollars plus the tax on shares prescribed by section one hundred eighty of the tax law.

(r) For filing a statement pursuant to section four hundred eight of this chapter, nine dollars.

(s) For filing any other certificate or instrument, sixty dollars.

S 105. Certificates; corrections.

Any certificate or other instrument relating to a domestic or foreign corporation filed by the department of state under this chapter may be corrected with respect to any informality or error apparent on the face, incorrect statement or defect in the execution thereof including the deletion of any matter not permitted to be stated therein. A certificate, entitled "Certificate of correction of............ (correct title of certificate and name of corporation)" shall be signed, verified and delivered to the department of state. It shall set forth the name of the corporation, the date the certificate to be corrected was filed by the department of state, a statement as to the nature of the informality, error, incorrect statement or defect, the provision in the certificate as corrected or eliminated and if the execution was defective, the proper execution. The filing of the certificate by the department of state shall not alter the effective time of the instrument being corrected, which shall remain as its original effective time, and shall not affect any right or liability accrued or incurred before such filing. A corporate name may not be changed or corrected under this section. The provisions of this section shall apply to all instruments and certificates heretofore and hereafter filed with the department of state.

S 106. Certificates as evidence.

(a) Any certificate or other instrument filed by the department of state relating to a domestic or foreign corporation and containing statements of fact required or permitted by law to be contained therein, shall be received in all courts, public offices and official bodies as prima facie evidence of such facts and of the execution of such instrument.

(b) Whenever by the laws of any jurisdiction other than this state, any certificate by any officer in such jurisdiction or a copy of any instruments certified or exemplified by any such officer, may be received as prima facie evidence of the incorporation, existence or capacity of any foreign corporation incorporated in such jurisdiction, or claiming so to be, such certificate when exemplified, or such copy of such instrument when exemplified shall be received in all courts, public offices and official bodies of this state, as prima facie evidence with the same force as in such jurisdiction. Such certificate or certified copy of such instrument shall be so received, without being exemplified, if it is certified by the secretary of state, or official performing the equivalent function as to corporate records, of such jurisdiction.

S 107. Corporate seal as evidence.

The presence of the corporate seal on a written instrument purporting to be executed by authority of a domestic or foreign corporation shall be prima facie evidence that the instrument was so executed.

S 108. When notice or lapse of time unnecessary; notices dispensed with when delivery is prohibited.

(a) Whenever, under this chapter or the certificate of incorporation or by-laws of any corporation or by the terms of any agreement or instrument, a corporation or the board or any committee thereof is authorized to take any action after notice to any person or persons or after the lapse of a prescribed period of time, such action may be taken without notice and without the lapse of such period of time, if at any time before or after such action is completed the person or persons entitled to such notice or entitled to participate in the action to be taken or, in the case of a shareholder, by his attorney-in-fact, submit a signed waiver of notice of such requirements.

(b) Whenever any notice or communication is required to be given to any person by this chapter, the certificate of incorporation or by-laws, or by the terms of any agreement or instrument, or as a condition precedent to taking any corporate action and communication with such person is then unlawful under any statute of this state or of the United States or any regulation, proclamation or order issued under said statutes, then the giving of such notice or communication to such person shall not be required and there shall be no duty to apply for license or other permission to do so. Any affidavit, certificate or other instrument which is required to be made or filed as proof of the giving of any notice or communication required under this chapter shall, if such notice or communication to any person is dispensed with under this paragraph, include a statement that such notice or communication was not given to any person with whom communication is unlawful. Such affidavit, certificate or other instrument shall be as effective for all purposes as though such notice or communication had been personally given to such person.

(c) Whenever any notice or communication is required or permitted by this chapter to be given by mail, it shall, except as otherwise expressly provided in this chapter, be mailed to the person to whom it is directed at the address designated by him for that purpose or, if none is designated, at his last known address. Such notice or communication is given when deposited, with postage thereon prepaid, in a post office or official depository under the exclusive care and custody of the United States Post Office department. Such mailing shall be by first class mail except where otherwise required by this chapter.

S 109. Actions or special proceedings by attorney-general.

(a) The attorney-general may maintain an action or special proceeding:
  (1) To annul the corporate existence or dissolve a corporation that has acted beyond its capacity or power or to restrain it from the doing of unauthorized business;
  (2) To annul the corporate existence or dissolve any corporation that has not been duly formed;
  (3) To restrain any person or persons from acting as a domestic or foreign corporation within this state without being duly incorporated or from exercising in this state any corporate rights, privileges or franchises not granted to them by the law of the state;
  (4) To procure a judgment removing a director of a corporation for cause under section 706 (Removal of directors);
  (5) To dissolve a corporation under article 11 (Judicial dissolution);
  (6) To restrain a foreign corporation or to annul its authority to do business in this state under section 1303 (Violations).
  (7) Upon written application, ex parte, for an order to the supreme court at a special term held within the judicial district where the office of the corporation is located, and if the court so orders, to inspect the books and records of the corporation to the extent that such inspection is available to shareholders and directors under the law of this state. Such application shall contain a statement that the inspection is necessary to protect the interests of the people of this state. This paragraph applies to every corporation, no shares of which are listed on a national securities exchange or regularly quoted in an over-the-counter market by one or more members of a national or an affiliated securities association. This paragraph does not apply to a corporation all shares of which are owned either directly or through a wholly owned subsidiary by a corporation or corporations to which this paragraph does not apply.
  (8) To collect any fines payable to the department of state pursuant to section four hundred nine of this chapter.

(b) In an action or special proceeding brought by the attorney-general under any of the provisions of this chapter:
  (1) If an action, it is triable by jury as a matter of right.
  (2) The court may confer immunity in accordance with the provisions of section 50.20 of the criminal procedure law.
  (3) A temporary restraining order to restrain the commission or continuance of the unlawful acts which form the basis of the action or special proceeding may be granted upon proof, by affidavit, that the defendant or defendants have committed or are about to commit such acts. Application for such restraining order may be made ex parte or upon such notice as the court may direct.
  (4) If the action or special proceeding is against a foreign corporation, the attorney-general may apply to the court at any stage thereof for the appointment of a temporary receiver of the assets in this state of such foreign corporation, whenever it has assets or property of any kind whatsoever, tangible or intangible, within this state.
  (5) When final judgment in such action or special proceeding is rendered against the defendant or defendants, the court may direct the costs to be collected by execution against any or all of the defendants or by order of attachment or other process against the person of any director or officer of a corporate defendant.
  (6) In connection with any such proposed action or special proceeding, the attorney-general may take proof and issue subpoenas in accordance with the civil practice law and rules.

(c) In any such action or special proceeding against a foreign corporation which has not designated the secretary of state as its agent for service of process under section 304 (Statutory designation of secretary of state as agent for service of process), any of the following acts in this state by such foreign corporation shall constitute the appointment by it of the secretary of state as its agent upon whom process against such foreign corporation may be served:
  (1) As used in this paragraph the term "resident" shall include individuals, domestic corporations and foreign corporations authorized to do business in the state.
  (2) Any act done, or representation made as part of a course of the solicitation of orders, or the issuance, or the delivery, of contracts for, or the sale of, property, or the performance of services to residents which involves or promotes a plan or scheme to defraud residents in violation of the laws or the public policy of the state.
  (3) Any act done as part of a course of conduct of business in the solicitation of orders from residents for property, goods or services, to be delivered or rendered within this state to, or on their behalf, where the orders or contracts are executed by such residents within this state and where such orders or contracts are accompanied or followed by an earnest money deposit or other down payment or any installment payment thereon or any other form of payment, which

payment is either delivered in or transmitted from the state.

(4) Any act done as part of the conduct of a course of business with residents which defrauds such residents or otherwise involves or promotes an attempt by such foreign corporation to circumvent the laws of this state.

(d) Paragraphs (b), (c), (d) and (e) of section 307 (Service of process on unauthorized foreign corporation) shall apply to process served under paragraph (c).

S 110. Reservation of power.

The legislature reserves the right, at pleasure, to alter, amend, suspend or repeal in whole or in part this chapter, or any certificate of incorporation or any authority to do business in this state, of any domestic or foreign corporation, whether or not existing or authorized on the effective date of this chapter.

S 111. Effect of invalidity of part of chapter; severability.

If any provision of this chapter or application thereof to any person or circumstances is held invalid, such invalidity shall not affect other provisions or applications of this chapter which can be given effect without the invalid provision or application, and to this end the provisions of this chapter are declared severable.

S 112. References.

Unless otherwise stated, all references in this chapter to articles or sections refer to the articles or sections of this chapter, and all references in any section of this chapter to a lettered or numbered paragraph or subparagraph refer to the paragraph or subparagraph so lettered or numbered in such section.

ARTICLE 2
CORPORATE PURPOSES AND POWERS

S. 201 Purposes.

(a) A corporation may be formed under this chapter for any lawful business purpose or purposes except to do in this state any business for which formation is permitted under any other statute of this state unless such statute permits formation under this chapter. If,immediately prior to the effective date of this chapter, a statute of this state permitted the formation of a corporation under the stock corporation law for a purpose or purposes specified in such other statute, such statute shall be deemed and construed to permit formation of such corporation under this chapter, and any conditions,limitations or restrictions in such other statute upon the formation of such corporation under the stock corporation law shall apply to the formation thereof under this chapter.

(b) The approval of the industrial board of appeals is required for the filing with the department of state of any certificate of incorporation, certificate of merger or consolidation or application of a foreign corporation for authority to do business in this state which states as the purpose or one of the purposes of the corporation the formation of an organization of groups of working men or women or wage earners, or the performance, rendition or sale of services as labor consultant or as advisor on labor-management relations or as arbitrator or negotiator in labor-management disputes.

(c) In time of war or other national emergency, a corporation may do any lawful business in aid thereof, notwithstanding the purpose or purposes set forth in its certificate of incorporation, at the request or direction of any competent governmental authority.

(d) A corporation may not include as its purpose or among its purposes the establishment or operation of a day care center for children, unless its certificate of incorporation shall so state and such certificate shall have annexed thereto the approval of the commissioner of social services.

(e) A corporation may not include as its purpose or among its purposes the establishment or maintenance of a hospital or facility providing health related services, as those terms are defined in article twenty-eight of the public health law unless its certificate of incorporation shall so state and such certificate shall have annexed thereto the approval of the public health council.

S 202. General powers.

(a) Each corporation, subject to any limitations provided in this chapter or any other statute of this state or its certificate of incorporation, shall have power in furtherance of its corporate purposes:

(1) To have perpetual duration.

(2) To sue and be sued in all courts and to participate in actions and proceedings, whether judicial, administrative, arbitrative or otherwise, in like cases as natural persons.

(3) To have a corporate seal, and to alter such seal at pleasure, and to use it by causing it or a facsimile to be affixed or impressed or reproduced in any other manner.

(4) To purchase, receive, take by grant, gift, devise, bequest or otherwise, lease, or otherwise acquire, own, hold, improve, employ,use and otherwise deal in and with, real or personal property, or any interest therein, wherever situated.

(5) To sell, convey, lease, exchange, transfer or otherwise dispose of, or mortgage or pledge, or create a security interest in, all or any of its property, or any interest therein, wherever situated.

(6) To purchase, take, receive, subscribe for, or otherwise acquire,own, hold, vote, employ, sell, lend, lease, exchange, transfer, or otherwise dispose of, mortgage, pledge, use and otherwise deal in and with, bonds and other obligations, shares, or other securities or interests issued by others,

whether engaged in similar or different business, governmental, or other activities.

(7) To make contracts, give guarantees and incur liabilities, borrow money at such rates of interest as the corporation may determine, issue its notes, bonds and other obligations, and secure any of its obligations by mortgage or pledge of all or any of its property or any interest therein, wherever situated.

(8) To lend money, invest and reinvest its funds, and take and hold real and personal property as security for the payment of funds so loaned or invested.

(9) To do business, carry on its operations, and have offices and exercise the powers granted by this chapter in any jurisdiction within or without the United States.

(10) To elect or appoint officers, employees and other agents of the corporation, define their duties, fix their compensation and the compensation of directors, and to indemnify corporate personnel.

(11) To adopt, amend or repeal by-laws, including emergency by-laws made pursuant to subdivision seventeen of section twelve of the state defense emergency act, relating to the business of the corporation, the conduct of its affairs, its rights or powers or the rights or powers of its shareholders, directors or officers.

(12) To make donations, irrespective of corporate benefit, for the public welfare or for community fund, hospital, charitable, educational, scientific, civic or similar purposes, and in time of war or other national emergency in aid thereof.

(13) To pay pensions, establish and carry out pension, profit-sharing, share bonus, share purchase, share option, savings, thrift and other retirement, incentive and benefit plans, trusts and provisions for any or all of its directors, officers and employees.

(14) To purchase, receive, take, or otherwise acquire, own, hold, sell, lend, exchange, transfer or otherwise dispose of, pledge, use and otherwise deal in and with its own shares.

(15) To be a promoter, partner, member, associate or manager of other business enterprises or ventures, or to the extent permitted in any other jurisdiction to be an incorporator of other corporations of any type or kind.

(16) To have and exercise all powers necessary or convenient to effect any or all of the purposes for which the corporation is formed.

(b) No corporation shall do business in New York state under any name, other than that appearing in its certificate of incorporation, without compliance with the filing provisions of section one hundred thirty of the general business law governing the conduct of business under an assumed name.

S 203. Defense of ultra vires.

(a) No act of a corporation and no transfer of real or personal property to or by a corporation, otherwise lawful, shall be invalid by reason of the fact that the corporation was without capacity or power to do such act or to make or receive such transfer, but such lack of capacity or power may be asserted:

(1) In an action by a shareholder against the corporation to enjoin the doing of any act or the transfer of real or personal property by or to the corporation. If the unauthorized act or transfer sought to been joined is being, or is to be, performed or made under any contract to which the corporation is a party, the court may, if all of the parties to the contract are parties to the action and if it deems the same to be equitable, set aside and enjoin the performance of such contract, and in so doing may allow to the corporation or to the other parties to the contract, as the case may be, such compensation as may be equitable for the loss or damage sustained by any of them from the action of the court in setting aside and enjoining the performance of such contract; provided that anticipated profits to be derived from the performance of the contract shall not be awarded by the court as a loss or damage sustained.

(2) In an action by or in the right of the corporation to procure a judgment in its favor against an incumbent or former officer or director of the corporation for loss or damage due to his unauthorized act.

(3) In an action or special proceeding by the attorney-general to annul or dissolve the corporation or to enjoin it from the doing of unauthorized business.

ARTICLE 3
CORPORATE NAME AND SERVICE OF PROCESS

S 301. Corporate name; general.

(a) Except as otherwise provided in this chapter, the name of a domestic or foreign corporation:

(1) Shall contain the word "corporation," "incorporated," or "limited," or an abbreviation of one of such words; or, in the case of a foreign corporation, it shall, for use in this state, add at the end of its name one of such words or an abbreviation thereof.

(2) Shall be such as to distinguish it from the names of corporations of any type or kind, or a fictitious name of an authorized foreign corporation filed pursuant to article thirteen of this chapter, as such names appear on the index of names of existing domestic and authorized foreign corporations of any type or kind, including fictitious names of authorized foreign corporations filed pursuant to article thirteen of this chapter, in the

department of state, division of corporations, or names the right to which are reserved.

(3) Shall not contain any word or phrase, or any abbreviation or derivative thereof, the use of which is prohibited or restricted by any other statute of this state, unless in the latter case the restrictions have been complied with.

(4) Shall not contain any word or phrase, or any abbreviation or derivative thereof, in a context which indicates or implies that the corporation, if domestic, is formed or, if foreign, is authorized for any purpose or is possessed in this state of any power other than a purpose for which, or a power with which, the domestic corporation maybe and is formed or the foreign corporation is authorized.

(5)(A) Shall not contain any of the following phrases, or any abbreviation or derivative thereof:

board of trade	state police
urban development	chamber of commerce
state trooper	urban relocation
community renewal	tenant relocation.

(B) Shall not contain any of the following words, or any abbreviation or derivative thereof:

acceptance	endowment	loan
annuity	fidelity	mortgage
assurance	finance	savings
bank	guaranty	surety
benefit	indemnity	title
bond	insurance	trust
casualty	investment	underwriter
doctor	lawyer	

unless the approval of the superintendent of banks or the superintendent of insurance, as appropriate, is attached to the certificate of incorporation, or application for authority or amendment thereof; or that the word "doctor" or "lawyer" or an abbreviation or derivation thereof is used in the name of a university faculty practice corporation formed pursuant to section fourteen hundred twelve of the not-for-profit corporation law or a professional service corporation formed pursuant to article fifteen of this chapter, or a foreign professional service corporation authorized to do business in this state pursuant to article fifteen-A of this chapter, the members or shareholders of which are composed exclusively of doctors or lawyers, respectively, or are used in a context which clearly denotes a purpose other than the practice of law or medicine.

(6) Shall not, unless the approval of the state board of standards and appeals is attached to the certificate of incorporation, or application for authority or amendment thereof, contain any of the following words or phrases, or any abbreviation or derivative thereof: union, labor, council, industrial organization, in a context which indicates or implies that the domestic corporation is formed or the foreign corporation authorized as an organization of working men or women or wage earners or for the performance, rendition or sale of services as labor or management consultant, adviser or specialist, or as negotiator or arbitrator in labor-management disputes.

(7) Shall not, unless the approval of the state department of social services is attached to the certificate of incorporation, or application for authority or amendment thereof, contain the word "blind" or "handicapped." Such approval shall be granted by the state department of social services, if in its opinion the word "blind" or"handicapped" as used in the corporate name proposed will not tend to mislead or confuse the public into believing that the corporation is organized for charitable or non-profit purposes related to the blind or the handicapped.

(8) Shall not contain any words or phrases, or any abbreviation or derivation thereof in a context which will tend to mislead the public into believing that the corporation is an agency or instrumentality of the United States or the state of New York or a subdivision thereof or is a public corporation.

(9) Shall not contain any word or phrase, or any abbreviation or derivation thereof, which, separately, or in context, shall be indecent or obscene, or shall ridicule or degrade any person, group, belief, business or agency of government, or indicate or imply any unlawful activity.

(10) Shall not, unless the approval of the attorney general is attached to the certificate of incorporation, or application for authority or amendment thereof, contain the word "exchange" or any abbreviation or derivative thereof. Such approval shall not be granted by the attorney general, if in his opinion the use of the word "exchange" in the proposed corporate name would falsely imply that the corporation conducts its business at a place where trade is carried on in securities or commodities by brokers, dealers, or merchants.

S 302. Corporate name; exceptions.

(a) Any reference to a corporation in this section except as otherwise provided herein shall include both domestic and foreign corporations.

(b) The provisions of section 301 (Corporate name; general):

(1) Shall not require any corporation, existing or authorized under any statute on the effective date of this chapter, to add to, modify or otherwise change its corporate name; provided, however, that any corporation organized or qualified to do business in this state under this chapter

which contains in its name any of the following words or phrases or any abbreviation or derivation thereof, "community renewal," "tenant relocation," "urban development" or "urban relocation," shall plainly and legibly state immediately following its name in any writing issued or authorized to be issued by it upon which its name appears, including, but not limited to, advertising material letterheads, business cards and building directories and signs, the phrase "not a governmental agency."

(2) Shall not prevent a corporation with which another corporation is merged, or which is formed by the reorganization or consolidation of one or more other corporations or upon a sale, lease, exchange or other disposition to a domestic corporation of all or substantially all the assets of another domestic corporation, including its name, as provided in paragraph (b) of Section 909 (Sale, lease, exchange or other disposition of assets), from having the same name as any of such corporations if at the time such other corporation was authorized or existing under any statute of this state.

(3) Shall not prevent a foreign corporation from being authorized under a name which is similar to the name of a corporation of any type or kind existing or authorized under any statute, if the department of state finds, upon proof by affidavit or otherwise as it may determine, that a difference between such names exists in the terms or abbreviations indicating corporate character or otherwise, that the applicant has engaged in business as a corporation under its said name for not less than ten consecutive years immediately prior to the date of its application that the business to be conducted in this state is not the same as or similar to the business conducted by the corporation with whose name it may conflict and that the public is not likely to be confused or deceived, and if the applicant shall agree in its application for authority to use with its corporate name, in this state, to be placed immediately under or following such name, the words "a .... (name of jurisdiction of incorporation)-corporation."

(4) Shall not prevent a "small business investment corporation" as defined in an act of congress entitled "Small Business Investment Act of 1958" from including the word "investment" as part of its name if such word is coupled with the words "small business."

(5) Shall not prevent an "investment company" as defined in an act of congress entitled "Investment Company Act of 1940" from including the word "finance" or "bond" as part of its name, if the approval of the superintendent of banks is attached to the certificate of incorporation, application for authority, or amendment thereof.

(6) Shall not prevent a broker or dealer in securities, as defined in an act of congress entitled "Securities Exchange Act of 1934," from including the word "investment" as part of its name if such word is coupled with the words "broker" or "brokers" and if such broker or dealer is registered with the securities and exchange commission under the provisions of section fifteen of the securities exchange act of nineteen hundred thirty-four and is also registered with the attorney general under the provisions of section three hundred fifty-nine-e of the general business law.

(7) Shall not prevent an association of banks or trust companies organized as a non-profit membership corporation for the promotion of the interests of member banks from including the word "bankers" as part of its corporate name.

(8) Shall not prevent a bank holding company, as long as it is required to be registered under article III-A of the banking law or under the federal Bank Holding Company Act, as each may be amended from time to time, from using the words "bank", "banker" or "trusts" or any abbreviation, derivative or combination thereof as part of its corporate name, if the approval of the superintendent of banks is attached to the certificate of incorporation, application for authority, or amendment thereof.

S 303. Reservation of name.
(a) A corporate name may be reserved by:
  (1) Any person intending to form a domestic corporation.
  (2) Any domestic corporation intending to change its name.
  (3) Any foreign corporation intending to apply for authority to do business in this state.
  (4) Any authorized foreign corporation intending to change its name.
  (5) Any person intending to incorporate a foreign corporation and to have it apply for authority to do business in this state.
(b) A fictitious name for use pursuant to section 1301 of this chapter, may be reserved by:
  (1) Any foreign corporation intending to apply for authority to do business in this state, pursuant to paragraph (d) of section 1301 of this chapter.
  (2) Any authorized foreign corporation intending to change its fictitious name under which it does business in this state.
  (3) Any authorized foreign corporation which has changed its corporate name in its jurisdiction, such new corporate name not being available in this state.

(c) Application to reserve a corporate name shall be delivered to the department of state. It shall set forth the name and address of the applicant, the name to be reserved and a statement of the basis under paragraph (a) or (b) for the application. The secretary of state may require that there be included in the application a statement as to the nature of the business to be conducted by the corporation. If the name is available for corporate use, the department of state shall reserve the name for the use of the applicant for a period of sixty days and issue a certificate of reservation. The restrictions and qualifications set forth in subparagraphs (a) (3), (4), (5), (6) and(7) of section 301 (Corporate name; general) are not waived by the issuance of a certificate of reservation. The certificate of reservation shall include the name of the applicant, the name reserved and the date of the reservation. The certificate of reservation (or in lieu thereof an affidavit by the applicant or by his agent or attorney that the certificate of reservation has been lost or destroyed) shall accompany the certificate of incorporation or the application for authority when either is delivered to the department of state.

(d) The secretary of state may extend the reservation for additional periods of not more than sixty days each, upon the written request of the applicant, his attorney or agent delivered to the department of state, to be filed before the expiration of the reservation period then in effect. Such request shall have attached to it the certificate of reservation of name. Not more than two such extensions shall be granted.

(e) Upon the request of the applicant, delivered to the department of state before the expiration of the reserved period, the department shall cancel the reservation.

(f) Any application or request under this section shall be signed by the applicant, his attorney or agent.

S 304. Statutory designation of secretary of state as agent for service of process.

(a) The secretary of state shall be the agent of every domestic corporation and every authorized foreign corporation upon whom process against the corporation may be served.

(b) No domestic or foreign corporation may be formed or authorized to do business in this state under this chapter unless in its certificate of incorporation or application for authority it designates the secretary of state as such agent.

(c) Any designation by a domestic or a foreign corporation of the secretary of state as such agent, which designation is in effect on the effective date of this chapter, shall continue. Every domestic or foreign corporation, existing or authorized on the effective date of this chapter, which has not designated the secretary of state as such agent, shall be deemed to have done so. Any designation prior to the effective date of this chapter by a foreign corporation of an agent other than the secretary of state shall terminate on the effective date of this chapter.

(d) Any designated post-office address to which the secretary of state shall mail a copy of process served upon him as agent of a domestic corporation or a foreign corporation, shall continue until the filing of a certificate under this chapter directing the mailing to a different post-office address.

S 305. Registered agent for service of process.

(a) In addition to such designation of the secretary of state, every domestic corporation or authorized foreign corporation may designate a registered agent in this state upon whom process against such corporation-ration may be served. The agent shall be a natural person who is a resident of or has a business address in this state or a domestic corporation-ration or foreign corporation of any type or kind formed, or authorized to do business in this state, under this chapter or under any other statute of this state.

(b) Any such designation of a registered agent may be made, revoked or changed as provided in this chapter.

(c) A registered agent may resign as such agent. A certificate, entitled "Certificate of resignation of registered agent of ....(name of designating corporation) under section 305 of the Business Corporation Law", shall be signed by him and delivered to the department of state. It shall set forth:

(1) That he resigns as registered agent for the designating corporation.

(2) The date the certificate of incorporation or the application for authority of the designating corporation was filed by the department of state.

(3) That he has sent a copy of the certificate of resignation by registered mail to the designating corporation at the post office address on file in the department of state specified for the mailing of process or if such address is the address of the registered agent, then to the office of the designating corporation in the jurisdiction of its formation or incorporation.

(d) The designation of a registered agent shall terminate thirty days after the filing by the department of state of a certificate of resignation or a certificate containing a revocation or change of the designation, whichever is filed earlier. A certificate designating a new registered agent may be delivered to the department of state by the corporation within the thirty days or thereafter.

S 306. Service of process.

(a) Service of process on a registered agent may be made in the manner provided by law for the service of a summons, as if the registered agent was a defendant.

(b) (1) Service of process on the secretary of state as agent of a domestic or authorized foreign corporation shall be made by personally delivering to and leaving with the secretary of state or a deputy, or with any person authorized by the secretary of state to receive such service, at the office of the department of state in the city of Albany, duplicate copies of such process together with the statutory fee, which fee shall be a taxable disbursement. Service of process on such corporation shall be complete when the secretary of state is so served. The secretary of state shall promptly send one of such copies by certified mail, return receipt requested, to such corporation, at the post office address, on file in the department of state, specified for the purpose. If a domestic or authorized foreign corporation has no such address on file in the department of state, the secretary of state shall so mail such copy, in the case of a domestic corporation, in care of any director named in its certificate of incorporation at the director's address stated therein or, in the case of an authorized foreign corporation, to such corporation at the address of its office within this state on file in the department.

(2) An additional service of the summons may be made pursuant to paragraph four of subdivision (f) of section thirty-two hundred fifteen of the civil practice law and rules.

(c) If an action or special proceeding is instituted in a court of limited jurisdiction, service of process may be made in the manner provided in this section if the office of the domestic or foreign corporation is within the territorial jurisdiction of the court.

(d) Nothing in this section shall affect the right to serve process in any other manner permitted by law.

S 306-A. Resignation for receipt of process.

(a) The party (or his/her legal representative) whose post office address has been supplied by a domestic corporation or authorized foreign corporation as its address for process may resign. A certificate entitled "Certificate of Resignation for Receipt of Process under Section 306-A of the Business Corporation Law" shall be signed by such party and delivered to the department of state. It shall set forth:

(1) The name of the corporation and the date that its certificate of incorporation or application of authority was filed by the department of state.

(2) That the address of the party has been designated by the corporation as the post office address to which the secretary of state shall mail a copy of any process served on the secretary of state as agent for such corporation, and that such party wishes to resign.

(3) That sixty days prior to the filing of the certificate of resignation with the department of state the party has sent a copy of the certificate of resignation for receipt of process by registered or certified mail to the address of the registered agent of the designating corporation, if other than the party filing the certificate of resignation, for receipt of process, or if the resigning corporation has no registered agent, then to the last address of the designating corporation known to the party, specifying the address to which the copy was sent. If there is no registered agent and no known address of the designating corporation, the party shall attach an affidavit to the certificate stating that a diligent but unsuccessful search was made by the party to locate the corporation, specifying what efforts were made.

(4) That the designating corporation is required to deliver to the department of state a certificate of amendment or change providing for the designation by the corporation of a new address and that upon its failure to file such certificate, its authority to do business in this state shall be suspended, unless the corporation has previously filed a statement of addresses and directors under section four hundred eight of this chapter, in which case the address of the principal executive office stated in the last filed statement of addresses and directors shall constitute the new address for process of the corporation, and no such certificate of amendment or change need be filed.

(b) Upon the failure of the designating corporation to file a certificate of amendment or change providing for the designation by the corporation of the new address after the filing of a certificate of resignation for receipt of process with the secretary of state, its authority to do business in this state shall be suspended unless the corporation has previously filed a statement of addresses and directors under section four hundred eight of this chapter, the address of the principal executive office stated in the last filed statement of addresses and directors shall constitute the new address for process of the corporation, and the corporation shall not be deemed suspended.

(c) The filing by the department of state of a certificate of amendment or change providing for a new address by a designating corporation shall annul the suspension and its authority to do business in this state shall be restored and continue as if no suspension had occurred.

(d) The resignation for receipt of process shall become effective upon the filing by the department of state of a certificate of resignation for receipt of process.

(e) (1) In any case in which a corporation suspended pursuant to this section would be subject to the personal or other jurisdiction of the courts of this state under article three of the civil practice law and rules, process against such corporation may be served upon the secretary of state as its agent pursuant to this section. Such process may issue in any court in this state having jurisdiction of the subject matter.

(2) Service of such process upon the secretary of state shall be made by personally delivering to and leaving with him or his deputy, or with any person authorized by the secretary of state to receive such service, at the office of the department of state in the city of Albany, a copy of such process together with the statutory fee, which fee shall be a taxable disbursement. Such service shall be sufficient if notice thereof and a copy of the process are:

(i) delivered personally within or without this state to such corporation by a person and in manner authorized to serve process by law of the jurisdiction in which service is made, or

(ii) sent by or on behalf of the plaintiff to such corporation by registered or certified mail with return receipt requested to the last address of such corporation known to the plaintiff.

(3) (i) Where service of a copy of process was effected by personal service, proof of service shall be by affidavit of compliance with this section filed, together with the process, within thirty days after such service, with the clerk of the court in which the action or special proceeding is pending. Service of process shall complete ten days after such papers are filed with the clerk of the court.

(ii) Where service of a copy of process was effected by mailing in accordance with this section, proof of service shall be by affidavit of compliance with this section filed, together with the process, within thirty days after receipt of the return receipt signed by the corporation, or other official proof of delivery or of the original envelope mailed. If a copy of the process is mailed in accordance with this section, there shall be filed with the affidavit of compliance either the return receipt signed by such corporation or other official proof of delivery, if acceptance was refused by it, the original envelope with annotation by the postal authorities that acceptance was refused. If acceptance was refused, a copy of the notice and process together with notice of the mailing by registered or certified mail and refusal to accept shall be promptly sent to such corporation at the same address by ordinary mail and the affidavit of compliance shall so state. Service of process shall be complete ten days after such papers are filed with the clerk of the court. The refusal to accept delivery of the registered or certified mail or to sign the return receipt shall not affect the validity of the service and such corporation refusing to accept such registered or certified mail shall be charged with knowledge of the contents thereof.

(4) Service made as provided in this section without the state shall have the same force as personal service made within this state.

(5) Nothing in this section shall affect the right to serve process in any other manner permitted by law.

S 307. Service of process on unauthorized foreign corporation.

(a) In any case in which a non-domiciliary would be subject to the personal or other jurisdiction of the courts of this state under article three of the civil practice law and rules, a foreign corporation not authorized to do business in this state is subject to a like jurisdiction. In any such case, process against such foreign corporation may be served upon the secretary of state as its agent. Such process may issue in any court in this state having jurisdiction of the subject matter.

(b) Service of such process upon the secretary of state shall be made by personally delivering to and leaving with him or his deputy, or with any person authorized by the secretary of state to receive such service, at the office of the department of state in the city of Albany, a copy of such process together with the statutory fee, which fee shall be a taxable disbursement. Such service shall be sufficient if notice thereof and a copy of the process are: (1) Delivered personally without this state to such foreign corporation by a person and in the manner authorized to serve process by law of the jurisdiction in which service is made, or (2) Sent by or on behalf of the plaintiff to such foreign corporation by registered mail with return receipt requested, at the post office address specified for the purpose of mailing process, on file in the department of state, or with any official or body performing the equivalent function, in the jurisdiction of its incorporation, or if no such address is there specified, to its registered or other office there specified, or if no such office is there specified, to the last address of such foreign corporation known to the plaintiff.

(c) (1) Where service of a copy of process was effected by personal service, proof of service shall be by affidavit of compliance with this section filed, together with the process, within thirty days after such service, with the clerk of the court in which the action or special proceeding is pending. Service of process shall be complete ten days after such papers are filed with the clerk of the court.

(2) Where service of a copy of process was effected by mailing in accordance with this section, proof of service shall be by affidavit of compliance with this section filed, together with the process, within thirty days after receipt of the return receipt signed by the foreign corporation, or other official proof of delivery or of the original envelope mailed. If a copy of the process is

mailed in accordance with this section, there shall be filed with the affidavit of compliance either the return receipt signed by such foreign corporation or other official proof of delivery or, if acceptance was refused by it, the original envelope with a notation by the postal authorities that acceptance was refused. If acceptance was refused, a copy of the notice and process together with notice of the mailing by registered mail and refusal to accept shall be promptly sent to such foreign corporation at the same address by ordinary mail and the affidavit of compliance shall so state. Service of process shall be complete ten days after such papers are filed with the clerk of the court. The refusal to accept delivery of the registered mail or to sign the return receipt shall not affect the validity of the service and such foreign corporation refusing to accept such registered mail shall be charged with knowledge of the contents thereof.

(d) Service made as provided in this section shall have the same force as personal service made within this state.

(e) Nothing in this section shall affect the right to serve process in any other manner permitted by law.

S 308. Records and certificates of department of state.

The department of state shall keep a record of each process served upon the secretary of state under this chapter, including the date of service. It shall, upon request made within ten years of such service, issue a certificate under its seal certifying as to the receipt of the process by an authorized person, the date and place of such service and the receipt of the statutory fee. Process served upon the secretary of state under this chapter shall be destroyed by him after a period of ten years from such service.

ARTICLE 4
FORMATION OF CORPORATIONS

S 401. Incorporators.

One or more natural persons of the age of eighteen years or over may act as incorporators of a corporation to be formed under this chapter.

S 402. Certificate of incorporation; contents.

(a) A certificate, entitled "Certificate of incorporation of (name of corporation) under section 402 of the Business Corporation Law", shall be signed by each incorporator, with his name and address included in such certificate and delivered to the department of state. It shall set forth:

(1) The name of the corporation.

(2) The purpose or purposes for which it is formed, it being sufficient to state, either alone or with other purposes, that the purpose of the corporation is to engage in any lawful act or activity for which corporations may be organized under this chapter, provided that it also state that it is not formed to engage in any act or activity requiring the consent or approval of any state official, department, board, agency or other body without such consent or approval first being obtained. By such statement all lawful acts and activities shall be within the purposes of the corporation, except for express limitations therein or in this chapter, if any.

(3) The county within this state in which the office of the corporation is to be located.

(4) The aggregate number of shares which the corporation shall have the authority to issue; if such shares are to consist of one class only, the par value of the shares or a statement that the shares are without par value; or, if the shares are to be divided into classes, the number of shares of each class and the par value of the shares having par value and a statement as to which shares, if any, are without par value.

(5) If the shares are to be divided into classes, the designation of each class and a statement of the relative rights, preferences and limitations of the shares of each class.

(6) If the shares of any preferred class are to be issued in series, the designation of each series and a statement of the variations in the relative rights, preferences and limitations as between series insofar as the same are to be fixed in the certificate of incorporation, a statement of any authority to be vested in the board to establish and designate series and to fix the variations in the relative rights, preferences and limitations as between series and a statement of any limit on the authority of the board of directors to change the number of shares of any series of preferred shares as provided in paragraph (e) of section 502 (Issue of any class of preferred shares in series).

(7) A designation of the secretary of state as agent of the corporation upon whom process against it may be served and the post office address within or without this state to which the secretary of state shall mail a copy of any process against it served upon him.

(8) If the corporation is to have a registered agent, his name and address within this state and a statement that the registered agent is to be the agent of the corporation upon whom process against it may be served.

(9) The duration of the corporation if other than perpetual.

(b) The certificate of incorporation may set forth a provision eliminating or limiting the personal liability of directors to the corporation or its shareholders for damages for any breach of duty in such capacity, provided that no such provision shall eliminate or limit:

(1) the liability of any director if a judgment or other final adjudication adverse to him establishes that his acts or omissions were in bad faith or involved intentional misconduct or a knowing violation of law or that he personally gained in fact a financial profit or other advantage to which he was not legally entitled or that his acts violated section 719, or

(2) the liability of any director for any act or omission prior to the adoption of a provision authorized by this paragraph.

(c) The certificate of incorporation may set forth any provision, not inconsistent with this chapter or any other statute of this state, relating to the business of the corporation, its affairs, its rights or powers, or the rights or powers of its shareholders, directors or officers including any provision relating to matters which under this chapter are required or permitted to be set forth in the by-laws. It is not necessary to set forth in the certificate of incorporation any of the powers enumerated in this chapter.

S 403. Certificate of incorporation; effect.

Upon the filing of the certificate of incorporation by the department of state, the corporate existence shall begin, and such certificate shall be conclusive evidence that all conditions precedent have been fulfilled and that the corporation has been formed under this chapter, except in an action or special proceeding brought by the attorney-general. Notwithstanding the above, a certificate of incorporation may set forth a date subsequent to filing, not to exceed ninety days after filing, upon which date corporate existence shall begin.

S 404. Organization meeting.

(a) After the corporate existence has begun, an organization meeting of the incorporator or incorporators shall be held within or without this state, for the purpose of adopting by-laws, electing directors to hold office until the first annual meeting of shareholders, except as authorized under section 704 (Classification of directors), and the transaction of such other business as may come before the meeting. If there are two or more incorporators, the meeting may be held at the call of any incorporator, who shall give at least five days' notice thereof by mail to each other incorporator, which notice shall set forth the time and place of the meeting. Notice need not be given to any incorporator who attends the meeting or submits a signed waiver of notice before or after the meeting. If there are more than two incorporators, a majority shall constitute a quorum and the act of the majority of the incorporators present at a meeting at which a quorum is present shall be the act of the incorporators. An incorporator may act in person or by proxy signed by the incorporator or his attorney-in-fact.

(b) Any action permitted to be taken at the organization meeting may be taken without a meeting if each incorporator or his attorney-in-fact signs an instrument setting forth the action so taken.

(c) If an incorporator dies or is for any reason unable to act, action may be taken as provided in such event in paragraph (c) of section 615 (Written consent of shareholders, subscribers or incorporators without a meeting).

S 405. Day care center for children; approval of certificate.

Every certificate of incorporation which includes among its corporate purposes the establishment or operation of a day care center for children shall have endorsed thereon or annexed thereto the approval of the state department of social services. S 405-a. Institution for children; approval of certificate. Every certificate of incorporation which includes among its corporate purposes, the authority to care for children through the establishment or operation of an institution for destitute, delinquent, abandoned, neglected or dependent children shall have endorsed thereon or annexed thereto the approval of the state department of social services. Provided, however, nothing herein shall authorize such corporation to place out or board out children, as those terms are defined in the social services law, or to care for children in a facility other than an institution possessing an operating certificate issued by the state department of social services.

S 406. Filing of a certificate of incorporation; facility for alcoholism or alcohol abuse.

Every certificate of incorporation which includes among its corporate purposes the establishment or operation of a program of services for alcoholism or alcohol abuse shall have endorsed thereon or annexed thereto the approval of the director of the state division of alcoholism and alcohol abuse.

S 407. Substance abuse program; consent to certificate.

Every certificate of incorporation which includes among the purposes of the corporation, the establishment or operation of a substance abuse program shall have endorsed thereon or annexed thereto the consent of the director of the division of substance abuse services to its filing by the department of state.

S 408. Biennial statement; filing.

(1) Each domestic corporation, and each foreign corporation authorized to do business in this state, shall, during the applicable filing period as determined by subdivision three of this section, file a statement setting forth:

(a) The name and respective business address of its chief executive officer.

(b) The street address of its principal executive office.

(c) The post office address within or without this state to which the secretary of state shall mail a copy of any process against it served upon him or her. Such address shall supersede any previous address on file with the department of state for this purpose.

(2) Such statement shall be made on forms prescribed by the secretary of state, and the information therein contained shall be given as of the date of the execution of the statement. Such statement shall only request reporting of information required under subdivision one of this section. It shall be signed, verified and delivered to the department of state.

(3) For the purpose of this section the applicable filing period for a corporation shall be the calendar month during which its original certificate of incorporation or application for authority were filed or the effective date thereof if stated. The applicable filing period shall only occur: (a) annually, during the period starting on April 1, 1992 and ending on March 31, 1994; and (b) biennially, during a period starting on April 1 and ending on March 31 thereafter. Those corporations that filed between April 1, 1992 and June 30, 1994 shall not be required to file such statements again until such time as they would have filed, had this subdivision not been amended.

(4) The provisions of subdivision eleven of section ninety-six of the executive law and paragraph (g) of section one hundred four of this chapter shall not be applicable to filings pursuant to this section.

(5) The provisions of this section and section 409 of this article shall not apply to a farm corporation. For the purposes of this subdivision, the term "farm corporation" shall mean any domestic corporation or foreign corporation authorized to do business in this state under this chapter engaged in the production of crops, livestock and livestock products on land used in agricultural production, as defined in section 301 of the agriculture and markets law.

(6) No such statement shall be accepted for filing when a certificate of resignation for receipt of process has been filed under section three hundred six-A of this chapter unless the corporation has stated a different address for process which does not include the name of the party previously designated in the address for process in such certificate.

S 409. Penalty for failure to file; cure.

(1) Each corporation which has failed to file its statement within the time required by this chapter after thirty days shall be shown to be past due on the records of the department of state.

(2) Each corporation which has failed to file its statement for two years shall be shown to be delinquent on the records of the department of state sixty days after a notice of delinquency has been mailed to the last known address of such corporation. Such delinquency shall be removed from the records of the department of state upon the filing of the current statement required by section four hundred eight of this article, and the payment of a fine of two hundred fifty dollars.

(3) The notice of delinquency shall state the cure and fine for such delinquency as determined by subdivision two of this section and the period during which such delinquency shall be forborne without the imposition of such fine.

ARTICLE 5
CORPORATE FINANCE

S 501. Authorized shares.

(a) Every corporation shall have power to create and issue the number of shares stated in its certificate of incorporation. Such shares may be all of one class or may be divided into two or more classes. Each class shall consist of either shares with par value or shares without par value, having such designation and such relative voting, dividend, liquidation and other rights, preferences and limitations, consistent with this chapter, as shall be stated in the certificate of incorporation. The certificate of incorporation may deny, limit or otherwise define the voting rights and may limit or otherwise define the dividend or liquidation rights of shares of any class, but no such denial, limitations or definition of voting rights shall be effective unless at the time one or more classes of outstanding shares or bonds, singly or in the aggregate, are entitled to full voting rights, and no such limitation or definition of dividend or liquidation rights shall be effective unless at the time one or more classes of outstanding shares, singly or in the aggregate, are entitled to unlimited dividend and liquidation rights.

(b) If the shares are divided into two or more classes, the shares of each class shall be designated to distinguish them from the shares of all other classes. Shares which are entitled to preference in the distribution of dividends or assets shall not be designated as common shares. Shares which are not entitled to preference in the distribution of dividends or assets shall be common shares, even if identified by a class or other designation, and shall not be designated as preferred shares.

(c) Subject to the designations, relative rights, preferences and limitations applicable to separate series and except as otherwise permitted by subparagraph two of paragraph (a) of section five hundred five of this article, each share shall be equal to every other share of the same class. With respect to corporations owning or leasing residential premises and operating the same on a cooperative basis, however, provided that (1) liquidation or other distribution rights are substantially equal per share, (2) changes in maintenance charges and general assessments pursuant to a proprietary lease have been and are hereafter fixed and determined on an equal per-share basis or on an equal per-room basis or as an equal percentage of the maintenance charges, and (3) voting rights are substantially equal per share or the certificate of incorporation provides that the shareholders holding the shares allocated to each apartment or dwelling unit owned by the corporation shall be entitled to one vote in the aggregate regardless of the number of shares allocated to the apartment or dwelling unit or the number of shareholders holding such shares, shares of the same class shall not be considered unequal because of variations in fees or charges payable to the corporation upon sale or transfer of shares and appurtenant proprietary leases that are provided for in proprietary leases, occupancy agreements or offering plans or properly approved amendments to the foregoing instruments.

S 502. Issue of any class of preferred shares in series.

(a) If the certificate of incorporation so provides, a corporation may issue any class of preferred shares in series. Shares of each such series when issued, shall be designated to distinguish them from shares of all other series.

(b) The number of shares included in any or all series of any classes of preferred shares and any or all of the designations, relative rights, preferences and limitations of any or all such series may be fixed in the certificate of incorporation, subject to the limitation that, unless the certificate of incorporation provides otherwise, if the stated dividends and amounts payable on liquidation are not paid in full, the shares of all series of the same class shall share ratable in the payment of dividends including accumulations, if any, in accordance with the sums which would be payable on such shares if all dividends were declared and paid in full, and in any distribution of assets other than by way of dividends in accordance with the sums which would be payable on such distribution if all sums payable were discharged in full.

(c) If any such number of shares or any such designation, relative right, preference or limitation of the shares of any series is not fixed in the certificate of incorporation, it may be fixed by the board, to the extent authorized by the certificate of incorporation. Unless otherwise provided in the certificate of incorporation, the number of preferred shares of any series so fixed by the board may be increased (but not above the total number of authorized shares of the class) or decreased (but not below the number of shares thereof then outstanding) by the board. In case the number of such shares shall be decreased, the number of shares by which the series is decreased shall, unless eliminated pursuant to paragraph (e) of this section, resume the status which they had prior to being designated as part of a series of preferred shares.

(d) Before the issue of any shares of a series established by the board, a certificate of amendment under section 805 (Certificate of amendment; contents) shall be delivered to the department of state. Such certificate shall set forth:

(1) The name of the corporation, and, if it has been changed, the name under which it was formed.

(2) The date the certificate of incorporation was filed by the department of state.

(3) That the certificate of incorporation is thereby amended by the addition of a provision stating the number, designation, relative rights, preferences, and limitations of the shares of the series as fixed by the board, setting forth in full the text of such provision.

(e) Action by the board to increase or decrease the number of preferred shares of any series pursuant to paragraph (c) of this section shall become effective by delivering to the department of state a certificate of amendment under section 805 (Certificate of amendment; contents) which shall set forth:

(1) The name of the corporation, and, if it has been changed, the name under which it was formed.

(2) The date its certificate of incorporation was filed with the department of state.

(3) That the certificate of incorporation is thereby amended to increase or decrease, as the case may be, the number of preferred shares of any series so fixed by the board, setting forth the specific terms of the amendment and the number of shares so authorized following the effectiveness of the amendment.

When no shares of any such series are outstanding, either because none were issued or because no issued shares of any such series remain outstanding, the certificate of amendment under section 805 may also set forth a statement that none of the authorized shares of such series are outstanding and that none will be issued subject to the certificate of incorporation, and, when such certificate becomes accepted for filing, it shall have the effect of eliminating from the certificate of incorporation all matters set forth therein with respect to such series of preferred shares.

S 503. Subscription for shares; time of payment, forfeiture for default.

(a) Unless otherwise provided by the terms of the subscription, a subscription for shares of a corporation to be formed shall be irrevocable, except with the consent of all other subscribers or the corporation, for a period of three months from its date.

(b) A subscription, whether made before or after the formation of a corporation, shall not be enforceable unless in writing and signed by the subscriber.

(c) Unless otherwise provided by the terms of the subscription, subscriptions for shares, whether made before or after the formation of a corporation, shall be paid in full at such time, or in such installments and at such times, as shall be determined by the board. Any call made by the board for payment on subscriptions shall be uniform as to all shares of the same class or of the same series. If a receiver of the corporation has been appointed, all unpaid subscriptions shall be paid at such times and in such installments as such receiver or the court may direct.

(d) In the event of default in the payment of any installment or call when due, the corporation may proceed to collect the amount due in the same manner as any debt due the corporation or the board may declare a forfeiture of the subscriptions. The subscription agreement may prescribe other penalties, not amounting to forfeiture, for failure to pay installments or calls that may become due. No forfeiture of the subscription shall be declared as against any subscriber unless the amount due thereon shall remain unpaid for a period of thirty days after written demand has been made therefor. If mailed, such written demand shall be deemed to be made when deposited in the United States mail in a sealed envelope addressed to the subscriber at his last post office address known to the corporation, with postage thereon prepaid. Upon forfeiture of the subscription, if at least fifty percent of the subscription price has been paid, the shares subscribed for shall be offered for sale for cash or a binding obligation to pay cash at a price at least sufficient to pay the full balance owed by the delinquent subscriber plus the expenses incidental to such sale, and any excess of net proceeds realized over the amount owed on such shares shall be paid to the delinquent subscriber or to his legal representative. If no prospective purchaser offers a cash price or a binding obligation to pay cash sufficient to pay the full balance owed by the delinquent subscriber plus the expenses incidental to such sale, or if less than fifty percent of the subscription price has been paid, the shares subscribed for shall be cancelled and restored to the status of authorized but unissued shares and all previous payments thereon shall be forfeited to the corporation and transferred to surplus.

(e) Notwithstanding the provisions of paragraph (d) of this section, in the event of default in payment or other performance under the instrument evidencing a subscriber's binding obligation to pay a portion of the subscription price or perform services, the corporation may pursue such remedies as are provided in such instrument or a related agreement or under law.

S 504. Consideration and payment for shares.

(a) Consideration for the issue of shares shall consist of money or other property, tangible or intangible; labor or services actually received by or performed for the corporation or for its benefit or in its formation or reorganization; a binding obligation to pay the purchase price or the subscription price in cash or other property; a binding obligation to perform services having an agreed value; or a combination thereof. In the absence of fraud in the transaction, the judgment of the board or shareholders, as the case may be, as to the value of the consideration received for shares shall be conclusive.

****

(c) Shares with par value may be issued for such consideration, not less than the par value thereof, as is fixed from time to time by the board.

(d) Shares without par value may be issued for such consideration as is fixed from time to time by the board unless the certificate of incorporation reserves to the shareholders the right to fix the consideration. If such right is reserved as to any shares, a vote of the shareholders shall either fix the consideration to be received for the shares or authorize the board to fix such consideration.

(e) Treasury shares may be disposed of by a corporation on such terms and conditions as are fixed from time to time by the board.

(f) Upon distribution of authorized but unissued shares to shareholders, that part of the surplus of a corporation which is concurrently transferred to stated capital shall be the consideration for the issue of such shares.

(g) In the event of a conversion of bonds or shares into shares, or in the event of an exchange of bonds or shares for shares, with or without par value, the consideration for the shares so issued in exchange or conversion shall be the sum of (1) either the principal sum of, and accrued interest on, the bonds so exchanged or converted, or the stated capital then represented by the shares so exchanged or converted, plus (2) any additional consideration paid to the corporation for the new shares, plus (3) any stated capital not theretofore allocated to any designated class or series which is thereupon allocated to the new shares, plus (4) any surplus thereupon transferred to stated capital and allocated to the new shares.

(h) Certificates for shares may not be issued until the amount of the consideration therefor determined to be stated capital pursuant to section 506 (Determination of stated capital) has been paid in the form of cash, services rendered, personal or real property or a combination thereof and consideration for the balance (if any) complying with paragraph (a) of this section has been provided, except as provided in paragraphs (e) and (f) of section 505 (Rights and options to purchase shares; issue of rights and options to directors, officers and employees).

(i) When the consideration for shares has been provided in compliance with paragraph (h) of this section, the subscriber shall be entitled to all the rights and privileges of a holder of such shares and to a certificate representing his shares, and such shares shall be fully paid and nonassessable.

(j) Notwithstanding that such shares may be fully paid and nonassessable, the corporation may place in escrow shares issued for a binding obligation to pay cash or other property or to perform future services, or make other arrangements to restrict the transfer of the shares, and may credit distributions in respect of the shares against the obligation, until the obligation is performed. If the obligation is not performed in whole or in part, the corporation may pursue such remedies as are provided in the instrument evidencing the obligation or a related agreement or under law.

S 505. Rights and options to purchase shares; issue of rights and options to directors, officers and employees.

(a) (1) Except as otherwise provided in this section or in the certificate of incorporation, a corporation may create and issue, whether or not in connection with the issue and sale of any of its shares or bonds, rights or options entitling the holders thereof to purchase from the corporation, upon such consideration, terms and conditions as may be fixed by the board, shares of any class or series, whether authorized but unissued shares, treasury shares or shares to be purchased or acquired or assets of the corporation.

    (2) (i) In the case of a domestic corporation that has a class of voting stock registered with the Securities and Exchange Commission pursuant to section twelve of the Exchange Act, the terms and conditions of such rights or options may include, without limitation, restrictions or conditions that preclude or limit the exercise, transfer or receipt of such rights or options by an interested shareholder or any transferee of any such interested shareholder or that invalidate or void such rights or options held by any such interested shareholder or any such transferee. For the purpose of this subparagraph, the terms "voting stock", "Exchange Act" and "interested shareholder" shall have the same meanings as set forth in section nine hundred twelve of this chapter;

        (ii) Determinations of the board of directors whether to impose, enforce or waive or otherwise render ineffective such limitations or conditions as are permitted by clause (i) of this subparagraph shall be subject to judicial review in an appropriate proceeding in which the courts formulate or apply appropriate standards in order to insure that such limitations or conditions are imposed, enforced or waived in the best long-term interests and short-term interests of the corporation and its shareholders considering, without limitation, the prospects for potential growth, development, productivity and profitability of the corporation.

(b) The consideration for shares to be purchased under any such right or option shall comply with the requirements of section 504 (Consideration and payment for shares).

(c) The terms and conditions of such rights or options, including the time or times at or within which and the price or prices at which they may be exercised and any limitations upon transferability, shall be set forth or incorporated by reference in the instrument or instruments evidencing such rights or options.

(d) The issue of such rights or options to one or more directors, officers or employees of the corporation or a subsidiary or affiliate thereof, as an incentive to service or continued service with the corporation, a subsidiary or affiliate thereof, or to a trustee on behalf of such directors, officers or employees, shall be authorized by a majority of the votes cast at a meeting of shareholders by the holders of shares entitled to vote thereon, or authorized by and consistent with a plan adopted by such vote of shareholders. If, under the certificate of incorporation, there are preemptive rights to any of the shares to be thus subject to rights or options to purchase, either such issue or such plan, if any shall also be approved by the vote or written consent of the holders of a majority of the shares entitled to exercise preemptive rights with respect to such shares and such vote or written consent shall operate to release the preemptive rights with respect thereto of the holders of all the shares that were entitled to exercise such preemptive rights. In the absence of preemptive rights, nothing in this paragraph shall require shareholder approval for the issuance of rights or options to purchase shares of the corporation in substitution for, or upon the assumption of, rights or options issued by another corporation, if such substitution or assumption is in connection with such other corporation's merger or consolidation with, or the acquisition of its shares or all or part of its assets by, the corporation or its subsidiary.

(e) A plan adopted by the shareholders for the issue of rights or options to directors, officers or employees shall include the material terms and conditions upon which such rights or options are to be issued, such as, but without limitation thereof, any restrictions on the number of shares that eligible individuals may have the right or option to purchase, the method of administering the plan, the terms and conditions of payment for shares in full or in installments, the issue of certificates for shares to be paid for in installments, any limitations upon the transferability of such shares and the voting and dividend rights to which the holders of such shares may be entitled, though the full amount of the consideration therefor has not been paid; provided that under this section no certificate for shares shall be delivered to a shareholder, prior to full payment therefor, unless the fact that the shares are partly paid is noted conspicuously on the face or back of such certificate.

(f) If there is shareholder approval for the issue of rights or options to individual directors, officers or employees, but not under an approved plan under paragraph (e), the terms and conditions of issue set forth in paragraph (e) shall be permissible except that the grantees of such rights or options shall not be granted voting or dividend rights until the consideration for the shares to which they are entitled under such rights or options has been fully paid.

(g) If there is shareholder approval for the issue of rights and options, such approval may provide that the board is authorized by certificate of amendment under section 805 (Certificate of amendment; contents) to increase the authorized shares of any class or series to such number as will be sufficient, when added to the previously authorized but unissued shares of such class or series, to satisfy any such rights or options entitling the holders thereof to purchase from the corporation authorized but unissued shares of such class or series.

(h) In the absence of fraud in the transaction, the judgment of the board shall be conclusive as to the adequacy of the consideration, tangible or intangible, received or to be received by the corporation for the issue of rights or options for the purchase from the corporation of its shares. (i) The provisions of this section are inapplicable to the rights of the holders of convertible shares or bonds to acquire shares upon the exercise of conversion privileges under section 519 (Convertible shares and bonds).

S 506. Determination of stated capital.

(a) Upon issue by a corporation of shares with a par value, the consideration received therefor shall constitute stated capital to the extent of the par value of such shares.

(b) Upon issue by a corporation of shares without par value, the entire consideration received therefor shall constitute stated capital unless the board within a period of sixty days after issue allocates to surplus a portion, but not all, of the consideration received for such shares. No such allocation shall be made of any portion of the consideration received for shares without par value having a preference in the assets of the corporation upon involuntary liquidation except all or part of the amount, if any, of such consideration in excess of such preference, nor shall such allocation be made of any portion of the consideration for the issue of shares without par value which is fixed by the shareholders pursuant to a right reserved in the certificate of incorporation, unless such allocation is authorized by vote of the shareholders.

(c) The stated capital of a corporation may be increased from time to time by resolution of the board transferring all or part of the surplus of the corporation to stated capital. The board may direct that the amount so transferred shall be stated capital in respect of any designated class or series of shares. Compensation for formation, reorganization and financing. The reasonable charges and expenses of formation or reorganization of a corporation, and the reasonable expenses of and compensation for the sale or underwriting of its shares may be paid or allowed by the corporation out of the consideration received by it in payment for its shares without thereby impairing the fully paid and nonassessable status of such shares.

S 508. Certificates representing shares.

(a) The shares of a corporation shall be represented by certificates or shall be uncertificated shares. Certificates shall be signed by the chairman or a vice-chairman of the board or the president or a vice-president and the secretary or an assistant secretary or the treasurer or an assistant treasurer of the corporation, and may be sealed with the seal of the corporation or a facsimile thereof. The signatures of the officers upon a certificate may be facsimiles if: (1) the certificate is countersigned by a transfer agent or registered by a registrar other than the corporation itself or its employee, or (2) the shares are listed on a registered national security exchange. In case any officer who has signed or whose facsimile signature has been placed upon a certificate shall have ceased to be such officer before such certificate is issued, it may be issued by the corporation with the same effect as if he were such officer at the date of issue.

(b) Each certificate representing shares issued by a corporation which is authorized to issue shares of more than one class shall set forth upon the face or back of the certificate, or shall state that the corporation will furnish to any shareholder upon request and without charge, a full statement of the designation, relative rights, preferences and limitations of the shares of each class authorized to be issued and, if the corporation is authorized to issue any class of preferred shares in series, the designation, relative rights, preferences and limitations of each such series so far as the same have been fixed and the authority of the board to designate and fix the relative rights, preferences and limitations of other series.

(c) Each certificate representing shares shall state upon the face thereof: (1) That the corporation is formed under the laws of this state. (2) The name of the person or persons to whom issued. (3) The number and class of shares, and the designation of the series, if any, which such certificate represents.

(d) Shares shall be transferable in the manner provided by law and in the by-laws.

(e) The corporation may issue a new certificate for shares in place of any certificate theretofore issued by it, alleged to have been lost or destroyed, and the board may require the owner of the lost or destroyed certificate, or his legal representative, to give the corporation a bond sufficient to indemnify the corporation against any claim that may be made against it on account of the alleged loss or destruction of any such certificate or the issuance of any such new certificate.

(f) Unless otherwise provided by the articles of incorporation or by-laws, the board of directors of a corporation may provide by resolution that some or all of any or all classes and series of its shares shall be uncertificated shares, provided that such resolution shall not apply to shares represented by a certificate until such certificate is surrendered to the corporation. Within a reasonable time after the issuance or transfer of uncertificated shares, the corporation shall send to the registered owner thereof a written notice containing the information required to be set forth or stated on certificates pursuant to paragraphs (b) and (c) of this section. Except as otherwise expressly provided by law, the rights and obligations of the holders of uncertificated shares and the rights and obligations of the holders of certificates representing shares of the same class and series shall be identical.

S 509. Fractions of a share or scrip authorized.

(a) A corporation may, but shall not be obliged to, issue fractions of a share either represented by a certificate or uncertificated, which shall entitle the holder, in proportion to his fractional holdings, to exercise voting rights, receive dividends and participate in liquidating distributions.

(b) As an alternative, a corporation may pay in cash the fair value of fractions of a share as of the time when those entitled to receive such fractions are determined.

(c) As an alternative, a corporation may issue scrip in registered or bearer form over the manual or facsimile signature of an officer of the corporation or of its agent, exchangeable as therein provided for full shares, but such scrip shall not entitle the holder to any rights of a shareholder except as therein provided. Such scrip may be issued subject to the condition that it shall become void if not exchanged for certificates representing full shares or uncertificated full shares before a specified date, or subject to the condition that the shares for which such scrip is exchangeable may be sold by the corporation and the proceeds thereof distributed to the holders of such scrip, or subject to any other conditions which the board may determine.

(d) A corporation may provide reasonable opportunity for persons entitled to fractions of a share or scrip to sell such fractions of a share or scrip or to purchase such additional fractions of a share or scrip as may be needed to acquire a full share.

S 510. Dividends or other distributions in cash or property.

(a) A corporation may declare and pay dividends or make other distributions in cash or its bonds or its property, including the shares or bonds of other corporations, on its outstanding shares, except when currently the corporation is insolvent or would thereby be made insolvent, or when the declaration, payment or distribution would be contrary to any restrictions contained in the certificate of incorporation.

(b) Dividends may be declared or paid and other distributions may be made out of surplus only, so that the net assets of the corporation remaining after such declaration, payment or distribution shall at least equal the amount of its stated capital; except that a corporation engaged in the exploitation of natural resources or other wasting assets, including patents, or formed primarily for the liquidation of specific assets, may declare and pay dividends or make other distributions in excess of its surplus, computed after taking due account of depletion and amortization, to the extent that the cost of the wasting or specific assets has been recovered by depletion reserves, amortization or sale, if the net assets remaining after such dividends or distributions are sufficient to cover the liquidation preferences of shares having such preferences in involuntary liquidation.

S 511. Share distributions and changes.

(a) A corporation may make pro rata distributions of its authorized but unissued shares to holders of any class or series of its outstanding shares, subject to the following conditions:

(1) If a distribution of shares having a par value is made, such shares shall be issued at not less than the par value thereof and there shall be transferred to stated capital at the time of such distribution an amount of surplus equal to the aggregate par value of such shares.

(2) If a distribution of shares without par value is made, the amount of stated capital to be represented by each such share shall be fixed by the board, unless the certificate of incorporation reserves to the shareholders the right to fix the consideration for the issue of such shares, and there shall be transferred to stated capital at the time of such distribution an amount of surplus equal to the aggregate stated capital represented by such shares.

(3) A distribution of shares of any class or series may be made to holders of the same or any other class or series of shares unless the certificate of incorporation provides otherwise, provided, however, that in the case of a corporation incorporated prior to the effective date of subparagraph. (4) of this paragraph, then so long as any shares of such class remain outstanding a distribution of shares of any class or series of shares of such corporation may be made only to holders of the same class or series of shares unless the certificate of incorporation permits distribution to holders of another class or series, or unless such distribution is approved by the affirmative vote or the written consent of the holders of a majority of the

outstanding shares of the class or series to be distributed.

(4) A distribution of any class or series of shares shall be subject to the preemptive rights, if any, applicable to such shares pursuant to this chapter.

(b) A corporation making a pro rata distribution of authorized but unissued shares to the holders of any class or series of outstanding shares may at its option make an equivalent distribution upon treasury shares of the same class or series, and any shares so distributed shall be treasury shares.

(c) A change of issued shares of any class which increases the stated capital represented by those shares may be made if the surplus of the corporation is sufficient to permit the transfer, and a transfer is concurrently made, from surplus to stated capital, of an amount equal to such increase.

(d) No transfer from surplus to stated capital need be made by a corporation making a distribution of its treasury shares to holders of any class of outstanding shares; nor upon a split up or division of issued shares of any class into a greater number of shares of the same class, or a combination of issued shares of any class into a lesser number of shares of the same class, if there is no increase in the aggregate stated capital represented by them.

(e) Nothing in this section shall prevent a corporation from making other transfers from surplus to stated capital in connection with share distributions or otherwise.

(f) Every distribution to shareholders of certificates representing a share distribution or a change of shares which affects stated capital or surplus shall be accompanied by a written notice (1) disclosing the amounts by which such distribution or change affects stated capital and surplus, or (2) if such amounts are not determinable at the time of such notice, disclosing the approximate effect of such distribution or change upon stated capital and surplus and stating that such amounts are not yet determinable.

(g) When issued shares are changed in any manner which affects stated capital or surplus, and no distribution to shareholders of certificates representing any shares resulting from such change is made, disclosure of the effect of such change upon the stated capital and surplus shall be made in the next financial statement covering the period in which such change is made that is furnished by the corporation to holders of shares of the class or series so changed or, if practicable, in the first notice of dividend or share distribution or change that is furnished to such shareholders between the date of the change of shares and the next such financial statement, and in any event within six months of the date of such change.

S 512. Redeemable shares.

(a) Subject to the restrictions contained in section 513 (Purchase, redemption and certain other transactions by a corporation with respect to its own shares) and paragraph (b) of this section, a corporation may provide in its certificate of incorporation for one or more classes or series of shares which are redeemable, in whole or in part, at the option of the corporation, the holder or another person or upon the happening of a specified event.

(b) No redeemable common shares, other than shares of an open-end investment company, as defined in an act of congress entitled "Investment Company Act of 1940", as amended, or of a member corporation of a national securities exchange registered under a statute of the United States such as the Securities Exchange Act of 1934, as amended, or of a corporation described in this paragraph, shall be issued or redeemed unless the corporation at the time has outstanding a class of common shares that is not subject to redemption. Any common shares of a corporation which directly or through a subsidiary has a license or franchise to conduct its business, which license or franchise is conditioned upon some or all of the holders of such corporation's common shares possessing prescribed qualifications, may be made subject to redemption by the corporation to the extent necessary to prevent the loss of, or to reinstate, such license or franchise.

(c) Shares of any class or series which may be made redeemable under this section may be redeemed for cash, other property, indebtedness or other securities of the same or another corporation, at such time or times, price or prices, or rate or rates, and with such adjustments, as shall be stated in the certificate of incorporation.

(d) Nothing in this section shall prevent a corporation from creating sinking funds for the redemption or purchase of its shares to the extent permitted by section 513 (Purchase, redemption and certain other transactions by a corporation with respect to its own shares).

S 513. Purchase, redemption and certain other transactions by a corporation with respect to its own shares.

(a) Notwithstanding any authority contained in the certificate of incorporation, the shares of a corporation may not be purchased by the corporation, or, if redeemable, convertible or exchangeable shares, may not be redeemed, converted or exchanged, in each case for or into cash, other property, indebtedness or other securities of the corporation (other than shares of the corporation and rights to acquire such shares) if the corporation is then insolvent or would thereby be made insolvent. Shares may be purchased or redeemed only out of surplus.

(b) When its redeemable, convertible or exchangeable shares are purchased by the corporation within the period during which such shares may be redeemed, converted or exchanged at the option of the corporation, the purchase price thereof shall not exceed the applicable redemption, conversion or exchange price stated in the certificate of incorporation. Upon a redemption, conversion or exchange, the amount payable by the corporation for shares having a cumulative preference on dividends may include the stated redemption, conversion or exchange price plus accrued dividends to the next dividend date following the date of redemption, conversion or exchange of such shares.

(c) No domestic corporation which is subject to the provisions of section nine hundred twelve of this chapter shall purchase or agree to purchase more than ten percent of the stock of the corporation from a shareholder for more than the market value thereof unless such purchase or agreement to purchase is approved by the affirmative vote of the board of directors and a majority of the votes of all outstanding shares entitled to vote thereon at a meeting of shareholders unless the certificate of incorporation requires a greater percentage of the votes of the outstanding shares to approve. The provisions of this paragraph shall not apply when the corporation offers to purchase shares from all holders of stock or for stock which the holder has been the beneficial owner of for more than two years. The terms "stock," "beneficial owner," and "market value" shall be as defined in section nine hundred twelve of this chapter.

S 514. Agreements for purchase by a corporation of its own shares.

(a) An agreement for the purchase by a corporation of its own shares shall be enforceable by the shareholder and the corporation to the extent such purchase is permitted at the time of purchase by section 513 (purchase or redemption by a corporation of its own shares).

(b) The possibility that a corporation may not be able to purchase its shares under section 513 shall not be a ground for denying to either party specific performance of an agreement for the purchase by a corporation of its own shares, if at the time for performance the corporation can purchase all or part of such shares under section 513.

S 515. Reacquired shares.

(a) Shares that have been issued and have been purchased, redeemed or otherwise reacquired by a corporation shall be cancelled if they are reacquired out of stated capital, or if they are converted shares, or if the certificate of incorporation requires that such shares be cancelled upon reacquisition.

(b) Any shares reacquired by the corporation and not required to be cancelled may be either retained as treasury shares or cancelled by the board at the time of reacquisition or at any time thereafter.

(c) Neither the retention of reacquired shares as treasury shares, nor their subsequent distribution to shareholders or disposition for a consideration shall change the stated capital. When treasury shares are disposed of for a consideration, the surplus shall be increased by the full amount of the consideration received.

(d) Shares cancelled under this section are restored to the status of authorized but unissued shares. However, if the certificate of incorporation prohibits the reissue of any shares required or permitted to be cancelled under this section, the board by certificate of amendment under section 805 (Certificate of amendment; contents) shall reduce the number of authorized shares accordingly.

S 516. Reduction of stated capital in certain cases.

(a) Except as otherwise provided in the certificate of incorporation, the board may at any time reduce the stated capital of a corporation in any of the following ways: (1) by eliminating from stated capital any portion of amounts previously transferred by the board from surplus to stated capital and not allocated to any designated class or series of shares; (2) by reducing or eliminating any amount of stated capital represented by issued shares having a par value which exceeds the aggregate par value of such shares; (3) by reducing the amount of stated capital represented by issued shares without par value; or (4) by applying to an otherwise authorized purchase, redemption, conversion or exchange of outstanding shares some or all of the stated capital represented by the shares being purchased, redeemed, converted or exchanged, or some or all of any stated capital that has not been allocated to any particular shares, or both. Notwithstanding the foregoing, if the consideration for the issue of shares without par value was fixed by the shareholders under section 504 (Consideration and payment for shares), the board shall not reduce the stated capital represented by such shares except to the extent, if any, that the board was authorized by the shareholders to allocate any portion of such consideration to surplus.

(b) No reduction of stated capital shall be made under this section unless after such reduction the stated capital exceeds the aggregate preferential amounts payable upon involuntary liquidation upon all issued shares having preferential rights in the assets plus the par value of all other issued shares with par value.

(c) When a reduction of stated capital has been effected under this section, the amount of such reduction shall be disclosed in the next financial statement covering the period in which such reduction is made that is furnished by the corporation to all its shareholders or, if practicable, in the first notice of dividend or share distribution that is furnished to the holders of each class or series of its shares between the date of such reduction and the next such financial statement, and in any event to all its shareholders within six months of the date of such reduction.

S 518. Corporate bonds.

(a) No corporation shall issue bonds except for money or other property, tangible or intangible; labor or services actually received by or performed for the corporation or for its benefit or in its formation or reorganization; a binding obligation to pay the purchase price thereof in cash or other property; a binding obligation to perform services having an agreed value; or a combination thereof. In the absence of fraud in the transaction, the judgment of the board as to the value of the consideration received shall be conclusive.

(b) If a distribution of its own bonds is made by a corporation to holders of any class or series of its outstanding shares, there shall be concurrently transferred to the liabilities of the corporation in respect of such bonds an amount of surplus equal to the principal amount of, and any accrued interest on, such bonds. The amount of the surplus so transferred shall be the consideration for the issue of such bonds.

(c) A corporation may, in its certificate of incorporation, confer upon the holders of any bonds issued or to be issued by the corporation, rights to inspect the corporate books and records and to vote in the election of directors and on any other matters on which shareholders of the corporation may vote.

S 519. Convertible or exchangeable shares and bonds.

(a) Unless otherwise provided in the certificate of incorporation, and subject to the restrictions in section 513 (Purchase, redemption and certain other transactions by a corporation with respect to its own shares) and paragraphs (c) and (d) of this section, a corporation may issue shares or bonds convertible into or exchangeable for, at the option of the holder, the corporation or another person, or upon the happening of a specified event, shares of any class or shares of any series of any class or cash, other property, indebtedness or other securities of the same or another corporation.

(b) If there is shareholder approval for the issue of bonds or shares convertible into, or exchangeable for, shares of the corporation, such approval may provide that the board is authorized by certificate of amendment under section 805 (Certificate of amendment; contents) to increase the authorized shares of any class or series to such number as will be sufficient, when added to the previously authorized but unissued shares of such class or series, to satisfy the conversion or exchange privileges of any such bonds or shares convertible into, or exchangeable for, shares of such class or series.

(c) No issue of bonds or shares convertible into, or exchangeable for, shares of the corporation shall be made unless: (1) A sufficient number of authorized but unissued shares, or treasury shares, of the appropriate class or series are reserved by the board to be issued only in satisfaction of the conversion or exchange privileges of such convertible or exchangeable bonds or shares when issued; (2) The aggregate conversion or exchange privileges of such convertible or exchangeable bonds or shares when issued do not exceed the aggregate gate of any shares reserved under subparagraph (1) and any additional shares which may be authorized by the board under paragraph (b); or (3) In the case of the conversion or exchange of shares of common stock other than into other shares of common stock, there remains outstanding a class or series of common stock not subject to conversion or exchange other than into other shares of common stock, except in the case of corporations of the type described in the exceptions to the provisions of paragraph (b) of section 512 (Redeemable shares).

(d) No privilege of conversion may be conferred upon, or altered in respect to, any shares or bonds that would result in the receipt by the corporation of less than the minimum consideration required to be received upon the issue of new shares. The consideration for shares issued upon the exercise of a conversion or exchange privilege shall be that provided in paragraph (g) of section 504 (Consideration and payment for shares).

(e) When shares have been converted or exchanged, they shall be cancelled. When bonds have been converted or exchanged, they shall be cancelled and not reissued except upon compliance with the provisions governing the issue of convertible or exchangeable bonds.

S 520. Liability for failure to disclose required information.

Failure of the corporation to comply in good faith with the notice or disclosure provisions of paragraphs (f) and (g) of section 511 (Share distributions and changes), or paragraph (c) of section 516 (Reduction of stated capital in certain cases), shall make the corporation liable for any damage sustained by any shareholder in consequence thereof.

ARTICLE 6
SHAREHOLDERS

S 601. By-laws.

(a) The initial by-laws of a corporation shall be adopted by its incorporator or incorporators at the organization meeting. Thereafter, subject to section 613 (Limitations on right to vote), by-laws may be adopted, amended or repealed by a majority of the votes cast by the shares at the time entitled to vote in the election of any directors. When so provided in the certificate of incorporation or a by-law adopted by the shareholders, by-laws may also be adopted, amended or repealed by the board by such vote as may be therein specified, which may be greater than the vote otherwise prescribed by this chapter, but any by-law adopted by the board may be amended or repealed by the shareholders entitled to vote thereon as herein provided. Any reference in this chapter to a "by-law adopted by the shareholders" shall include a by-law adopted by the incorporator or incorporators.

(b) The by-laws may contain any provision relating to the business of the corporation, the conduct of its affairs, its rights or powers or the rights or powers of its shareholders, directors or officers, not inconsistent with this chapter or any other statute of this state or the certificate of incorporation.

S 602. Meetings of shareholders.

(a) Meetings of shareholders may be held at such place, within or without this state, as may be fixed by or under the by-laws, or if not so fixed, at the office of the corporation in this state.

(b) A meeting of shareholders shall be held annually for the election of directors and the transaction of other business on a date fixed by or under the by-laws. A failure to hold the annual meeting on the date so fixed or to elect a sufficient number of directors to conduct the business of the corporation shall not work a forfeiture or give cause for dissolution of the corporation, except as provided in paragraph (c) of section 1104 (Petition in case of deadlock among directors or shareholders).

(c) Special meetings of the shareholders may be called by the board and by such person or persons as may be so authorized by the certificate of incorporation or the by-laws. At any such special meeting only such business may be transacted which is related to the purpose or purposes set forth in the notice required by section 605 (Notice of meetings of shareholders).

(d) Except as otherwise required by this chapter, the by-laws may designate reasonable procedures for the calling and conduct of a meeting of shareholders, including but not limited to specifying: (i) who may call and who may conduct the meeting, (ii) the means by which the order of business to be conducted shall be established, (iii) the procedures and requirements for the nomination of directors, (iv) the procedures with respect to the making of shareholder proposals, and (v) the procedures to be established for the adjournment of any meeting of shareholders. No amendment of the by-laws pertaining to the election of directors or the procedures for the calling and conduct of a meeting of shareholders shall affect the election of directors or the procedures for the calling or conduct in respect of any meeting of shareholders unless adequate notice thereof is given to the shareholders in a manner reasonably calculated to provide shareholders with sufficient time to respond thereto prior to such meeting.

S 603. Special meeting for election of directors.

(a) If, for a period of one month after the date fixed by or under the by-laws for the annual meeting of shareholders, or if no date has been so fixed, for a period of thirteen months after the formation of the corporation or the last annual meeting, there is a failure to elect a sufficient number of directors to conduct the business of the corporation, the board shall call a special meeting for the election of directors. If such special meeting is not called by the board within two weeks after the expiration of such period or if it is so called but there is a failure to elect such directors for a period of two months after the expiration of such period, holders of ten percent of the votes of the shares entitled to vote in an election of directors may, in writing, demand the call of a special meeting for the election of directors specifying the date and month thereof, which shall not be less than sixty nor more than ninety days from the date of such written demand. The secretary of the corporation upon receiving the written demand shall promptly give notice of such meeting, or if he fails to do so within five business days thereafter, any shareholder signing such demand may give such notice. The meeting shall be held at the place fixed in the by-laws or, if not so fixed, at the office of the corporation.

(b) At any such special meeting called on demand of shareholders, notwithstanding section 608 (Quorum of shareholders), the shareholders attending, in person or by proxy, and entitled to vote in an election of directors shall constitute a quorum for the purpose of electing directors, but not for the transaction of any other business.

S 604. Fixing record date.

(a) For the purpose of determining the shareholders entitled to notice of or to vote at any meeting of shareholders or any adjournment thereof, or to express consent to or dissent from any proposal without a meeting, or for the purpose of determining shareholders entitled to receive payment of any dividend or the allotment of any rights, or for the purpose of any other action, the by-laws may provide for fixing or, in the absence of such provision, the board may fix, in advance, a date as the record date for any such determination of shareholders. Such date shall not be more than sixty nor less than ten days before the date of such meeting, nor more than sixty days prior to any other action.

(b) If no record date is fixed:

(1) The record date for the determination of shareholders entitled to notice of or to vote at a meeting of shareholders shall be at the close of business on the day next preceding the day on which notice is given, or, if no notice is given, the day on which the meeting is held.

(2) The record date for determining shareholders for any purpose other than that specified in

subparagraph (1) shall be at the close of business on the day on which the resolution of the board relating thereto is adopted.

(c) When a determination of shareholders of record entitled to notice of or to vote at any meeting of shareholders has been made as provided in this section, such determination shall apply to any adjournment thereof, unless the board fixes a new record date under this section for the adjourned meeting.

S 605. Notice of meetings of shareholders.

(a) Whenever under the provisions of this chapter shareholders are required or permitted to take any action at a meeting, written notice shall be given stating the place, date and hour of the meeting and, unless it is the annual meeting, indicating that it is being issued by or at the direction of the person or persons calling the meeting. Notice of a special meeting shall also state the purpose or purposes for which the meeting is called. If, at any meeting, action is proposed to be taken which would, if taken, entitle shareholders fulfilling the requirements of section 623 (Procedure to enforce shareholder's right to receive payment for shares) to receive payment for their shares, the notice of such meeting shall include a statement of that purpose and to that effect and shall be accompanied by a copy of section 623 or an outline of its material terms. A copy of the notice of any meeting shall be given, personally or by first class mail, not fewer than ten nor more than sixty days before the date of the meeting, provided, however, that a copy of such notice may be given by third class mail not fewer than twenty-four nor more than sixty days before the date of the meeting, to each shareholder entitled to vote at such meeting. If mailed, such notice is given when deposited in the United States mail, with postage thereon prepaid, directed to the shareholder at his address as it appears on the record of shareholders, or, if he shall have filed with the secretary of the corporation a written request that notices to him be mailed to some other address, then directed to him at such other address. An affidavit of the secretary or other person giving the notice or of a transfer agent of the corporation that the notice required by this section has been given shall, in the absence of fraud, be prima facie evidence of the facts therein stated.

(b) When a meeting is adjourned to another time or place, it shall not be necessary, unless the by-laws require otherwise, to give any notice of the adjourned meeting if the time and place to which the meeting is adjourned are announced at the meeting at which the adjournment is taken, and at the adjourned meeting any business may be transacted that might have been transacted on the original date of the meeting. However, if after the adjournment the board fixes a new record date for the adjourned meeting, a notice of the adjourned meeting shall be given to each shareholder of record on the new record date entitled to notice under paragraph (a).

S 606. Waivers of notice.

Notice of meeting need not be given to any shareholder who submits a signed waiver of notice, in person or by proxy, whether before or after the meeting. The attendance of any shareholder at a meeting, in person or by proxy, without protesting prior to the conclusion of the meeting the lack of notice of such meeting, shall constitute a waiver of notice by him.

S 607. List of shareholders at meetings.

A list of shareholders as of the record date, certified by the corporate officer responsible for its preparation or by a transfer agent, shall be produced at any meeting of shareholders upon the request thereat or prior thereto of any shareholder. If the right to vote at any meeting is challenged, the inspectors of election, or person presiding thereat, shall require such list of shareholders to be produced as evidence of the right of the persons challenged to vote at such meeting, and all persons who appear from such list to be shareholders entitled to vote thereat may vote at such meeting.

S 608. Quorum of shareholders.

(a) The holders of a majority of the votes of shares entitled to vote thereat shall constitute a quorum at a meeting of shareholders for the transaction of any business, provided that when a specified item of business is required to be voted on by a particular class or series of shares, voting as a class, the holders of a majority of the votes of shares of such class or series shall constitute a quorum for the transaction of such specified item of business.

(b) The certificate of incorporation or by-laws may provide for any lesser quorum not less than one-third of the votes of shares entitled to vote, and the certificate of incorporation may, under section 616 (Greater requirement as to quorum and vote of shareholders), provide for a greater quorum.

(c) When a quorum is once present to organize a meeting, it is not broken by the subsequent withdrawal of any shareholders.

(d) The shareholders present may adjourn the meeting despite the absence of a quorum.

S 609. Proxies.

(a) Every shareholder entitled to vote at a meeting of shareholders or to express consent or dissent without a meeting may authorize another person or persons to act for him by proxy.

(b) No proxy shall be valid after the expiration of eleven months from the date thereof unless otherwise provided in the proxy. Every proxy shall be revocable at the pleasure of the shareholder executing it, except as otherwise provided in this section.

(c) The authority of the holder of a proxy to act shall not be revoked by the incompetence or death of the shareholder who executed the proxy unless, before the authority is exercised, written notice of an adjudication of such incompetence or of such death is received by the corporate officer responsible for maintaining the list of shareholders.

(d) Except when other provision shall have been made by written agreement between the parties, the record holder of shares which he holds as pledgee or otherwise as security or which belong to another, shall issue to the pledgor or to such owner of such shares, upon demand therefor and payment of necessary expenses thereof, a proxy to vote or take other action thereon.

(e) A shareholder shall not sell his vote or issue a proxy to vote to any person for any sum of money or anything of value, except as authorized in this section and section 620 (Agreements as to voting; provision in certificate of incorporation as to control of directors); provided, however, that this paragraph shall not apply to votes, proxies or consents given by holders of preferred shares in connection with a proxy or consent solicitation made available on identical terms to all holders of shares of the same class or series and remaining open for acceptance for at least twenty business days.

(f) A proxy which is entitled "irrevocable proxy" and which states that it is irrevocable, is irrevocable when it is held by any of the following or a nominee of any of the following:
  (1) A pledgee;
  (2) A person who has purchased or agreed to purchase the shares;
  (3) A creditor or creditors of the corporation who extend or continue credit to the corporation in consideration of the proxy if the proxy states that it was given in consideration of such extension or continuation of credit, the amount thereof, and the name of the person extending or continuing credit;
  (4) A person who has contracted to perform services as an officer of the corporation, if a proxy is required by the contract of employment, if the proxy states that it was given in consideration of such contract of employment, the name of the employee and the period of employment contracted for;
  (5) A person designated by or under an agreement under paragraph (a) of section 620.

(g) Notwithstanding a provision in a proxy, stating that it is irrevocable, the proxy becomes revocable after the pledge is redeemed, or the debt of the corporation is paid, or the period of employment provided for in the contract of employment has terminated, or the agreement under paragraph (a) of section 620 has terminated; and, in a case provided for in subparagraphs (f) (3) or (4), becomes revocable three years after the date of the proxy or at the end of the period, if any, specified therein, whichever period is less, unless the period of irrevocability is renewed from time to time by the execution of a new irrevocable proxy as provided in this section. This paragraph does not affect the duration of a proxy under paragraph (b).

(h) A proxy may be revoked, notwithstanding a provision making it irrevocable, by a purchaser of shares without knowledge of the existence of the provision unless the existence of the proxy and its irrevocability is noted conspicuously on the face or back of the certificate representing such shares.

(i) Without limiting the manner in which a shareholder may authorize another person or persons to act for him as proxy pursuant to paragraph (a) of this section, the following shall constitute a valid means by which a shareholder may grant such authority.
  (1) A shareholder may execute a writing authorizing another person or persons to act from him as proxy. Execution may be accomplished by the shareholder or the shareholder's authorized officer, director, employee or agent signing such writing or causing his or her signature to be affixed to such writing by any reasonable means including, but not limited to, by facsimile signature.
  (2) A shareholder may authorize another person or persons to act for the shareholder as proxy by transmitting or authorizing the transmission of a telegram, cablegram or other means of electronic transmission to the person who will be the holder of the proxy or to a proxy solicitation firm, proxy support service organization or like agent duly authorized by the person who will be the holder of the proxy to receive such transmission, provided that any such telegram, cablegram or other means of electronic transmission must either set forth or be submitted with information from which it can be reasonably determined that the telegram, cablegram or other electronic transmission was authorized by the shareholder. If it is determined that such telegrams, cablegrams or other electronic transmissions are valid, the inspectors or, if there are no inspectors, such other persons making that determination shall specify the nature of the information upon which they relied.

(j) Any copy, facsimile telecommunication or other reliable reproduction of the writing or transmission created pursuant to paragraph (i) of this section may be substituted or used in lieu of the original writing or transmission for any and all purposes for which the original writing or transmission could be used, provided that such copy, facsimile telecommunication or other reproduction shall be a complete reproduction of the entire original writing or transmission.

S 610. Selection of inspectors at shareholders` meetings.

(a) The board of directors shall appoint one or more inspectors to act at the meeting or any adjournment thereof and make a written report thereof. The board of directors may designate one or more persons as alternate inspectors to replace any inspector who fails to act. If no inspector or alternate has been appointed, or if such persons are unable to act at a meeting of shareholders, the person presiding at the meeting shall appoint one or more inspectors to act at the meeting. Each inspector, before entering upon the discharge of his duties, shall take and sign an oath faithfully to execute the duties of inspector at such meeting with strict impartiality and according to the best of his ability.

(b) Unless otherwise provided in the certificate of incorporation or by-laws, paragraph (a) of this section shall not apply to a corporation that does not have a class of voting stock that is listed on a national securities exchange or authorized for quotation on an inter-dealer quotation system of a registered national securities association. Notwithstanding the foregoing, any corporation may take the actions set forth in paragraph (a) of this section.

S 611. Duties of inspectors at shareholders` meetings.

(a) The inspectors shall determine the number of shares outstanding and the voting power of each, the shares represented at the meeting, the existence of a quorum, the validity and effect of proxies, and shall receive votes, ballots or consents, hear and determine all challenges and questions arising in connection with the right to vote, count and tabulate all votes, ballots or consents, determine the result, and do such acts as are proper to conduct the election or vote with fairness to all shareholders. On request of the person presiding at the meeting or any shareholder entitled to vote thereat, the inspectors shall make a report in writing of any challenge, question or matter determined by them and execute a certificate of any fact found by them. Any report or certificate made by them shall be prima facie evidence of the facts stated and of the vote as certified by them.

(b) In determining the validity and counting of proxies, ballots and consents, the inspectors shall be limited to an examination of the proxies, any envelopes submitted with those proxies and consents, any information provided in accordance with section 609 (Proxies), ballots and the regular books and records of the corporation, except that the inspectors may consider other reliable information for the limited purpose of reconciling proxies, ballots and consents submitted by or on behalf of banks, brokers, their nominees or similar persons which represent more votes than the holder of a proxy is authorized by the record owner to cast or more votes than the stockholder holds of record. If the inspectors consider other reliable information for the limited purpose permitted herein, the inspectors at the time they make their certification pursuant to paragraph (a) of this section shall specify the precise information considered by them including the person or persons from whom they obtained the information, when the information was obtained, the means by which the information was obtained and the basis for the inspectors` belief that such information is reliable.

(c) The date and time (which need not be a particular time of day) of the opening and the closing of the polls for each matter upon which the shareholders will vote at a meeting shall be announced by the person presiding at the meeting at the beginning of the meeting and, if no date and time is so announced, the polls shall close at the end of the meeting, including any adjournment thereof. No ballot, proxies or consents, nor any revocation thereof or changes thereto, shall be accepted by the inspectors after the closing of polls in accordance with section 605 (Notice of meetings of shareholders) unless the supreme court at a special term held within the judicial district where the office of the corporation is located upon application by a shareholder shall determine otherwise.

(d) Unless otherwise provided in the certificate of incorporation or by-laws, paragraphs (a) and (c) of this section shall not apply to a corporation that does not have a class of voting stock that is listed on a national securities exchange or authorized for quotation on an interdealer quotation system of a registered national securities association. Notwithstanding the foregoing, any corporation may take the actions set forth in paragraphs (a) and (c) of this section.

S 612. Qualification of voters.

(a) Every shareholder of record shall be entitled at every meeting of shareholders to one vote for every share standing in his name on the record of shareholders, unless otherwise provided in the certificate of incorporation.

(b) Treasury shares and shares held by another domestic or foreign corporation of any type or kind, if a majority of the shares entitled to vote in the election of directors of such other corporation is held by the corporation, shall not be shares entitled to vote or to be counted in determining the total number of outstanding shares.

(c) Shares held by an administrator, executor, guardian, conservator, committee, or other fiduciary, except a trustee, may be voted by him, either in person or by proxy, without transfer of such shares into his name. Shares held by a trustee may be voted by him, either in person or by proxy, only after the shares have been transferred into his name as trustee or into the name of his nominee.

(d) Shares held by or under the control of a receiver may be voted by him without the transfer thereof into his name if authority so to do is contained in an order of the court by which such receiver was appointed.

(e) A shareholder whose shares are pledged shall be entitled to vote such shares until the shares have been transferred into the name of the pledgee, or a nominee of the pledgee.

(f) Redeemable shares which have been called for redemption shall not be deemed to be outstanding shares for the purpose of voting or determining the total number of shares entitled to vote on any matter on and after the date on which written notice of redemption has been sent to holders thereof and a sum sufficient to redeem such shares has been deposited with a bank or trust company with irrevocable instruction and authority to pay the redemption price to the holders of the shares upon surrender of certificates therefor.

(g) Shares standing in the name of another domestic or foreign corporation of any type or kind may be voted by such officer, agent or proxy as the by-laws of such corporation may provide, or, in the absence of such provision, as the board of such corporation may determine.

(h) If shares are registered on the record of shareholders of a corporation in the name of two or more persons, whether fiduciaries, members of a partnership, joint tenants, tenants in common, tenants by the entirety or otherwise, or if two or more persons have the same fiduciary relationship respecting the same shares, unless the secretary of the corporation is given written notice to the contrary and is furnished with a copy of the instrument or order appointing them or creating the relationship wherein it is so provided, their acts with respect to voting shall have the following effect:

(1) If only one votes, the vote shall be accepted by the corporation as the vote of all;

(2) If more than one vote, the act of the majority so voting shall be accepted by the corporation as the vote of all;

(3) If more than one vote, but the vote is equally divided on any particular matter, the vote shall be accepted by the corporation as a proportionate vote of the shares; unless the corporation has evidence, on the record of shareholders or otherwise, that the shares are held in a fiduciary capacity. Nothing in this paragraph shall alter any requirement that the exercise of fiduciary powers be by act of a majority, contained in any law applicable to such exercise of powers (including section 10-10.7 of the estates, powers and trusts law);

(4) When shares as to which the vote is equally divided are registered on the record of shareholders of a corporation in the name of, or have passed by operation of law or by virtue of any deed of trust or other instrument to two or more fiduciaries, any court having jurisdiction of their accounts, upon petition by any of such fiduciaries or by any party in interest, may direct the voting of such shares for the best interest of the beneficiaries. This subparagraph shall not apply in any case where the instrument or order of the court appointing fiduciaries shall otherwise direct how such shares shall be voted; and

(5) If the instrument or order furnished to the secretary of a corporation shows that a tenancy is held in unequal interests, a majority or equal division for the purposes of this paragraph shall be a majority or equal division in interest.

(i) Notwithstanding the foregoing paragraphs, a corporation shall be protected in treating the persons in whose names shares stand on the record of shareholders as the owners thereof for all purposes.

S 613. Limitations on right to vote.

The certificate of incorporation may provide, except as limited by section 501 (Authorized shares), either absolutely or conditionally, that the holders of any designated class or series of shares shall not be entitled to vote, or it may otherwise limit or define the respective voting powers of the several classes or series of shares, and, except as otherwise provided in this chapter, such provisions of such certificate shall prevail, according to their tenor, in all elections and in all proceedings, over the provisions of this chapter which authorizes any action by the shareholders.

S 614. Vote of shareholders.

(a) Directors shall, except as otherwise required by this chapter or by the certificate of incorporation as permitted by this chapter, be elected by a plurality of the votes cast at a meeting of shareholders by the holders of shares entitled to vote in the election.

(b) Whenever any corporate action, other than the election of directors, is to be taken under this chapter by vote of the shareholders, it shall, except as otherwise required by this chapter or by the certificate of incorporation as permitted by this chapter or by the specific provisions of a by-law adopted by the shareholders, be authorized by a majority of the votes cast in favor of or against such action at a meeting of shareholders by the holders of shares entitled to vote thereon. Except as otherwise provided in the certificate of incorporation or the specific provision of a by-law adopted by the shareholders, an abstention shall not constitute a vote cast.

S 615. Written consent of shareholders, subscribers or incorporators without a meeting.

(a) Whenever under this chapter shareholders are required or permitted to take any action by vote, such action may be taken without a meeting on written consent, setting forth the action so taken, signed by the holders of all outstanding shares entitled to vote thereon or, if the certificate of incorporation so permits, signed by the holders of outstanding shares having not less than the minimum number of votes that would be necessary to authorize or take such action at a meeting at which all shares entitled to vote thereon were present and voted.

In addition, this paragraph shall not be construed to alter or modify the provisions of any section or any provision in a certificate of incorporation not inconsistent with this chapter under which the written consent of the holders of less than all outstanding shares is sufficient for corporate action.

(b) No written consent shall be effective to take the corporate action referred to therein unless, within sixty days of the earliest dated consent delivered in the manner required by this paragraph to the corporation, written consents signed by a sufficient number of holders to take action are delivered to the corporation by delivery to its registered office in this state, its principal place of business, or an officer or agent of the corporation having custody of the book in which proceedings of meetings of shareholders are recorded. Delivery made to a corporation's registered office shall be by hand or by certified or registered mail, return receipt requested.

(c) Prompt notice of the taking of the corporate action without a meeting by less than unanimous written consent shall be given to those shareholders who have not consented in writing.

(d) Written consent thus given by the holders of such number of shares as is required under paragraph (a) of this section shall have the same effect as a valid vote of holders of such number of shares, and any certificate with respect to the authorization or taking of any such action which is to be delivered to the department of state shall recite that written consent has been given in accordance with this section and that written notice has been given as and to the extent required by this section.

(e) When there are no shareholders of record, such action may be taken on the written consent signed by a majority in interest of the subscribers for shares whose subscriptions have been accepted or their successors in interest or, if no subscription has been accepted, on the written consent signed by the incorporator or a majority of the incorporators. When there are two or more incorporators, if any dies or is for any reason unable to act, the other or others may act. If there is no incorporator able to act, any person for whom an incorporator was acting as agent may act in his stead, or if such other person also dies or is for any reason unable to act, his legal representative may act.

S 616. Greater requirement as to quorum and vote of shareholders.

(a) The certificate of incorporation may contain provisions specifying either or both of the following:

(1) That the proportion of votes of shares, or the proportion of votes of shares of any class or series thereof, the holders of which shall be present in person or by proxy at any meeting of shareholders, including a special meeting for election of directors under section 603 (Special meeting for election of directors), in order to constitute a quorum for the transaction of any business or of any specified item of business, including amendments to the certificate of incorporation, shall be greater than the proportion prescribed by this chapter in the absence of such provision.

(2) That the proportion of votes of shares, or votes of shares of a particular class or series of shares, that shall be necessary at any meeting of shareholders for the transaction of any business or of any specified item of business, including amendments to the certificate of incorporation, shall be greater than the proportion prescribed by this chapter in the absence of such provision.

(b) An amendment of the certificate of incorporation which changes or strikes out a provision permitted by this section, shall be authorized at a meeting of shareholders by two-thirds of the votes of the shares entitled to vote thereon, or of such greater proportion of votes of shares, or votes of shares of a particular class or series of shares, as may be provided specifically in the certificate of incorporation for changing or striking out a provision permitted by this section.

(c) If the certificate of incorporation of any corporation contains a provision authorized by this section, the existence of such provision shall be noted conspicuously on the face or back of every certificate for shares issued by such corporation, except that this requirement shall not apply to any corporation having any class of any equity security registered pursuant to Section twelve of the Securities Exchange Act of 1934, as amended.

S 617. Voting by class or classes of shares.

(a) The certificate of incorporation may contain provisions specifying that any class or classes of shares or of any series thereof shall vote as a class in connection with the transaction of any business or of any specified item of business at a meeting of shareholders, including amendments to the certificate of incorporation.

(b) Where voting as a class is provided in the certificate of incorporation, it shall be by the proportionate vote so provided or, if no proportionate vote is provided, in the election of directors, by a plurality of the votes cast at such meeting by the holders of shares of such class entitled to vote in the election, or for any other corporate action, by a majority of the votes cast at such meeting by the holders of shares of such class entitled to vote thereon.

(c) Such voting by class shall be in addition to any other vote, including vote by class, required by this chapter and by the certificate of incorporation as permitted by this chapter.

S 618. Cumulative voting.

The certificate of incorporation of any corporation may provide that in all elections of directors of such corporation each shareholder shall be entitled to as many votes as shall equal the number of votes which, except for such provisions as to cumulative voting, he would be entitled to cast for the election of directors with respect to his shares multiplied by the number of directors to be elected, and that he may cast all of such votes for a single director or may distribute them among the number to be voted for, or any two or more of them, as he may see fit, which right, when exercised, shall be termed cumulative voting.

S 619. Powers of supreme court respecting elections.

Upon the petition of any shareholder aggrieved by an election, and upon notice to the persons declared elected thereat, the corporation and such other persons as the court may direct, the supreme court at a special term held within the judicial district where the office of the corporation is located shall forthwith hear the proofs and allegations of the parties, and confirm the election, order a new election, or take such other action as justice may require.

S 620. Agreements as to voting; provision in certificate of incorporation as to control of directors.

(a) An agreement between two or more shareholders, if in writing and signed by the parties thereto, may provide that in exercising any voting rights, the shares held by them shall be voted as therein provided, or as they may agree, or as determined in accordance with a procedure agreed upon by them.

(b) A provision in the certificate of incorporation otherwise prohibited by law because it improperly restricts the board in its management of the business of the corporation, or improperly transfers to one or more shareholders or to one or more persons or corporations to be selected by him or them, all or any part of such management otherwise within the authority of the board under this chapter, shall nevertheless be valid:

(1) If all the incorporators or holders of record of all outstanding shares, whether or not having voting power, have authorized such provision in the certificate of incorporation or an amendment thereof; and

(2) If, subsequent to the adoption of such provision, shares are transferred or issued only to persons who had knowledge or notice thereof or consented in writing to such provision.

(c) A provision authorized by paragraph (b) shall be valid only so long as no shares of the corporation are listed on a national securities exchange or regularly quoted in an over-the-counter market by one or more members of a national or affiliated securities association.

(d) (1) Except as provided in paragraph (e), an amendment to strike out a provision authorized by paragraph (b) shall be authorized at a meeting of shareholders by (A) (i) for any corporation in existence on the effective date of subparagraph (2) of this paragraph, two-thirds of the votes of the shares entitled to vote thereon and (ii) for any corporation in existence on the effective date of this clause the certificate of incorporation of which expressly provides such and for any corporation incorporated after the effective date of subparagraph (2) of this paragraph, a majority of the votes of the shares entitled to vote thereon or (B) in either case, by such greater proportion of votes of shares as may be required by the certificate of incorporation for that purpose.

(2) Any corporation may adopt an amendment of the certificate of incorporation in accordance with the applicable clause or subclause of subparagraph (1) of this paragraph to provide that any further amendment of the certificate of incorporation that strikes out a provision authorized by paragraph (b) of this section shall be authorized at a meeting of the shareholders by a specified proportion of votes of the shares, or votes of a particular class or series of shares, entitled to vote thereon, provided that such proportion may not be less than a majority.

(e) Alternatively, if a provision authorized by paragraph (b) shall have ceased to be valid under this section, the board may authorize a certificate of amendment under section 805 (Certificate of amendment; contents) striking out such provision. Such certificate shall set forth the event by reason of which the provision ceased to be valid.

(f) The effect of any such provision authorized by paragraph (b) shall be to relieve the directors and impose upon the shareholders authorizing the same or consenting thereto the liability for managerial acts or omissions that is imposed on directors by this chapter to the extent that and so long as the discretion or powers of the board in its management of corporate affairs is controlled by any such provision.

(g) If the certificate of incorporation of any corporation contains a provision authorized by paragraph (b), the existence of such provision shall be noted conspicuously on the face or back of every certificate for shares issued by such corporation.

S 621. Voting trust agreements.

(a) Any shareholder or shareholders, under an agreement in writing, may transfer his or their shares to a voting trustee or trustees for the purpose of conferring the right to vote thereon for a period not exceeding ten years upon the terms and conditions therein stated. The certificates for shares so transferred shall be surrendered and cancelled and new certificates therefor issued to such trustee or trustees stating that they are issued under such agreement, and in the entry of such ownership in the record of the corporation that fact shall also be noted, and such trustee or trustees may vote the shares so transferred during the term of such agreement.

(b) The trustee or trustees shall keep available for inspection by holders of voting trust certificates at his or their office or at a place designated in such agreement or of which the holders of voting trust certificates have been notified in writing, correct and complete books and records of account relating to the trust, and a record containing the names and addresses of all persons who are holders of voting trust certificates and the number and class of shares represented by the certificates held by them and the dates when they became the owners thereof. The record may be in written form or any other form capable of being converted into written form within a reasonable time.

(c) A duplicate of every such agreement shall be filed in the office of the corporation and it and the record of voting trust certificate holders shall be subject to the same right of inspection by a shareholder of record or a holder of a voting trust certificate, in person or by agent or attorney, as are the records of the corporation under section 624 (Books and records; right of inspection, prima facie evidence). The shareholder or holder of a voting trust certificate shall be entitled to the remedies provided in that section.

(d) At any time within six months before the expiration of such voting trust agreement as originally fixed or as extended one or more times under this paragraph, one or more holders of voting trust certificates may, by agreement in writing, extend the duration of such voting trust agreement, nominating the same or substitute trustee or trustees, for an additional period not exceeding ten years. Such extension agreement shall not affect the rights or obligations of persons not parties thereto and shall in every respect comply with and be subject to all the provisions of this section applicable to the original voting trust agreement.

S 622. Preemptive rights.

(a) As used in this section, the term:
  (1) "Unlimited dividend rights" means the right without limitation as to amount either to all or to a share of the balance of current or liquidating dividends after the payment of dividends on any shares entitled to a preference.
  (2) "Equity shares" means shares of any class, whether or not preferred as to dividends or assets, which have unlimited dividend rights.
  (3) "Voting rights" means the right to vote for the election of one or more directors, excluding a right so to vote which is dependent on the happening of an event specified in the certificate of incorporation which would change the voting rights of any class of shares.
  (4) "Voting shares" means shares of any class which have voting rights, but does not include bonds on which voting rights are conferred under section 518 (Corporate bonds).
  (5) "Preemptive right" means the right to purchase shares or other securities to be issued or subjected to rights or options to purchase, as such right is defined in this section.

(b) (1) With respect to any corporation incorporated prior to the effective date of subparagraph (2) of this paragraph, except as otherwise provided in the certificate of incorporation, and except as provided in this section, the holders of equity shares of any class, in case of the proposed issuance by the corporation of, or the proposed granting by the corporation of rights or options to purchase, its equity shares of any class or any shares or other securities convertible into or carrying rights or options to purchase its equity shares of any class, shall, if the issuance of the equity shares proposed to be issued or issuable upon exercise of such rights or options or upon conversion of such other securities would adversely affect the unlimited dividend rights of such holders, have the right during a reasonable time and on reasonable conditions, both to be fixed by the board, to purchase such shares or other securities in such proportions as shall be determined as provided in this section.

  (2) With respect to any corporation incorporated on or after the effective date of this subparagraph, the holders of such shares shall not have any preemptive right, except as otherwise expressly provided in the certificate of incorporation.

(c) Except as otherwise provided in the certificate of incorporation, and except as provided in this section, the holders of voting shares of any class having any preemptive right under this paragraph on the date immediately prior to the effective date of subparagraph (2) of paragraph (b) of this section, in case of the proposed issuance by the corporation of, or the proposed granting by the corporation of rights or options to purchase, its voting shares of any class or any shares or other securities convertible into or carrying rights or options to purchase its voting shares of any class, shall, if the issuance of the voting shares proposed to be issued or issuable upon exercise of such rights or options or upon conversion of such other securities would adversely affect the voting rights of such holders, have the right during a reasonable time and on reasonable conditions, both to be fixed by the board, to purchase such shares or other securities in such proportions as shall be determined as provided in this section.

(d) The preemptive right provided for in paragraphs (b) and (c) shall entitle shareholders having such rights to purchase the shares or other securities to be offered or optioned for sale as nearly as practicable in such proportions as would, if such preemptive right were exercised, preserve the relative unlimited dividend rights and voting rights of such holders and at a price or prices not less favorable than the price or prices at which such shares or other securities are proposed to be offered for sale to others, without deduction of such reasonable expenses of and compensation for the sale, underwriting or purchase of such shares or other securities by underwriters or dealers as may lawfully be paid by the corporation. In case each of the shares entitling the holders thereof to preemptive rights does not confer the same unlimited dividend right or voting right, the board shall apportion the shares or other securities to be offered or optioned for sale among the shareholders having preemptive rights to purchase them in such proportions as in the opinion of the board shall preserve as far as practicable the relative unlimited dividend rights and voting rights of the holders at the time of such offering. The apportionment made by the board shall, in the absence of fraud or bad faith, be binding upon all shareholders.

(e) Unless otherwise provided in the certificate of incorporation, shares or other securities offered for sale or subjected to rights or options to purchase shall not be subject to preemptive rights under paragraph (b) or (c) of this section if they:
  (1) Are to be issued by the board to effect a merger or consolidation or offered or subjected to rights or options for consideration other than cash;
  (2) Are to be issued or subjected to rights or options under paragraph (d) of section 505 (Rights and options to purchase shares; issue of rights and options to directors, officers and employees);
  (3) Are to be issued to satisfy conversion or option rights theretofore granted by the corporation;
  (4) Are treasury shares;
  (5) Are part of the shares or other securities of the corporation authorized in its original certificate of incorporation and are issued, sold or optioned within two years from the date of filing such certificate; or
  (6) Are to be issued under a plan of reorganization approved in a proceeding under any applicable act of congress relating to reorganization of corporations.

(f) Shareholders of record entitled to preemptive rights on the record date fixed by the board under section 604 (Fixing record date), or, if no record date is fixed, then on the record date determined under section 604, and no others shall be entitled to the right defined in this section.

(g) The board shall cause to be given to each shareholder entitled to purchase shares or other securities in accordance with this section, a notice directed to him in the manner provided in section 605 (Notice of meetings of shareholders) setting forth the time within which and the terms and conditions upon which the shareholder may purchase such shares or other securities and also the apportionment made of the right to purchase among the shareholders entitled to preemptive rights. Such notice shall be given personally or by mail at least fifteen days prior to the expiration of the period during which the shareholder shall have the right to purchase. All shareholders entitled to preemptive rights to whom notice shall have been given as aforesaid shall be deemed conclusively to have had a reasonable time in which to exercise their preemptive rights.

(h) Shares or other securities which have been offered to shareholders having preemptive rights to purchase and which have not been purchased by them within the time fixed by the board may thereafter, for a period of not exceeding one year following the expiration of the time during which shareholders might have exercised such preemptive rights, be issued, sold or subjected to rights or options to any other person or persons at a price, without deduction of such reasonable expenses of and compensation for the sale, underwriting or purchase of such shares by underwriters or dealers as may lawfully be paid by the corporation, not less than that at which they were offered to such shareholders. Any such shares or other securities not so issued, sold or subjected to rights or options to others during such one year period shall thereafter again be subject to the preemptive rights of shareholders.

(i) Except as otherwise provided in the certificate of incorporation and except as provided in this section, no holder of any shares of any class shall as such holder have any preemptive right to purchase any other shares or securities of any class which at any time may be sold or offered for sale by the corporation. Unless otherwise provided in the certificate of incorporation, holders of bonds on which voting rights are conferred under section 518 shall have no preemptive rights.

S 623. Procedure to enforce shareholder's right to receive payment for shares.

(a) A shareholder intending to enforce his right under a section of this chapter to receive payment for his shares if the proposed corporate action referred to therein is taken shall file with the corporation, before the meeting of shareholders at which the action is submitted to a vote, or at such meeting but before the vote, written objection to the action. The objection shall include a notice of his election to dissent, his name and residence address, the number and classes of shares as to which he dissents and a demand for payment of the fair value of his shares if the action is taken. Such objection is not required from any shareholder to whom the corporation did not give notice of such meeting in accordance with this chapter or where the proposed action is authorized by written consent of shareholders without a meeting.

(b) Within ten days after the shareholders' authorization date, which term as used in this section means the date on which the shareholders' vote authorizing such action was taken, or the date on which such consent without a meeting was obtained from the requisite shareholders, the corporation shall give written notice of such authorization or consent by registered mail to each shareholder who filed written objection or from whom written objection was not required, excepting any shareholder who voted for or consented in writing to the proposed action and who thereby is deemed to have elected not to enforce his right to receive payment for his shares.

(c) Within twenty days after the giving of notice to him, any shareholder from whom written objection was not required and who elects to dissent shall file with the corporation a written notice of such election, stating his name and residence address, the number and classes of shares as to which he dissents and a demand for payment of the fair value of his shares. Any shareholder who elects to dissent from a merger under section 905 (Merger of subsidiary corporation) or paragraph (c) of section 907 (Merger or consolidation of domestic and foreign corporations) or from a share exchange under paragraph (g) of section 913 (Share exchanges) shall file a written notice of such election to dissent within twenty days after the giving to him of a copy of the plan of merger or exchange or an outline of the material features thereof under section 905 or 913.

(d) A shareholder may not dissent as to less than all of the shares, as to which he has a right to dissent, held by him of record, that he owns beneficially. A nominee or fiduciary may not dissent on behalf of any beneficial owner as to less than all of the shares of such owner, as to which such nominee or fiduciary has a right to dissent, held of record by such nominee or fiduciary.

(e) Upon consummation of the corporate action, the shareholder shall cease to have any of the rights of a shareholder except the right to be paid the fair value of his shares and any other rights under this section. A notice of election may be withdrawn by the shareholder at any time prior to his acceptance in writing of an offer made by the corporation, as provided in paragraph (g), but in no case later than sixty days from the date of consummation of the corporate action except that if the corporation fails to make a timely offer, as provided in paragraph (g), the time for withdrawing a notice of election shall be extended until sixty days from the date an offer is made. Upon expiration of such time, withdrawal of a notice of election shall require the written consent of the corporation. In order to be effective, withdrawal of a notice of election must be accompanied by the return to the corporation of any advance payment made to the shareholder as provided in paragraph (g). If a notice of election is withdrawn, or the corporate action is rescinded, or a court shall determine that the shareholder is not entitled to receive payment for his shares, or the shareholder shall otherwise lose his dissenters' rights, he shall not have the right to receive payment for his shares and he shall be reinstated to all his rights as a shareholder as of the consummation of the corporate action, including any intervening preemptive rights and the right to payment of any intervening dividend or other distribution or, if any such rights have expired or any such dividend or distribution other than in cash has been completed, in lieu thereof, at the election of the corporation, the fair value thereof in cash as determined by the board as of the time of such expiration or completion, but without prejudice otherwise to any corporate proceedings that may have been taken in the interim.

(f) At the time of filing the notice of election to dissent or within one month thereafter the shareholder of shares represented by certificates shall submit the certificates representing his shares to the corporation, or to its transfer agent, which shall forthwith note conspicuously thereon that a notice of election has been filed and shall return the certificates to the shareholder or other person who submitted them on his behalf. Any shareholder of shares represented by certificates who fails to submit his certificates for such notation as herein specified shall, at the option of the corporation exercised by written notice to him within forty-five days from the date of filing of such notice of election to dissent, lose his dissenter's rights unless a court, for good cause shown, shall otherwise direct. Upon transfer of a certificate bearing such notation, each new certificate issued therefor shall bear a similar notation together with the name of the original dissenting holder of the shares and a transferee shall acquire no rights in the corporation except those which the original dissenting shareholder had at the time of transfer.

(g) Within fifteen days after the expiration of the period within which shareholders may file their notices of election to dissent, or within fifteen days after the proposed corporate action is consummated, whichever is later (but in no case later than ninety days from the shareholders' authorization date), the corporation or, in the case of a merger or consolidation, the surviving or new corporation, shall make a written offer by registered mail to each shareholder who has filed such notice of election to pay for his shares at a specified price which the corporation considers to be their fair value. Such offer shall be accompanied by a statement setting forth the aggregate number of shares with respect to which notices of election to dissent have been received and the aggregate number of holders of such shares. If the corporate action has been consummated, such offer shall also be accompanied by (1) advance payment to each such shareholder who has submitted the certificates representing his shares to the corporation, as provided in paragraph (f), of an amount equal to eighty percent of the amount of such offer, or (2) as to each shareholder who has not yet submitted his certificates a statement that advance payment to him of an amount equal to eighty percent of the amount of such offer will be made by the corporation promptly upon submission of his certificates. If the corporate action has not been consummated at the time of the making of the offer, such advance payment or statement as to advance payment shall be sent to each shareholder entitled thereto forthwith upon consummation of the corporate action. Every advance payment or statement as to advance payment shall include advice to the shareholder to the effect that acceptance of such payment does not constitute a waiver of any dissenters' rights. If the corporate action has not been consummated upon the expiration of the ninety day period after the shareholders' authorization date, the offer may be conditioned upon the consummation of such action. Such offer shall be made at the same price per share to all dissenting shareholders of the same class, or if divided into series, of the same series and shall be accompanied by a balance sheet of the corporation whose shares the dissenting shareholder holds as of the latest available date, which shall not be earlier than twelve months before the making of such offer, and a profit and loss statement or statements for not less than a twelve month period ended on the date of such balance sheet or, if the corporation was not in existence throughout such twelve month period, for the portion thereof during which it was in existence. Notwithstanding the foregoing, the corporation shall not be required to furnish a balance sheet or profit and loss statement or statements to any shareholder to whom such balance sheet or profit and loss statement or statements were previously furnished, nor if in connection with obtaining the shareholders' authorization for or consent to the proposed corporate action the shareholders were furnished with a proxy or information statement, which included financial statements, pursuant to Regulation 14A or Regulation 14C of the United States Securities and Exchange Commission. If within thirty days after the making of such offer, the corporation making the offer and any shareholder agree upon the price to be paid for his shares, payment therefor shall be made within sixty days after the making of such offer or the consummation of the proposed corporate action, whichever is later, upon the surrender of the certificates for any such shares represented by certificates.

(h) The following procedure shall apply if the corporation fails to make such offer within such period of fifteen days, or if it makes the offer and any dissenting shareholder or shareholders fail to agree with it within the period of thirty days thereafter upon the price to be paid for their shares:

(1) The corporation shall, within twenty days after the expiration of whichever is applicable of the two periods last mentioned, institute a special proceeding in the supreme court in the judicial district in which the office of the corporation is located to determine the rights of dissenting shareholders and to fix the fair value of their shares. If, in the case of merger or consolidation, the surviving or new corporation is a foreign corporation without an office in this state, such proceeding shall be brought in the county where the office of the domestic corporation, whose shares are to be valued, was located.

(2) If the corporation fails to institute such proceeding within such period of twenty days, any dissenting shareholder may institute such proceeding for the same purpose not later than thirty days after the expiration of such twenty day period. If such proceeding is not instituted within such thirty day period, all dissenter's rights shall be lost unless the supreme court, for good cause shown, shall otherwise direct.

(3) All dissenting shareholders, excepting those who, as provided in paragraph (g), have agreed with the corporation upon the price to be paid for their shares, shall be made parties to such proceeding, which shall have the effect of an action quasi in rem against their shares. The corporation shall serve a copy of the petition in such proceeding upon each dissenting shareholder who is a resident of this state in the manner provided by law for the service of a summons, and upon each nonresident dissenting shareholder either by registered mail and publication, or in such other manner as is permitted by law. The jurisdiction of the court shall be plenary and exclusive.

(4) The court shall determine whether each dissenting shareholder, as to whom the corporation requests the court to make such determination, is entitled to receive payment for his shares. If the corporation does not request any such determination or if the court finds that any dissenting shareholder is so entitled, it shall proceed to fix the value of the shares, which, for the purposes of this section, shall be the fair value as of the close of business on the day prior to the shareholders' authorization date. In fixing the fair value of the shares, the court shall consider the nature of the transaction giving rise to the shareholder's right to receive payment for shares and its effects on the corporation and its shareholders, the concepts and methods then customary in

the relevant securities and financial markets for determining fair value of shares of a corporation engaging in a similar transaction under comparable circumstances and all other relevant factors. The court shall determine the fair value of the shares without a jury and without referral to an appraiser or referee. Upon application by the corporation or by any shareholder who is a party to the proceeding, the court may, in its discretion, permit pretrial disclosure, including, but not limited to, disclosure of any expert's reports relating to the fair value of the shares whether or not intended for use at the trial in the proceeding and notwithstanding subdivision (d) of section 3101 of the civil practice law and rules.

(5) The final order in the proceeding shall be entered against the corporation in favor of each dissenting shareholder who is a party to the proceeding and is entitled thereto for the value of his shares so determined.

(6) The final order shall include an allowance for interest at such rate as the court finds to be equitable, from the date the corporate action was consummated to the date of payment. In determining the rate of interest, the court shall consider all relevant factors, including the rate of interest which the corporation would have had to pay to borrow money during the pendency of the proceeding. If the court finds that the refusal of any shareholder to accept the corporate offer of payment for his shares was arbitrary, vexatious or otherwise not in good faith, no interest shall be allowed to him.

(7) Each party to such proceeding shall bear its own costs and expenses, including the fees and expenses of its counsel and of any experts employed by it. Notwithstanding the foregoing, the court may, in its discretion, apportion and assess all or any part of the costs, expenses and fees incurred by the corporation against any or all of the dissenting shareholders who are parties to the proceeding, including any who have withdrawn their notices of election as provided in paragraph (e), if the court finds that their refusal to accept the corporate offer was arbitrary, vexatious or otherwise not in good faith. The court may, in its discretion, apportion and assess all or any part of the costs, expenses and fees incurred by any or all of the dissenting shareholders who are parties to the proceeding against the corporation if the court finds any of the following: (A) that the fair value of the shares as determined materially exceeds the amount which the corporation offered to pay; (B) that no offer or required advance payment was made by the corporation; (C) that the corporation failed to institute the special proceeding within the period specified therefor; or (D) that the action of the corporation in complying with its obligations as provided in this section was arbitrary, vexatious or otherwise not in good faith. In making any determination as provided in clause (A), the court may consider the dollar amount or the percentage, or both, by which the fair value of the shares as determined exceeds the corporate offer.

(8) Within sixty days after final determination of the proceeding, the corporation shall pay to each dissenting shareholder the amount found to be due him, upon surrender of the certificates for any such shares represented by certificates.

(i) Shares acquired by the corporation upon the payment of the agreed value therefor or of the amount due under the final order, as provided in this section, shall become treasury shares or be cancelled as provided in section 515 (Reacquired shares), except that, in the case of a merger or consolidation, they may be held and disposed of as the plan of merger or consolidation may otherwise provide.

(j) No payment shall be made to a dissenting shareholder under this section at a time when the corporation is insolvent or when such payment would make it insolvent. In such event, the dissenting shareholder shall, at his option:

(1) Withdraw his notice of election, which shall in such event be deemed withdrawn with the written consent of the corporation; or

(2) Retain his status as a claimant against the corporation and, if it is liquidated, be subordinated to the rights of creditors of the corporation, but have rights superior to the non-dissenting shareholders, and if it is not liquidated, retain his right to be paid for his shares, which right the corporation shall be obliged to satisfy when the restrictions of this paragraph do not apply.

(3) The dissenting shareholder shall exercise such option under subparagraph (1) or (2) by written notice filed with the corporation within thirty days after the corporation has given him written notice that payment for his shares cannot be made because of the restrictions of this paragraph. If the dissenting shareholder fails to exercise such option as provided, the corporation shall exercise the option by written notice given to him within twenty days after the expiration of such period of thirty days.

(k) The enforcement by a shareholder of his right to receive payment for his shares in the manner provided herein shall exclude the enforcement by such shareholder of any other right to which he might otherwise be entitled by virtue of share ownership, except as provided in paragraph (e), and except that this section shall not exclude the right of such shareholder to bring or maintain an appropriate action to obtain relief on the ground that such corporate action will be or is unlawful or fraudulent as to him.

(l) Except as otherwise expressly provided in this section, any notice to be given by a corporation to a shareholder under this section shall be given in the manner provided in section 605 (Notice of meetings of shareholders).

(m) This section shall not apply to foreign corporations except as provided in subparagraph (e) (2) of section 907 (Merger or consolidation of domestic and foreign corporations).

S 624. Books and records; right of inspection, prima facie evidence.

(a) Each corporation shall keep correct and complete books and records of account and shall keep minutes of the proceedings of its shareholders, board and executive committee, if any, and shall keep at the office of the corporation in this state or at the office of its transfer agent or registrar in this state, a record containing the names and addresses of all shareholders, the number and class of shares held by each and the dates when they respectively became the owners of record thereof. Any of the foregoing books, minutes or records may be in written form or in any other form capable of being converted into written form within a reasonable time.

(b) Any person who shall have been a shareholder of record of a corporation upon at least five days' written demand shall have the right to examine in person or by agent or attorney, during usual business hours, its minutes of the proceedings of its shareholders and record of shareholders and to make extracts therefrom for any purpose reasonably related to such person's interest as a shareholder. Holders of voting trust certificates representing shares of the corporation shall be regarded as shareholders for the purpose of this section. Any such agent or attorney shall be authorized in a writing that satisfies the requirements of a writing under paragraph (b) of section 609 (Proxies). A corporation requested to provide information pursuant to this paragraph shall make available such information in written form and in any other format in which such information is maintained by the corporation and shall not be required to provide such information in any other format. If a request made pursuant to this paragraph includes a request to furnish information regarding beneficial owners, the corporation shall make available such information in its possession regarding beneficial owners as is provided to the corporation by a registered broker or dealer or a bank, association or other entity that exercises fiduciary powers in connection with the forwarding of information to such owners. The corporation shall not be required to obtain information about beneficial owners not in its possession.

(c) An inspection authorized by paragraph (b) may be denied to such shareholder or other person upon his refusal to furnish to the corporation, its transfer agent or registrar an affidavit that such inspection is not desired for a purpose which is in the interest of a business or object other than the business of the corporation and that he has not within five years sold or offered for sale any list of shareholders of any corporation of any type or kind, whether or not formed under the laws of this state, or aided or abetted any person in procuring any such record of shareholders for any such purpose.

(d) Upon refusal by the corporation or by an officer or agent of the corporation to permit an inspection of the minutes of the proceedings of its shareholders or of the record of shareholders as herein provided, the person making the demand for inspection may apply to the supreme court in the judicial district where the office of the corporation is located, upon such notice as the court may direct, for an order directing the corporation, its officer or agent to show cause why an order should not be granted permitting such inspection by the applicant. Upon the return day of the order to show cause, the court shall hear the parties summarily, by affidavit or otherwise, and if it appears that the applicant is qualified and entitled to such inspection, the court shall grant an order compelling such inspection and awarding such further relief as to the court may seem just and proper.

(e) Upon the written request of any shareholder, the corporation shall give or mail to such shareholder an annual balance sheet and profit and loss statement for the preceding fiscal year, and, if any interim balance sheet or profit and loss statement has been distributed to its shareholders or otherwise made available to the public, the most recent such interim balance sheet or profit and loss statement. The corporation shall be allowed a reasonable time to prepare such annual balance sheet and profit and loss statement.

(f) Nothing herein contained shall impair the power of courts to compel the production for examination of the books and records of a corporation.

(g) The books and records specified in paragraph (a) shall be prima facie evidence of the facts therein stated in favor of the plaintiff in any action or special proceeding against such corporation or any of its officers, directors or shareholders.

S 625. Infant shareholders and bondholders.

(a) A corporation may treat an infant who holds shares or bonds of such corporation as having capacity to receive and to empower others to receive dividends, interest, principal and other payments and distributions, to vote or express consent or dissent, in person or by proxy, and to make elections and exercise rights relating to such shares or bonds, unless, in the case of shares, the corporate officer responsible for maintaining the list of shareholders or the transfer agent of the corporation or, in the case of bonds, the treasurer or paying officer or agent has received written notice that such holder is an infant.

(b) An infant holder of shares or bonds of a corporation who has received or empowered others to receive payments or distributions, voted or expressed consent or dissent, or made an election or exercised a right relating thereto, shall have no right thereafter to disaffirm or avoid, as against the corporation, any such act on his part, unless prior to such receipt, vote, consent, dissent, election or exercise, as to shares, the corporate officer responsible for maintaining the list of shareholders or its transfer agent or, in the case of bonds, the treasurer or paying officer had received written notice that such holder was an infant.

(c) This section does not limit any other statute which authorizes any corporation to deal with an infant or limits the right of an infant to disaffirm his acts.

S 626. Shareholders' derivative action brought in the right of the corporation to procure a judgment in its favor.

(a) An action may be brought in the right of a domestic or foreign corporation to procure a judgment in its favor, by a holder of shares or of voting trust certificates of the corporation or of a beneficial interest in such shares or certificates.

(b) In any such action, it shall be made to appear that the plaintiff is such a holder at the time of bringing the action and that he was such a holder at the time of the transaction of which he complains, or that his shares or his interest therein devolved upon him by operation of law.

(c) In any such action, the complaint shall set forth with particularity the efforts of the plaintiff to secure the initiation of such action by the board or the reasons for not making such effort.

(d) Such action shall not be discontinued, compromised or settled, without the approval of the court having jurisdiction of the action. If the court shall determine that the interests of the shareholders or any class or classes thereof will be substantially affected by such discontinuance, compromise, or settlement, the court, in its discretion, may direct that notice, by publication or otherwise, shall be given to the shareholders or class or classes thereof whose interests it determines will be so affected; if notice is so directed to be given, the court may determine which one or more of the parties to the action shall bear the expense of giving the same, in such amount as the court shall determine and find to be reasonable in the circumstances, and the amount of such expense shall be awarded as special costs of the action and recoverable in the same manner as statutory taxable costs.

(e) If the action on behalf of the corporation was successful, in whole or in part, or if anything was received by the plaintiff or plaintiffs or a claimant or claimants as the result of a judgment, compromise or settlement of an action or claim, the court may award the plaintiff or plaintiffs, claimant or claimants, reasonable expenses, including reasonable attorney's fees, and shall direct him or them to account to the corporation for the remainder of the proceeds so received by him or them. This paragraph shall not apply to any judgment rendered for the benefit of injured shareholders only and limited to a recovery of the loss or damage sustained by them.

S 627. Security for expenses in shareholders' derivative action brought in the right of the corporation to procure a judgment in its favor.

In any action specified in section 626 (Shareholders' derivative action brought in the right of the corporation to procure a judgment in its favor), unless the plaintiff or plaintiffs hold five percent or more of any class of the outstanding shares or hold voting trust certificates or a beneficial interest in shares representing five percent or more of any class of such shares, or the shares, voting trust certificates and beneficial interest of such plaintiff or plaintiffs have a fair value in excess of fifty thousand dollars, the corporation in whose right such action is brought shall be entitled at any stage of the proceedings before final judgment to require the plaintiff or plaintiffs to give security for the reasonable expenses, including attorney's fees, which may be incurred by it in connection with such action and by the other parties defendant in connection therewith for which the corporation may become liable under this chapter, under any contract or otherwise under law, to which the corporation shall have recourse in such amount as the court having jurisdiction of such action shall determine upon the termination of such action. The amount of such security may thereafter from time to time be increased or decreased in the discretion of the court having jurisdiction of such action upon showing that the security provided has or may become inadequate or excessive.

S 628. Liability of subscribers and shareholders.

(a) A holder of or subscriber for shares of a corporation shall be under no obligation to the corporation for payment for such shares other than the obligation to pay the unpaid portion of his subscription which in no event shall be less than the amount of the consideration for which such shares could be issued lawfully.

(b) Any person becoming an assignee or transferee of shares or of a subscription for shares in good faith and without knowledge or notice that the full consideration therefor has not been paid shall not be personally liable for any unpaid portion of such consideration, but the transferor shall remain liable therefor.

(c) No person holding shares in any corporation as collateral security shall be personally liable as a shareholder but the person pledging such shares shall be considered the holder thereof and shall be so liable. No executor, administrator, guardian, trustee or other fiduciary shall be personally liable as a shareholder, but the estate and funds in the hands of such executor, administrator, guardian, trustee or other fiduciary shall be liable.

S 629. Certain transfers or assignments by shareholders or subscribers; effect.

Any transfer or assignment by a shareholder of his shares, or by a subscriber for shares of his interest in the corporation, shall not relieve him of any liability as a shareholder or subscriber if at the time of such transfer or assignment the aggregate of the corporation's property, exclusive of any property which it may have conveyed, transferred, concealed, removed, or permitted to be concealed or removed, with intent to defraud, hinder or delay its creditors, is not at a fair valuation sufficient in amount to pay its debts, or if such condition is imminent.

S 630. Liability of shareholders for wages due to laborers, servants or employees.

(a) The ten largest shareholders, as determined by the fair value of their beneficial interest as of the beginning of the period during which the unpaid services referred to in this section are performed, of every corporation (other than an investment company registered as such under an act of congress entitled "Investment Company Act of 1940"), no shares of which are listed on a national securities exchange or regularly quoted in an over-the-counter market by one or more members of a national or an affiliated securities association, shall jointly and severally be personally liable for all debts, wages or salaries due and owing to any of its laborers, servants or employees other than contractors, for services performed by them for such corporation. Before such laborer, servant or employee shall charge such shareholder for such services, he shall give notice in writing to such shareholder that he intends to hold him liable under this section. Such notice shall be given within one hundred and eighty days after termination of such services, except that if, within such period, the laborer, servant or employee demands an examination of the record of shareholders under paragraph (b) of section 624 (Books and records; right of inspection, prima facie evidence), such notice may be given within sixty days after he has been given the opportunity to examine the record of shareholders. An action to enforce such liability shall be commenced within ninety days after the return of an execution unsatisfied against the corporation upon a judgment recovered against it for such services.

(b) For the purposes of this section, wages or salaries shall mean all compensation and benefits payable by an employer to or for the account of the employee for personal services rendered by such employee. These shall specifically include but not be limited to salaries, overtime, vacation, holiday and severance pay; employer contributions to or payments of insurance or welfare benefits; employer contributions to pension or annuity funds; and any other moneys properly due or payable for services rendered by such employee.

(c) A shareholder who has paid more than his pro rata share under this section shall be entitled to contribution pro rata from the other shareholders liable under this section with respect to the excess so paid, over and above his pro rata share, and may sue them jointly or severally or any number of them to recover the amount due from them. Such recovery may be had in a separate action. As used in this paragraph, "pro rata" means in proportion to beneficial share interest. Before a shareholder may claim contribution from other shareholders under this paragraph, he shall, unless they have been given notice by a laborer, servant or employee under paragraph (a), give them notice in writing that he intends to hold them so liable to him. Such notice shall be given by him within twenty days after the date that notice was given to him by a laborer, servant or employee under paragraph (a).

ARTICLE 7
DIRECTORS AND OFFICERS

S 701. Board of directors.

Subject to any provision in the certificate of incorporation authorized by paragraph (b) of section 620 (Agreements as to voting; provision in certificate of incorporation as to control of directors) or by paragraph (b) of section 715 (Officers), the business of a corporation shall be managed under the direction of its board of directors, each of whom shall be at least eighteen years of age. The certificate of incorporation or the by-laws may prescribe other qualifications for directors.

S 702. Number of directors.

(a) The board of directors shall consist of one or more members. The number of directors constituting the board may be fixed by the by-laws, or by action of the shareholders or of the board under the specific provisions of a by-law adopted by the shareholders. If not otherwise fixed under this paragraph, the number shall be one. As used in this article, "entire board" means the total number of directors which the corporation would have if there were no vacancies.

(b) The number of directors may be increased or decreased by amendment of the by-laws, or by action of the shareholders or of the board under the specific provisions of a by-law adopted by the shareholders, subject to the following limitations:

(1) If the board is authorized by the by-laws to change the number of directors, whether by amending the by-laws or by taking action under the specific provisions of a by-law adopted by the shareholders, such amendment or action shall require the vote of a majority of the entire board.

(2) No decrease shall shorten the term of any incumbent director.

S 703. Election and term of directors.

(a) At each annual meeting of shareholders, directors shall be elected to hold office until the next annual meeting except as authorized by section 704 (Classification of directors). The certificate of incorporation may provide for the election of one or more directors by the holders of the shares of any class or series, or by the holders of bonds entitled to vote in the election of directors pursuant to section 518 (Corporate bonds), voting as a class.

(b) Each director shall hold office until the expiration of the term for which he is elected, and until his successor has been elected and qualified.

S 704. Classification of directors.

(a) The certificate of incorporation or the specific provisions of a by-law adopted by the shareholders may provide that the directors be divided into either two, three or four classes. All classes shall be as nearly equal in number as possible. The terms of office of the directors initially classified shall be as follows: that of the first class shall expire at the next annual meeting of shareholders, the second class at the second succeeding annual meeting, the third class, if any, at the third succeeding annual meeting, and the fourth class, if any, at the fourth succeeding annual meeting.

(b) At each annual meeting after such initial classification, directors to replace those whose terms expire at such annual meeting shall be elected to hold office until the second succeeding annual meeting if there are two classes, the third succeeding annual meeting if there are three classes, or the fourth succeeding annual meeting if there are four classes.

(c) If directors are classified and the number of directors is thereafter changed: (1) Any newly created directorships or any decrease in directorships shall be so apportioned among the classes as to make all classes as nearly equal in number as possible. (2) When the number of directors is increased by the board and any newly created directorships are filled by the board, there shall be no classification of the additional directors until the next annual meeting of shareholders.

S 705. Newly created directorships and vacancies.

(a) Newly created directorships resulting from an increase in the number of directors and vacancies occurring in the board for any reason except the removal of directors without cause may be filled by vote of the board. If the number of the directors then in office is less than a quorum, such newly created directorships and vacancies may be filled by vote of a majority of the directors then in office. Nothing in this paragraph shall affect any provision of the certificate of incorporation or the by-laws which provides that such newly created directorships or vacancies shall be filled by vote of the shareholders, or any provision of the certificate of incorporation specifying greater requirements as permitted under section 709 (Greater requirements as to quorum and vote of directors).

(b) Unless the certificate of incorporation or the specific provisions of a by-law adopted by the shareholders provide that the board may fill vacancies occurring in the board by reason of the removal of directors without cause, such vacancies may be filled only by vote of the shareholders.

(c) A director elected to fill a vacancy, unless elected by the shareholders, shall hold office until the next meeting of shareholders at which the election of directors is in the regular order of business, and until his successor has been elected and qualified.

(d) Unless otherwise provided in the certificate of incorporation or by-laws, notwithstanding the provisions of paragraphs (a) and (b) of this section, whenever the holders of any class or classes of shares or series thereof are entitled to elect one or more directors by the certificate of incorporation, any vacancy that may be filled by the board or a majority of the directors then in office, as the case may be, shall be filled by a majority of the directors elected by such class or classes or series thereof then in office, or, if no such director is in office, then as provided in paragraph (a) or (b) of this section, as the case may be.

S 706. Removal of directors.

(a) Any or all of the directors may be removed for cause by vote of the shareholders. The certificate of incorporation or the specific provisions of a by-law adopted by the shareholders may provide for such removal by action of the board, except in the case of any director elected by cumulative voting, or by the holders of the shares of any class or series, or holders of bonds, voting as a class, when so entitled by the provisions of the certificate of incorporation.

(b) If the certificate of incorporation or the by-laws so provide, any or all of the directors may be removed without cause by vote of the shareholders.

(c) The removal of directors, with or without cause, as provided in paragraphs (a) and (b) is subject to the following: (1) In the case of a corporation having cumulative voting, no director may be removed when the votes cast against his removal would be sufficient to elect him if voted cumulatively at an election at which the same total number of votes were cast and the entire board, or the entire class of directors of which he is a member, were then being elected; and (2) When by the provisions of the certificate of incorporation the holders of the shares of any class or series, or holders of bonds, voting as a class, are entitled to elect one or more directors, any director so elected may be removed only by the applicable vote of the holders of the shares of that class or series, or the holders of such bonds, voting as a class.

(d) An action to procure a judgment removing a director for cause may be brought by the attorney-general or by the holders of ten percent of the outstanding shares, whether or not entitled to vote. The court may bar from re-election any director so removed for a period fixed by the court.

S 707. Quorum of directors.

Unless a greater proportion is required by the certificate of incorporation, a majority of the entire board shall constitute a quorum for the transaction of business or of any specified item of business, except that the certificate of incorporation or the by-laws may fix the quorum at less than a majority of the entire board but not less than one-third thereof.

S 708. Action by the board.

(a) Except as otherwise provided in this chapter, any reference in this chapter to corporate action to be taken by the board shall mean such action at a meeting of the board.

(b) Unless otherwise restricted by the certificate of incorporation or the by-laws, any action required or permitted to be taken by the board or any committee thereof may be taken without a meeting if all members of the board or the committee consent in writing to the adoption of a resolution authorizing the action. The resolution and the written consents thereto by the members of the board or committee shall be filed with the minutes of the proceedings of the board or committee.

(c) Unless otherwise restricted by the certificate of incorporation or the by-laws, any one or more members of the board or any committee thereof may participate in a meeting of such board or committee by means of a conference telephone or similar communications equipment allowing all persons participating in the meeting to hear each other at the same time. Participation by such means shall constitute presence in person at a meeting.

(d) Except as otherwise provided in this chapter, the vote of a majority of the directors present at the time of the vote, if a quorum is present at such time, shall be the act of the board.

S 709. Greater requirement as to quorum and vote of directors.

(a) The certificate of incorporation may contain provisions specifying either or both of the following: (1) That the proportion of directors that shall constitute a quorum for the transaction of business or of any specified item of business shall be greater than the proportion prescribed by this chapter in the absence of such provision. (2) That the proportion of votes of directors that shall be necessary for the transaction of business or of any specified item of business shall be greater than the proportion prescribed by this chapter in the absence of such provision.

(b) (1) An amendment of the certificate of incorporation which changes or strikes out a provision permitted by this section shall be authorized at a meeting of shareholders by (A) (i) for any corporation in existence on the effective date of subparagraph (2) of this paragraph, two-thirds of the votes of all outstanding shares entitled to vote thereon, and (ii) for any corporation in existence on the effective date of this clause the certificate of incorporation of which expressly provides such and for any corporation incorporated after the effective date of subparagraph (2) of this paragraph, a majority of the votes of all outstanding shares entitled to vote thereon or (B) in either case, such greater proportion of votes of shares, or votes of a class or series of shares, as may be provided specifically in the certificate of incorporation for changing or striking out a provision permitted by this section.

(2) Any corporation may adopt an amendment of the certificate of incorporation in accordance with any applicable clause or subclause of subparagraph (1) of this paragraph to provide that any further amendment of the certificate of incorporation that changes or strikes out a provision permitted by this section shall be authorized at a meeting of the shareholders by a specified proportion of the votes of the shares, or particular class or series of shares, entitled to vote thereon, provided that such proportion may not be less than a majority.

S 710. Place and time of meetings of the board.

Meetings of the board, regular or special, may be held at any place within or without this state, unless otherwise provided by the certificate of incorporation or the by-laws. The time and place for holding meetings of the board may be fixed by or under the by-laws, or, if not so fixed, by the board.

S 711. Notice of meetings of the board.

(a) Unless otherwise provided by the by-laws, regular meetings of the board may be held without notice if the time and place of such meetings are fixed by the by-laws or the board. Special meetings of the board shall be held upon notice to the directors.

(b) The by-laws may prescribe what shall constitute notice of meeting of the board. A notice, or waiver of notice, need not specify the purpose of any regular or special meeting of the board, unless required by the by-laws.

(c) Notice of a meeting need not be given to any director who submits a signed waiver of notice whether before or after the meeting, or who attends the meeting without protesting, prior thereto or at its commencement, the lack of notice to him.

(d) A majority of the directors present, whether or not a quorum is present, may adjourn any meeting to another time and place. If the by-laws so provide, notice of any adjournment of a meeting of the board to another time or place shall be given to the directors who were not present at the time of the adjournment and, unless such time and place are announced at the meeting, to the other directors.

S 712. Executive committee and other committees.

(a) If the certificate of incorporation or the by-laws so provide, the board, by resolution adopted by a majority of the entire board, may designate from among its members an executive committee and other committees, each consisting of one or more directors, and each of which, to the extent provided in the resolution or in the certificate of incorporation or by-laws, shall have all the authority of the board, except that no such committee shall have authority as to the following matters: (1) The submission to shareholders of any action that needs shareholders' approval under this chapter. (2) The filling of vacancies in the board of directors or in any committee. (3) The fixing of compensation of the directors for serving on the board or on any committee. (4) The amendment or repeal of the by-laws, or the adoption of new by-laws. (5) The amendment or repeal of any resolution of the board which by its terms shall not be so amendable or repealable.

(b) The board may designate one or more directors as alternate members of any such committee, who may replace any absent or disqualified member or members at any meeting of such committee.

(c) Each such committee shall serve at the pleasure of the board. The designation of any such committee, the delegation thereto of authority, or action by any such committee pursuant to such authority shall not alone constitute performance by any member of the board who is not a member of the committee in question, of his duty to the corporation under section 717 (Duty of directors).

S 713. Interested directors.

(a) No contract or other transaction between a corporation and one or more of its directors, or between a corporation and any other corporation, firm, association or other entity in which one or more of its directors are directors or officers, or have a substantial financial interest, shall be either void or voidable for this reason alone or by reason alone that such director or directors are present at the meeting of the board, or of a committee thereof, which approves such contract or transaction, or that his or their votes are counted for such purpose: (1) If the material facts as to such director's interest in such contract or transaction and as to any such common directorship, officership or financial interest are disclosed in good faith or known to the board or committee, and the board or committee approves such contract or transaction by a vote sufficient for such purpose without counting the vote of such interested director or, if the votes of the disinterested directors are insufficient to constitute an act of the board as defined in section 708 (Action by the board), by unanimous vote of the disinterested directors; or (2) If the material facts as to such director's interest in such contract or transaction and as to any such common directorship, officership or financial interest are disclosed in good faith or known to the shareholders entitled to vote thereon, and such contract or transaction is approved by vote of such shareholders.

(b) If a contract or other transaction between a corporation and one or more of its directors, or between a corporation and any other corporation, firm, association or other entity in which one or more of its directors are directors or officers, or have a substantial financial interest, is not approved in accordance with paragraph (a), the corporation may avoid the contract or transaction unless the party or parties thereto shall establish affirmatively that the contract or transaction was fair and reasonable as to the corporation at the time it was approved by the board, a committee or the shareholders.

(c) Common or interested directors may be counted in determining the presence of a quorum at a meeting of the board or of a committee which approves such contract or transaction.

(d) The certificate of incorporation may contain additional restrictions on contracts or transactions between a corporation and its directors and may provide that contracts or transactions in violation of such restrictions shall be void or voidable by the corporation.

(e) Unless otherwise provided in the certificate of incorporation or the by-laws, the board shall have authority to fix the compensation of directors for services in any capacity.

S 714. Loans to directors.

(a) A corporation may not lend money to or guarantee the obligation of a director of the corporation unless: (1) the particular loan or guarantee is approved by the shareholders, with the holders of a majority of the votes of the shares entitled to vote thereon constituting a quorum, but shares held of record or beneficially by directors who are benefitted by such loan or guarantee shall not be entitled to vote or to be included in the determination of a quorum; or (2) with respect to any corporation in existence on the effective date of this subparagraph (2) the certificate of incorporation of which expressly provides such and with respect to any corporation incorporated after the effective date of this subparagraph (2), the board determines that the loan or guarantee benefits the corporation and either approves the specific loan or guarantee or a general plan authorizing loans and guarantees.

(b) The fact that a loan or guarantee is made in violation of this section does not affect the borrower's liability on the loan.

S 715. Officers.

(a) The board may elect or appoint a president, one or more vice-presidents, a secretary and a treasurer, and such other officers as it may determine, or as may be provided in the by-laws.

(b) The certificate of incorporation may provide that all officers or that specified officers shall be elected by the shareholders instead of by the board.

(c) Unless otherwise provided in the certificate of incorporation or the by-laws, all officers shall be elected or appointed to hold office until the meeting of the board following the next annual meeting of shareholders or, in the case of officers elected by the shareholders, until the next annual meeting of shareholders.

(d) Each officer shall hold office for the term for which he is elected or appointed, and until his successor has been elected or appointed and qualified.

(e) Any two or more offices may be held by the same person. When all of the issued and outstanding stock of the corporation is owned by one person, such person may hold all or any combination of offices.

(f) The board may require any officer to give security for the faithful performance of his duties

(g) All officers as between themselves and the corporation shall have such authority and perform such duties in the management of the corporation as may be provided in the by-laws or, to the extent not so provided, by the board.

(h) An officer shall perform his duties as an officer in good faith and with that degree of care which an ordinarily prudent person in a like position would use under similar circumstances. In performing his duties, an officer shall be entitled to rely on information, opinions, reports or statements including financial statements and other financial data, in each case prepared or presented by: (1) one or more other officers or employees of the corporation or of any other corporation of which at least fifty percent of the outstanding shares of stock entitling the holders thereof to vote for the election of directors is owned directly or indirectly by the corporation, whom the officer believes to be reliable and competent in the matters presented, or (2) counsel, public accountants or other persons as to matters which the officer believes to be within such person's professional or expert competence, so long as in so relying he shall be acting in good faith and with such degree of care, but he shall not be considered to be acting in good faith if he has knowledge concerning the matter in question that would cause such reliance to be unwarranted. A person who so performs his duties shall have no liability by reason of being or having been an officer of the corporation.

S 716. Removal of officers.

(a) Any officer elected or appointed by the board may be removed by the board with or without cause. An officer elected by the shareholders may be removed, with or without cause, only by vote of the shareholders, but his authority to act as an officer may be suspended by the board for cause.

(b) The removal of an officer without cause shall be without prejudice to his contract rights, if any. The election or appointment of an officer shall not of itself create contract rights.

(c) An action to procure a judgment removing an officer for cause may be brought by the attorney-general or by ten percent of the votes of the outstanding shares, whether or not entitled to vote. The court may bar from re-election or reappointment any officer so removed for a period fixed by the court.

S 717. Duty of directors.

(a) A director shall perform his duties as a director, including his duties as a member of any committee of the board upon which he may serve, in good faith and with that degree of care which an ordinarily prudent person in a like position would use under similar circumstances.In performing his duties, a director shall be entitled to rely on information, opinions, reports or statements including financial statements and other financial data, in each case prepared or presented by: (1) one or more officers or employees of the corporation or of any other corporation of which at least fifty percent of the outstanding shares of stock entitling the holders thereof to vote for the election of directors is owned directly or indirectly by the corporation, whom the director believes to be reliable and competent in the matters presented, (2) counsel, public accountants or other persons as to matters which the director believes to be within such person's professional or expert competence, or (3) a committee of the board upon which he does not serve, duly designated in accordance with a provision of the certificate of incorporation or the by-laws, as to matters within its designated authority, which committee the director believes to merit confidence, so long as in so relying he shall be acting in good faith and with such degree of care, but he shall not be considered to be acting in good faith if he has knowledge concerning the matter in question that would cause such reliance to be unwarranted. A person who so performs his duties shall have no liability by reason of being or having been a director of the corporation.

(b) In taking action, including, without limitation, action which may involve or relate to a change or potential change in the control of the corporation, a director shall be entitled to consider, without limitation, (1) both the long-term and the short-term interests of the corporation and its shareholders and (2) the effects that the corporation's actions may have in the short-term or in the long-term upon any of the following: (i) the prospects for potential growth, development, productivity and profitability of the corporation; (ii) the corporation's current employees; (iii) the corporation's retired employees and other beneficiaries receiving or entitled to receive retirement, welfare or similar benefits from or pursuant to any plan sponsored, or agreement entered into, by the corporation; (iv) the corporation's customers and creditors; and (v) the ability of the corporation to provide, as a going concern, goods, services, employment opportunities and employment benefits and otherwise to contribute to the communities in which it does business. Nothing in this paragraph shall create any duties owed by any director to any person or entity to consider or afford any particular weight to any of the foregoing or abrogate any duty of the directors, either statutory or recognized by common law or court decisions. For purposes of this paragraph, "control" shall mean the possession, directly or indirectly, of the power to direct or cause the direction of the management and policies of the corporation, whether through the ownership of voting stock, by contract, or otherwise.

S 718. List of directors and officers.

(a) If a shareholder of a corporation, in person or by his attorney or agent, or a representative of the district attorney or of the secretary of state, the attorney general, or other state official, makes a written demand on a corporation to inspect a current list of its directors and officers, the corporation shall, within two business days after receipt of the demand and for a period of one week thereafter, make the list available for such inspection at its office during usual business hours.

(b) Upon refusal by the corporation to make a current list of its directors and officers available, as provided in paragraph (a), the person making a demand for such list may apply, ex parte, to the supreme court at a special term held within the judicial district where the office of the corporation is located for an order directing the corporation to make such list available. The court may grant such order or take such other action as it may deem just and proper.

S 719. Liability of directors in certain cases.

(a) Directors of a corporation who vote for or concur in any of the following corporate actions shall be jointly and severally liable to the corporation for the benefit of its creditors or shareholders, to the extent of any injury suffered by such persons, respectively, as a result of such action: (1) The declaration of any dividend or other distribution to the extent that it is contrary to the provisions of paragraphs (a) and (b) of section 510 (Dividends or other distributions in cash or property). (2) The purchase of the shares of the corporation to the extent that it is contrary to the provisions of section 513 (Purchase or redemption by a corporation of its own shares). (3) The distribution of assets to shareholders after dissolution of the corporation without paying or adequately providing for all known liabilities of the corporation, excluding any claims not filed by creditors within the time limit set in a notice given to creditors under articles 10 (Nonjudicial dissolution) or 11 (Judicial dissolution). (4) The making of any loan contrary to section 714 (Loans to directors).

(b) A director who is present at a meeting of the board, or any committee thereof, when action specified in paragraph (a) is taken shall be presumed to have concurred in the action unless his dissent thereto shall be entered in the minutes of the meeting, or unless he shall submit his written dissent to the person acting as the secretary of the meeting before the adjournment thereof, or shall deliver or send by registered mail such dissent to the secretary of the corporation promptly after the adjournment of the meeting. Such right to dissent shall not apply to a director who voted in favor of such action. A director who is absent from a meeting of the board, or any committee thereof, when such action is taken shall be presumed to have concurred in the action unless he shall deliver or send by registered mail his dissent thereto to the secretary of the corporation or shall cause such dissent to be filed with the minutes of the proceedings of the board or committee within a reasonable time after learning of such action.

(c) Any director against whom a claim is successfully asserted under this section shall be entitled to contribution from the other directors who voted for or concurred in the action upon which the claim is asserted.

(d) Directors against whom a claim is successfully asserted under this section shall be entitled, to the extent of the amounts paid by them to the corporation as a result of such claims: (1) Upon payment to the corporation of any amount of an improper dividend or distribution, to be subrogated to the rights of the corporation against shareholders who received such dividend or distribution with knowledge of facts indicating that it was not authorized by section 510, in proportion to the amounts received by them respectively. (2) Upon payment to the corporation of any amount of the purchase price of an improper purchase of shares, to have the corporation rescind such purchase of shares and recover for their benefit, but at their expense, the amount of such purchase price from any seller who sold such shares with knowledge of facts indicating that such purchase of shares by the corporation was not authorized by section 513. (3) Upon payment to the corporation of the claim of any creditor by reason of a violation of subparagraph (a) (3), to be subrogated to the rights of the corporation against shareholders who received an improper distribution of assets. (4) Upon payment to the corporation of the amount of any loan made contrary to section 714, to be subrogated to the rights of the corporation against a director who received the improper loan.

(e) A director shall not be liable under this section if, in the circumstances, he performed his duty to the corporation under paragraph (a) of section 717.

(f) This section shall not affect any liability otherwise imposed by law upon any director.

S 720. Action against directors and officers for misconduct.

(a) An action may be brought against one or more directors or officers of a corporation to procure a judgment for the following relief: (1) Subject to any provision of the certificate of incorporation authorized pursuant to paragraph (b) of section 402, to compel the defendant to account for his official conduct in the following cases: (A) The neglect of, or failure to perform, or other violation of his duties in the management and disposition of corporate assets committed to his charge. (B) The acquisition by himself, transfer to others, loss or waste of corporate assets due to any neglect of, or failure to perform, or other violation of his duties. (2) To set aside an unlawful conveyance, assignment or transfer of corporate assets, where the transferee knew of its unlawfulness. (3) To enjoin a proposed unlawful conveyance, assignment or transfer of corporate assets, where there is sufficient evidence that it will be made.

(b) An action may be brought for the relief provided in this section, and in paragraph (a) of section 719 (Liability of directors in certain cases) by a corporation, or a receiver, trustee in bankruptcy, officer, director or judgment creditor thereof, or, under section 626 (Shareholders' derivative action brought in the right of the corporation to procure a judgment in its favor), by a shareholder, voting trust certificate holder, or the owner of a beneficial interest in shares thereof.

(c) This section shall not affect any liability otherwise imposed by law upon any director or officer.

S 721. Nonexclusivity of statutory provisions for indemnification of directors and officers.

The indemnification and advancement of expenses granted pursuant to, or provided by, this article shall not be deemed exclusive of any other rights to which a director or officer seeking indemnification or advancement of expenses may be entitled, whether contained in the certificate of incorporation or the by-laws or, when authorized by such certificate of incorporation or by-laws, (i) a resolution of shareholders, (ii) a resolution of directors, or (iii) an agreement providing for such indemnification, provided that no indemnification may be made to or on behalf of any director or officer if a judgment or other final adjudication adverse to the director or officer establishes that his acts were committed in bad faith or were the result of active and deliberate dishonesty and were material to the cause of action so adjudicated, or that he personally gained in fact a financial profit or other advantage to which he was not legally entitled. Nothing contained in this article shall affect any rights to indemnification to which corporate personnel other than directors and officers may be entitled by contract or otherwise under law.

S 722. Authorization for indemnification of directors and officers.

(a) A corporation may indemnify any person made, or threatened to be made, a party to an action or proceeding (other than one by or in the right of the corporation to procure a judgment in its favor), whether civil or criminal, including an action by or in the right of any other corporation of any type or kind, domestic or foreign, or any partnership, joint venture, trust, employee benefit plan or other enterprise, which any director or officer of the corporation served in any capacity at the request of the corporation, by reason of the fact that he, his testator or intestate, was a director or officer of the corporation, or served such other corporation, partnership, joint venture, trust, employee benefit plan or other enterprise in any capacity, against judgments, fines, amounts paid in settlement and reasonable expenses, including attorneys' fees actually and necessarily incurred as a result of such action or proceeding, or any appeal therein, if such director or officer acted, in good faith, for a purpose which he reasonably believed to be in, or, in the case of service for any other corporation or any partnership, joint venture, trust, employee benefit plan or other enterprise, not opposed to, the best interests of the corporation and, in criminal actions or proceedings, in addition, had no reasonable cause to believe that his conduct was unlawful.

(b) The termination of any such civil or criminal action or proceeding by judgment, settlement, conviction or upon a plea of nolo contendere, or its equivalent, shall not in itself create a presumption that any such director or officer did not act, in good faith, for a purpose which he reasonably believed to be in, or, in the case of service for any other corporation or any partnership, joint venture, trust, employee benefit plan or other enterprise, not opposed to, the best interests of the corporation or that he had reasonable cause to believe that his conduct was unlawful.

(c) A corporation may indemnify any person made, or threatened to be made, a party to an action by or in the right of the corporation to procure a judgment in its favor by reason of the fact that he, his testator or intestate, is or was a director or officer of the corporation, or is or was serving at the request of the corporation as a director or officer of any other corporation of any type or kind, domestic or foreign, of any partnership, joint venture, trust, employee benefit plan or other enterprise, against amounts paid in settlement and reasonable expenses, including attorneys' fees, actually and necessarily incurred by him in connection with the defense or settlement of such action, or in connection with an appeal therein, if such director or officer acted, in good faith, for a purpose which he reasonably believed to be in, or, in the case of service for any other corporation or any partnership, joint venture, trust, employee benefit plan or other enterprise, not opposed to, the best interests of the corporation, except that no indemnification under this paragraph shall be made in respect of (1) a threatened action, or a pending action which is settled or otherwise disposed of, or (2) any claim, issue or matter as to which such person shall have been adjudged to be liable to the corporation, unless and only to the extent that the court in which the action was brought, or, if no action was brought, any court of competent jurisdiction, determines upon application that, in view of all the circumstances of the case, the person is fairly and reasonably entitled to indemnity for such portion of the settlement amount and expenses as the court deems proper.

(d) For the purpose of this section, a corporation shall be deemed to have requested a person to serve an employee benefit plan where the performance by such person of his duties to the corporation also imposes duties on, or otherwise involves services by, such person to the plan or participants or beneficiaries of the plan; excise taxes assessed on a person with respect to an employee benefit plan pursuant to applicable law shall be considered fines; and action taken or omitted by a person with respect to an employee benefit plan in the performance of such person's duties for a purpose reasonably believed by such person to be in the interest of the participants and beneficiaries of the plan shall be deemed to be for a purpose which is not opposed to the best interests of the corporation.

S 723. Payment of indemnification other than by court award.

(a) A person who has been successful, on the merits or otherwise, in the defense of a civil or criminal action or proceeding of the character described in section 722 shall be entitled to indemnification as authorized in such section.

(b) Except as provided in paragraph (a), any indemnification under section 722 or otherwise permitted by section 721, unless ordered by a court under section 724 (Indemnification of directors and officers by a court), shall be made by the corporation, only if authorized in the specific case: (1) By the board acting by a quorum consisting of directors who are not parties to such action or proceeding upon a finding that the director or officer has met the standard of conduct set forth in section 722 or established pursuant to section 721, as the case may be, or, (2) If a quorum under subparagraph (1) is not obtainable or, even if obtainable, a quorum of disinterested directors so directs; (A) By the board upon the opinion in writing of independent legal counsel that indemnification is proper in the circumstances because the applicable standard of conduct set forth in such sections has been met by such director or officer, or (B) By the shareholders upon a finding that the director or officer has met the applicable standard of conduct set forth in such sections.

(c) Expenses incurred in defending a civil or criminal action or proceeding may be paid by the corporation in advance of the final disposition of such action or proceeding upon receipt of an undertaking by or on behalf of such director or officer to repay such amount as, and to the extent, required by paragraph (a) of section 725.

S 724. Indemnification of directors and officers by a court.

(a) Notwithstanding the failure of a corporation to provide indemnification, and despite any contrary resolution of the board or of the shareholders in the specific case under section 723 (Payment of indemnification other than by court award), indemnification shall be awarded by a court to the extent authorized under section 722 (Authorization for indemnification of directors and officers), and paragraph (a) of section 723. Application therefor may be made, in every case, either: (1) In the civil action or proceeding in which the expenses were incurred or other amounts were paid, or (2) To the supreme court in a separate proceeding, in which case the application shall set forth the disposition of any previous application made to any court for the same or similar relief and also reasonable cause for the failure to make application for such relief in the action or proceeding in which the expenses were incurred or other amounts were paid.

(b) The application shall be made in such manner and form as may be required by the applicable rules of court or, in the absence thereof, by direction of a court to which it is made. Such application shall be upon notice to the corporation. The court may also direct that notice be given at the expense of the corporation to the shareholders and such other persons as it may designate in such manner as it may require.

(c) Where indemnification is sought by judicial action, the court may allow a person such reasonable expenses, including attorneys' fees, during the pendency of the litigation as are necessary in connection with his defense therein, if the court shall find that the defendant has by his pleadings or during the course of the litigation raised genuine issues of fact or law.

S 725. Other provisions affecting indemnification of directors and officers.

(a) All expenses incurred in defending a civil or criminal action or proceeding which are advanced by the corporation under paragraph (c) of section 723 (Payment of indemnification other than by court award) or allowed by a court under paragraph (c) of section 724 (Indemnification of directors and officers by a court) shall be repaid in case the person receiving such advancement or allowance is ultimately found, under the procedure set forth in this article, not to be entitled to indemnification or, where indemnification is granted, to the extent the expenses so advanced by the corporation or allowed by the court exceed the indemnification to which he is entitled.

(b) No indemnification, advancement or allowance shall be made under this article in any circumstance where it appears: (1) That the indemnification would be inconsistent with the law of the jurisdiction of incorporation of a foreign corporation which prohibits or otherwise limits such indemnification; (2) That the indemnification would be inconsistent with a provision of the certificate of incorporation, a by-law, a resolution of the board or of the shareholders, an agreement or other proper corporate action, in effect at the time of the accrual of the alleged cause of action asserted in the threatened or pending action or proceeding in which the expenses were incurred or other amounts were paid, which prohibits or otherwise limits indemnification; or (3) If there has been a settlement approved by the court, that the indemnification would be inconsistent with any condition with respect to indemnification expressly imposed by the court in approving the settlement.

(c) If any expenses or other amounts are paid by way of indemnification, otherwise than by court order or action by the shareholders, the corporation shall, not later than the next annual meeting of shareholders unless such meeting is held within three months from the date of such payment, and, in any event, within fifteen months from the date of such payment, mail to its shareholders of record at the time entitled to vote for the election of directors a statement specifying the persons paid, the amounts paid, and the nature and status at the time of such payment of the litigation or threatened litigation.

(d) If any action with respect to indemnification of directors and officers is taken by way of amendment of the by-laws, resolution of directors, or by agreement, then the corporation shall, not later than the next annual meeting of shareholders, unless such meeting is held within three months from the date of such action, and, in any event, within fifteen months from the date of such action, mail to its shareholders of record at the time entitled to vote for the election of directors a statement specifying the action taken.

(e) Any notification required to be made pursuant to the foregoing paragraph (c) or (d) of this section by any domestic mutual insurer shall be satisfied by compliance with the corresponding provisions of section one thousand two hundred sixteen of the insurance law.

(f) The provisions of this article relating to indemnification of directors and officers and insurance therefor shall apply to domestic corporations and foreign corporations doing business in this state, except as provided in section 1320 (Exemption from certain provisions).

S 726. Insurance for indemnification of directors and officers.

(a) Subject to paragraph (b), a corporation shall have power to purchase and maintain insurance: (1) To indemnify the corporation for any obligation which it incurs as a result of the indemnification of directors and officers under the provisions of this article, and (2) To indemnify directors and officers in instances in which they may be indemnified by the corporation under the provisions of this article, and (3) To indemnify directors and officers in instances in which they may not otherwise be indemnified by the corporation under the provisions of this article provided the contract of insurance covering such directors and officers provides, in a manner acceptable to the superintendent of insurance, for a retention amount and for co-insurance.

(b) No insurance under paragraph (a) may provide for any payment, other than cost of defense, to or on behalf of any director or officer: (1) if a judgment or other final adjudication adverse to the insured director or officer establishes that his acts of active and deliberate dishonesty were material to the cause of action so adjudicated, or that he personally gained in fact a financial profit or other advantage to which he was not legally entitled, or (2) in relation to any risk the insurance of which is prohibited under the insurance law of this state.

(c) Insurance under any or all subparagraphs of paragraph (a) may be included in a single contract or supplement thereto. Retrospective rated contracts are prohibited.

(d) The corporation shall, within the time and to the persons provided in paragraph (c) of section 725 (Other provisions affecting indemnification of directors or officers), mail a statement in respect of any insurance it has purchased or renewed under this section, specifying the insurance carrier, date of the contract, cost of the insurance, corporate positions insured, and a statement explaining all sums, not previously reported in a statement to shareholders, paid under any indemnification insurance contract.

(e) This section is the public policy of this state to spread the risk of corporate management, notwithstanding any other general or special law of this state or of any other jurisdiction including the federal government.

ARTICLE 8
AMENDMENTS AND CHANGES

S 801. Right to amend certificate of incorporation.

(a) A corporation may amend its certificate of incorporation, from time to time, in any and as many respects as may be desired, if such amendment contains only such provisions as might be lawfully contained in an original certificate of incorporation filed at the time of making such amendment.

(b) In particular, and without limitation upon such general power of amendment, a corporation may amend its certificate of incorporation, from time to time, so as: (1) To change its corporate name. (2) To enlarge, limit or otherwise change its corporate purposes. (3) To specify or change the location of the office of the corporation. (4) To specify or change the post office address to which the secretary of state shall mail a copy of any process against the corporation served upon him. (5) To make, revoke or change the designation of a registered agent, or to specify or change the address of its registered agent. (6) To extend the duration of the corporation or, if the corporation ceased to exist because of the expiration of the duration specified in its certificate of incorporation, to revive its existence. (7) To increase or decrease the aggregate number of shares, or shares of any class or series, with or without par value, which the corporation shall have authority to issue. (8) To remove from authorized shares any class of shares, or any shares of any class, whether issued or unissued. (9) To increase the par value of any authorized shares of any class with par value, whether issued or unissued. (10) To reduce the par value of any authorized shares of any class with par value, whether issued or unissued. (11) To change any authorized shares, with or without par value, whether issued or unissued, into a different number of shares of the same class or into the same or a different number of shares of any one or more classes or any series thereof, either with or without par value. (12) To fix, change or abolish the designation of any authorized class or any series thereof or any of the relative rights, preferences and limitations of any shares of any authorized class or any series thereof, whether issued or unissued, including any provisions in respect of any undeclared dividends, whether or not cumulative or accrued, or the redemption of any shares, or any sinking fund for the redemption or purchase of any shares, or any preemptive right to acquire shares or other securities. (13) As to the shares of any preferred class, then or theretofore authorized, which may be issued in series, to grant authority to the board or to change or revoke the authority of the board to establish and designate series and to fix the number of shares and the relative rights, preferences and limitation as between series. (14) To strike out, change or add any provision, not inconsistent with this chapter or any other statute, relating to the business of the corporation, its affairs, its rights or powers, or the rights or powers of its shareholders, directors or officers, including any provision which under this chapter is required or permitted to be set forth in the by-laws, except that a certificate of amendment may not be filed wherein the duration of the corporation shall be reduced.

(c) A corporation created by special act may accomplish any or all amendments permitted in this article, in the manner and subject to the conditions provided in this article.

S 802. Reduction of stated capital by amendment.

(a) A corporation may reduce its stated capital by an amendment of its certificate of incorporation under section 801 (Right to amend certificate of incorporation) which: (1) Reduces the par value of any issued shares with par value. (2) Changes issued shares under subparagraph (b) (11) of section 801 that results in a reduction of stated capital. (3) Removes from authorized shares, shares that have been issued, reacquired and cancelled by the corporation.

(b) This section shall not prevent a corporation from reducing its stated capital in any other manner permitted by this chapter.

S 803. Authorization of amendment or change.

(a) Amendment or change of the certificate of incorporation may be authorized by vote of the board, followed by vote of a majority of all outstanding shares entitled to vote thereon at a meeting of shareholders, provided, however, that whenever the certificate of incorporation shall require action by the board of directors, by the holders of any class or series of shares or by the holders of any other securities having voting power, the vote of a greater number or proportion than is required by any section of this article, the provision of the certificates of incorporation requiring such greater vote shall not be altered, amended or repealed except by such greater vote.

(b) Alternatively, any one or more of the following changes may be authorized by or pursuant to authorization of the board: (1) To specify or change the location of the corporation's office. (2) To specify or change the post office address to which the secretary of state shall mail a copy of any process against the corporation served upon him. (3) To make, revoke or change the designation of a registered agent, or to specify or change the address of its registered agent.

(c) This section shall not alter the vote required under any other section for the authorization of an amendment referred to therein, nor alter the authority of the board to authorize amendments under any other section.

(d) Amendment or change of the certificate of incorporation of a corporation which has no shareholders of record, no subscribers for shares whose subscriptions have been accepted and no directors may be authorized by the sole incorporator or a majority of the incorporators.

S 804. Class voting on amendment.

(a) Notwithstanding any provision in the certificate of incorporation, the holders of shares of a class shall be entitled to vote and to vote as a class upon the authorization of an amendment and, in addition to the authorization of the amendment by a majority of the votes of all outstanding shares entitled to vote thereon, the amendment shall be authorized by a majority of the votes of all outstanding shares of the class when a proposed amendment would: (1) Exclude or limit their right to vote on any matter, except as such right may be limited by voting rights given to new shares then being authorized of any existing or new class or series. (2) Change their shares under subparagraphs (b) (10), (11) or (12) of section 801 (Right to amend certificate of incorporation) or provide that their shares may be converted into shares of any other class or into shares of any other series of the same class, or alter the terms or conditions upon which their shares are convertible or change the shares issuable upon conversion of their shares, if such action would adversely affect such holders, or (3) Subordinate their rights, by authorizing shares having preferences which would be in any respect superior to their rights.

(b) If any proposed amendment referred to in paragraph (a) would adversely affect the rights of the holders of shares of only one or more series of any class, but not the entire class, then only the holders of those series whose rights would be affected shall be considered a separate class for the purposes of this section.

S 805. Certificate of amendment; contents.

(a) To accomplish any amendment, a certificate of amendment, entitled "Certificate of amendment of the certificate of incorporation of ....(name of corporation) under section 805 of the Business Corporation Law", shall be signed and delivered to the department of state. It shall set forth: (1) The name of the corporation and, if it has been changed, the name under which it was formed. (2) The date its certificate of incorporation was filed by the department of state. (3) Each amendment effected thereby, setting forth the subject matter of each provision of the certificate of incorporation which is to be amended or eliminated and the full text of the provision or provisions, if any, which are to be substituted or added. (4) If an amendment provides for a change of shares, the number, par value and class of issued shares changed, the number, par value and class of issued shares resulting from such change, the number, par value and class of unissued shares changed, the number, par value and class of unissued shares resulting from such change and the terms of each such change. If an amendment makes two or more such changes, a like statement shall be included in respect to each change. (5) If any amendment reduces stated capital, then a statement of the manner in which the same is effected and the amounts from which and to which stated capital is reduced. (6) The manner in which the amendment of the certificate of incorporation was authorized. If the amendment was authorized under paragraph (d) of section eight hundred three of this chapter, then a statement that the corporation does not have any shareholders of record or any subscribers for shares whose subscriptions have been accepted and no directors.

(b) Any number of amendments or changes may be included in one certificate under this section. Such certificate may also include any amendments or changes permitted by other sections and in that case the certificate shall set forth any additional statement required by any other section specifying the contents of a certificate to effect such amendment or change.

(c) In the case of a change of shares, the shares resulting from such change, shall upon the filing of the certificate of amendment, be deemed substituted for the shares changed, in accordance with the stated terms of change.

S 805-A. Certificate of change; contents.

(a) Any one or more of the changes authorized by paragraph (b) of section 803 (Authorization of amendment or change) may be accomplished by filing a certificate of change which shall be entitled "Certificate of change of. (name of corporation) under section 805-A of the Business Corporation Law" and shall be signed and delivered to the department of state. It shall set forth: (1) The name of the corporation, and if it has been changed, the name under which it was formed. (2) The date its certificate of incorporation was filed by the department of state. (3) Each change effected thereby. (4) The manner in which the change was authorized.

(b) A certificate of change which changes only the post office address to which the secretary of state shall mail a copy of any process against a corporation served upon him or the address of the registered agent, provided such address being changed is the address of a person, partnership or other corporation whose address, as agent, is the address to be changed or who has been designated as registered agent for such corporation, may be signed, verified and delivered to the department of state by such agent. The certificate of change shall set forth the statements required under subparagraphs (a) (1), (2) and (3) of this section; that a notice of the proposed change was mailed to the corporation by the party signing the certificate not less than thirty days prior to the date of delivery to the department and that such corporation has not objected thereto; and that the party signing the certificate is the agent of such corporation to whose address the secretary of state is required to mail copies of process or the registered agent, if such be the case. A certificate signed, verified and delivered under this paragraph shall not be deemed to effect a change of location of the office of the corporation in whose behalf such certificate is filed.

S 806. **Provisions as to certain proceedings.**

(a) The department of state shall not file a certificate of amendment reviving the existence of a corporation unless the consent of the state tax commission to the revival is delivered to the department. If the name of the corporation being revived is not available under section 301 (Corporate name; general) for use by a corporation then being formed under this chapter, the certificate of amendment shall change the name to one which is available for such use.

(b) The following provisions shall apply to amendments and changes under this article, except under section 808 (Reorganization under act of congress): (1) The stated capital in respect of any shares without par value resulting from a change of issued shares shall be the amount of stated capital in respect of the shares changed or, if such stated capital is reduced by the amendment, the reduced amount stated in the certificate of amendment. No corporation shall change issued shares into both shares with par value and shares without par value unless the stated capital in respect of the shares so changed or, if such stated capital is reduced by the amendment, the reduced amount of stated capital stated in the certificate of amendment, exceeds the par value of the shares with par value resulting from such change; and the amount of such excess shall be the stated capital in respect of the shares without par value resulting from such change. (2) No corporation shall increase the aggregate par value of its issued shares with par value, unless, after giving effect to such increase, the stated capital is at least equal to the amount required by subparagraph (a) (12) of section 102 (Definitions). (3) No reduction of stated capital shall be made by amendment unless after such reduction the stated capital exceeds the aggregate preferential amount payable upon involuntary liquidation upon all issued shares having preferential rights in assets plus the par value of all other issued shares with par value. (4) Any changes that may be made in the relative rights, preferences and limitations of the authorized shares of any class by any certificate of amendment which does not eliminate such shares from authorized shares or change them into shares of another class, shall not for the purpose of any statute or rule of law effect an issue of a new class of shares. (5) No amendment or change shall affect any existing cause of action in favor of or against the corporation, or any pending suit to which it shall be a party, or the existing rights of persons other than shareholders; and in the event the corporate name shall be changed, no suit brought by or against the corporation under its former name shall abate for that reason. (6) A holder of any adversely affected shares who does not vote for or consent in writing to the taking of such action shall, subject to and by complying with the provisions of section 623 (Procedure to enforce shareholder's right to receive payment for shares), have the right to dissent and to receive payment for such shares, if the certificate of amendment (A) alters or abolishes any preferential right of such shares having preferences; or (B) creates, alters or abolishes any provision or right in respect of the redemption of such shares or any sinking fund for the redemption or purchase of such shares; or (C) alters or abolishes any preemptive right of such holder to acquire shares or other securities; or (D) excludes or limits the right of such holder to vote on any matter, except as such right may be limited by the voting rights given to new shares then being authorized of any existing or new class.

S 807. **Restated certificate of incorporation.**

(a) A corporation, when authorized by the board, may restate in a single certificate the text of its certificate of incorporation without making any amendment or change thereby, except that it may include any one or more of the amendments or changes which may be authorized by the board without a vote of shareholders under this chapter. Alternatively, a corporation may restate in a single certificate the text of its certificate of incorporation as amended thereby to effect any one or more of the amendments or changes authorized by this chapter, when authorized by the required vote of the holders of shares entitled to vote thereon.

(b) A restated certificate of incorporation, entitled "Restated certificate of incorporation .... (name of corporation) under section 807 of the Business Corporation Law", shall be signed and delivered to the department of state. It shall set forth: (1) The name of the corporation and, if it has been changed, the name under which it was formed. (2) The date its certificate of incorporation was filed by the department of state. (3) If the restated certificate restates the text of the certificate of incorporation without making any amendment or change, then a statement that the text of the certificate of incorporation is thereby restated without amendment or change to read as therein set forth in full. (4) If the restated certificate restates the text of the certificate of incorporation as amended or changed thereby, then a statement that the certificate of incorporation is amended or changed to effect one or more of the amendments or changes authorized by this chapter, specifying each such amendment or change and that the text of the certificate of incorporation is thereby restated as amended or changed to read as therein set forth in full. (5) If an amendment, effected by the restated certificate, provides for a change of issued shares, the number and kind of shares changed, the number and kind of shares resulting from such change and the terms of change. If any amendment makes two or more such changes, a like statement shall be included in respect to each such change. (6) If the restated certificate contains an amendment which effects a reduction of stated capital, then a statement of the manner in which the same is effected and the amounts from which and to which stated capital is reduced. (7) The manner in which the restatement of the certificate of incorporation was authorized.

(c) A restated certificate need not include statements as to the incorporator or incorporators, the original subscribers for shares or the first directors.

(d) Any amendment or change under this section shall be subject to any other section, not inconsistent with this section, which would be applicable if a separate certificate were filed to effect such amendment or change.

(e) Notwithstanding that the corporation would be required by any statute to secure from any state official, department, board, agency or other body, any consent or approval to the filing of its certificate of incorporation or a certificate of amendment, such consent or approval shall not be required with respect to the restated certificate if such certificate makes no amendment and if any previously required consent or approval had been secured. (f) Upon filing by the department, the original certificate of incorporation shall be superseded and the restated certificate of incorporation, including any amendments and changes made thereby, shall be the certificate of incorporation of the corporation.

S 808. Reorganization under act of congress.

(a) Whenever a plan of reorganization of a corporation has been confirmed by a decree or order of a court in proceedings under any applicable act of congress relating to reorganization of corporations, the corporation shall have authority, without action of its shareholders or board, to put into effect and carry out the plan and decree and orders of the court relative thereto, and take any proceeding and any action for which provision is made in any statute governing the corporation or for which provision is or might be made in its certificate of incorporation or by-laws and which is provided for in such plan or directed by any such decree or order.

(b) Such authority may be exercised, and such proceedings and actions may be taken, as may be directed by any such decree or order, by the trustee or trustees of such corporation appointed in the reorganization proceedings, or if none is acting, by any person or persons designated or appointed for the purpose by any such decree or order, with like effect as if exercised and taken by unanimous action of the board and shareholders of the corporation.

(c) Any certificate, required or permitted by law to be filed or recorded to accomplish any corporate purpose, shall be signed, and verified or acknowledged, under any such decree or order, by such trustee or trustees or the person or persons referred to in paragraph (b), and shall certify that provision for such certificate is contained in the plan of reorganization or in a decree or order of the court relative thereto, and that the plan has been confirmed, as provided in an applicable act of congress, specified in the certificate, with the title and venue of the proceeding and the date when the decree or order confirming the plan was made, and such certificate shall be delivered to the department of state.

(d) A shareholder of any such corporation shall have no right to receive payment for his shares and only such rights, if any, as are provided in the plan of reorganization.

(e) Notwithstanding section 504 (Consideration and payment for shares), such corporation may, after the confirmation of such plan, issue its shares, bonds and other securities for the consideration specified in the plan of reorganization and may issue warrants or other optional rights for the purchase of shares upon such terms and conditions as may be set forth in such plan.

(f) If after the filing of any such certificate by the department of state, the decree or order of confirmation of the plan of reorganization is reversed or vacated or such plan is modified, such other or further certificates shall be executed and delivered to the department of state as may be required to conform to the plan of reorganization as finally confirmed or to the decree or order as finally made.

(g) Except as otherwise provided in this section, no certificate filed by the department of state hereunder shall confer on any corporation any powers other than those permitted to be conferred on a corporation formed under this chapter.

(h) If, in any proceeding under any applicable act of congress relating to reorganization of corporations, a decree or order provides for the formation of a new domestic corporation or for the authorization of a new foreign corporation to do business in this state under a name the same as or similar to that of the corporation being reorganized, the certificate of incorporation of the new domestic corporation or the application of the new foreign corporation shall set forth that it is being delivered pursuant to such decree or order and be endorsed with the consent of the court having jurisdiction of the proceeding. After such certificate of incorporation or application has been filed, the corporation being reorganized shall not continue the use of its name except in connection with the reorganization proceeding and as may be necessary to adjust and wind up its affairs, and thirty days after such filing, the reorganized domestic corporation shall be automatically dissolved or the authority of the reorganized foreign corporation to transact business in this state shall cease. To the extent that the adjustment and winding up of the affairs of such dissolved corporation is not accomplished as a part of the proceeding or prescribed by the decree or order of such court, it shall proceed in accordance with the provisions of article 10 (Non-judicial dissolution).

(i) This section shall not relieve any corporation from securing from any state official, department, board, agency or other body, any consent or approval required by any statute.

ARTICLE 15
PROFESSIONAL SERVICE CORPORATIONS

S 1501. Definitions.

As used in this article, unless the context otherwise requires, the term:

(a) "Licensing authority" means the regents of the university of the state of New York or the state education department, as the case may be, in the case of all professions licensed under title eight of the education law, and the appropriate appellate division of the supreme court in the case of the profession of law.

(b) "Profession" includes any practice as an attorney and counselor-at-law, or as a licensed physician, and those occupations designated in title eight of the education law.

(c) "Professional service" means any type of service to the public which may be lawfully rendered by a member of a profession within the purview of his profession.

(d) "Professional service corporation" means a corporation organized under this article.

(e) "Officer" does not include the secretary or an assistant secretary of a corporation having only one shareholder.

S 1502. Corporations organized under other provisions of law.

The provisions of this article shall not apply to corporations heretofore or hereafter duly organized under any other provision of law.

S 1503. Organization.

(a) Notwithstanding any other provision of law, one or more individuals duly authorized by law to render the same professional service within the state may organize, or cause to be organized, a professional service corporation for pecuniary profit under this article for the purpose of rendering the same professional service, except that one or more individuals duly authorized by law to practice professional engineering, architecture, landscape architecture or land surveying within the state may organize, or cause to be organized, a professional service corporation for pecuniary profit under this article for the purpose of rendering such professional services as such individuals are authorized to practice.

(b) The certificate of incorporation of a professional service corporation shall meet the requirements of this chapter and (i) shall state the profession or professions to be practiced by such corporation and the names and residence addresses of all individuals who are to be the original shareholders, directors and officers of such corporation, and (ii) shall have attached thereto a certificate or certificates issued by the licensing authority certifying that each of the proposed shareholders, directors and officers is authorized by law to practice a profession which the corporation is being organized to practice and, if applicable, that one or more of such individuals is authorized to practice each profession which the corporation will be authorized to practice.

(c) A certified copy of the certificate of incorporation and of each amendment thereto shall be filed by the corporation with the licensing authority within thirty days after the filing of such certificate or amendment with the department of state.

(d) A professional service corporation, other than a corporation authorized to practice law, shall be under the supervision of the regents of the university of the state of New York and be subject to disciplinary proceedings and penalties, and its certificate of incorporation shall be subject to suspension, revocation or annulment for cause, in the same manner and to the same extent as is provided with respect to individuals and their licenses, certificates, and registrations in title eight of the education law relating to the applicable profession. Notwithstanding the provisions of this subdivision, a professional service corporation authorized to practice medicine shall be subject to the prehearing procedures and hearing procedures as is provided with respect to individual physicians and their licenses in Title II-A of article two of the public health law.

(e) A corporation authorized to practice law shall be subject to the regulation and control of, and its certificate of incorporation shall be subject to suspension, revocation or annulment for cause by, the appellate division of the supreme court and the court of appeals in the same manner and to the same extent provided in the judiciary law with respect to individual attorneys and counselors-at-law. Such corporation need not qualify for any certification under section four hundred sixty-four of the judiciary law, take an oath of office under section four hundred sixty-six of such law or register under section four hundred sixty-seven of such law.

(f) The order of suspension, revocation or annulment of the certificate of incorporation of a professional service corporation pursuant to subdivisions (e) and

(f) of this section shall be effective upon the filing of such order with the department of state.

S 1504. Rendering of professional service.

(a) No professional service corporation may render professional services except through individuals authorized by law to render such professional services as individuals.

(b) Each final plan and report made or issued by a corporation practicing professional engineering, architecture, landscape architecture or land surveying shall bear the name and seal of one or more professional engineers, architects, landscape architects, or land surveyors, respectively, who are in responsible charge of such plan or report.

(c) Each report, diagnosis, prognosis, and prescription made or issued by a corporation practicing medicine, dentistry, podiatry, optometry, ophthalmic dispensing, veterinary medicine, pharmacy, nursing, physiotherapy or chiropractic shall bear the signature of one or more physicians, dentists, podiatrists, optometrists, ophthalmic dispensers, veterinarians, pharmacists, nurses, physiotherapists, or chiropractors, respectively, who are in responsible charge of such report, diagnosis, prognosis, or prescription.

(d) Each record, transcript, report and hearing report prepared by a corporation practicing certified shorthand reporting shall bear the signature of one or more certified shorthand reporters who are in responsible charge of such record, transcript, report, or hearing report.

(e) Each corporation practicing public accounting or certified public accounting shall maintain records indicating the identity of each public accountant or certified public accountant, respectively, who was responsible for each report or statement which is issued prepared or examined by such corporation.

(f) Each opinion prepared by a corporation practicing law shall bear the signature of one or more attorneys and counselors-at-law who are in responsible charge of such opinion.

(g) In addition to the requirements in subdivisions (b) through (f), inclusive, each document prepared by a corporation which under the rules, regulations, laws or customs of the applicable profession is required to bear the signature of an individual in responsible charge of such document, shall be signed by one or more such individuals.

S 1505. Professional relationships and liabilities.

(a) Each shareholder, employee or agent of a professional service corporation shall be personally and fully liable and accountable for any negligent or wrongful act or misconduct committed by him or by any person under his direct supervision and control while rendering professional services on behalf of such corporation.

(b) The relationship of an individual to a professional service corporation with which such individual is associated, whether as shareholder, director, officer, employee or agent, shall not modify or diminish the jurisdiction over him of the licensing authority and in the case of an attorney and counselor-at-law, the other courts of this state.

S 1506. Purposes of incorporation.

No professional service corporation shall engage in any business other than the rendering of the professional services for which it was incorporated; provided that such corporation may invest its funds in real estate, mortgages, stocks, bonds or any other type of investments.

S 1507. Issuance of shares.

A professional service corporation may issue shares only to individuals who are authorized by law to practice in this state a profession which such corporation is authorized to practice and who are or have been engaged in the practice of such profession in such corporation or a predecessor entity, or who will engage in the practice of such profession in such corporation within thirty days of the date such shares are issued. No shareholder of a professional service corporation shall enter into a voting trust agreement, proxy, or any other type agreement vesting in another person, other than another shareholder of the same corporation or a person who would be eligible to become a shareholder if employed by the corporation, the authority to exercise voting power of any or all of his shares. All shares issued, agreements made, or proxies granted in violation of this section shall be void.

S 1508. Directors and officers.

No individual may be a director or officer of a professional service corporation unless he is authorized by law to practice in this state a profession which such corporation is authorized to practice and is either a shareholder of such corporation or engaged in the practice of his profession in such corporation.

S 1509. Disqualification of shareholders, directors, officers and employees.

If any shareholder, director, officer or employee of a professional service corporation who has been rendering professional service to the public becomes legally disqualified to practice his profession within this state, he shall sever all employment with, and financial interests (other than interests as a creditor) in, such corporation forthwith or as otherwise provided in section 1510. All provisions of law regulating the rendering of professional services by a person elected or appointed to a public office shall be applicable to a shareholder, director, officer and employee of such corporation in the same manner and to the same extent as if fully set forth herein. Such legal disqualification to practice his profession within this state shall be deemed to constitute an irrevocable offer by the disqualified shareholder to sell his shares to the corporation, pursuant to the provisions of section 1510 or of the certificate of incorporation, by-laws or agreement among the corporation and all shareholders, whichever is applicable. Compliance with the terms of such offer shall be specifically enforceable in the courts of this state. A professional service corporation's failure to enforce compliance with this provision shall constitute a ground for forfeiture of its certificate of incorporation and its dissolution.

S 1510. (a) Death or disqualification of shareholders.

A professional service corporation shall purchase or redeem the shares of a shareholder in case of his death or disqualification pursuant to the provisions of section 1509, within six months after the appointment of the executor or administrator or other legal representative of the estate of such deceased shareholder, or within six months after such disqualification, at the book value of such shares as of the end of the month immediately preceding the death or disqualification of the shareholder as determined from the books and records of the corporation in accordance with its regular method of accounting. The certificate of incorporation, the by-laws of the corporation or an agreement among the corporation and all shareholders may modify this section by providing for a shorter period of purchase or redemption, or an alternate method of determining the price to be paid for the shares, or both. If the corporation shall fail to purchase or redeem such shares within the required period, a successful plaintiff in an action to recover the purchase price of such shares shall also be awarded reasonable attorneys' fees and costs. Limitations on the purchase or redemption of shares set forth in section five hundred thirteen shall not apply to the purchase or redemption of shares pursuant to this section. Nothing herein contained shall prevent a corporation from paying pension benefits or other deferred compensation to or on behalf of a former or deceased officer, director or employee thereof as otherwise permitted by law. The provisions of this section shall not be deemed to require the purchase of the shares of a disqualified shareholder where the period of disqualification is for less than six months, and the shareholder again becomes eligible to practice his profession within six months from the date of disqualification.

(b) Notwithstanding the provisions of subdivision (a), the corporation shall not be required to purchase or redeem the shares of a deceased or disqualified shareholder if such shares, within the time limit prescribed by subdivision (a), are sold or transferred to another professional pursuant to the provisions of section 1511.

S 1511. Transfer of shares.

No shareholder of a professional service corporation may sell or transfer his shares in such corporation except to another individual who is eligible to have shares issued to him by such corporation or except in trust to another individual who would be eligible to receive shares if he were employed by the corporation. Nothing herein contained shall be construed to prohibit the transfer of shares by operation of law or by court decree. No transferee of shares by operation of law or court decree may vote the shares for any purpose whatsoever except with respect to corporate action under section nine hundred nine and section one thousand one. The restriction in the preceding sentence shall not apply, however, where such transferee would be eligible to have shares issued to him if he were an employee of the corporation and, if there are other shareholders, a majority of such other shareholders shall fail to redeem the shares so transferred, pursuant to section 1510, within sixty days of receiving written notice of such transfer. Any sale or transfer, except by operation of law or court decree or except for a corporation having only one shareholder, may be made only after the same shall have been approved by the board of directors, or at a shareholders' meeting specially called for such purpose by such proportion, not less than a majority, of the outstanding shares as may be provided in the certificate of incorporation or in the by-laws of such professional service corporation. At such shareholders' meeting the shares held by the shareholder proposing to sell or transfer his shares may not be voted or counted for any purpose, unless all shareholders consent that such shares be voted or counted. The certificate of incorporation or the by-laws of the professional service corporation, or the professional service corporation and the shareholders by private agreement, may provide, in lieu of or in addition to the foregoing provisions, for the alienation of shares and may require the redemption or purchase of such shares by such corporation at prices and in a manner specifically set forth therein. The existence of the restrictions on the sale or transfer of shares, as contained in this article and, if applicable, in the certificate of incorporation, by-laws, stock purchase or stock redemption agreement, shall be noted conspicuously on the face or back of every certificate for shares issued by a professional service corporation. Any sale or transfer in violation of such restrictions shall be void.

S 1512. Corporate name.

(a) Notwithstanding any other provision of law, the name of a professional service corporation may contain any word which, at the time of incorporation, could be used in the name of a partnership practicing a profession which the corporation is authorized to practice, and may not contain any word which could not be used by such a partnership. Provided, however, the name of a professional service corporation may not contain the name of a deceased person unless (1) such person's name was part of the corporate name at the time of such person's death; or (2) such person's name was part of the name of an existing partnership and at least two-thirds of such partnership's partners become shareholders of the corporation.

(b) Such corporate name shall end with the words "Professional Corporation" or the abbreviation "P.C." The provisions of paragraph one of subdivision (a) of section three hundred one shall not apply to a professional service corporation.

S 1513. Business corporation law applicable.

This chapter, except article thirteen and article fifteen-A, shall be applicable to a professional service corporation except to the extent that the provisions thereof conflict with this article. A professional service corporation may consolidate or merge only with another corporation organized under this article or authorized to do business in this state under article fifteen-A of this chapter or authorized and registered to practice the same profession pursuant to the applicable provisions of subdivision six of section seventy-two hundred nine of the education law or subdivision four of section seventy-three hundred seven of the education law, or may be a member of a professional service limited liability company, a foreign professional service limited liability company, a registered limited liability partnership or foreign limited liability partnership, and only if all of the professions practiced by such corporations, limited liability companies or limited liability partnerships could be practiced by a single corporation organized under this article.

S 1514. Triennial statement.

Each professional service corporation shall, on or before the first day of July every three years, furnish a statement to the licensing authority listing the name and residence address of each shareholder, director and officer of such corporation and certifying that all such individuals are authorized by law in this state to practice a profession which such corporation is authorized to practice. The statement shall be signed by the president or any vice-president of the corporation and attested to by the secretary or any assistant secretary of the corporation.

S 1515. Regulation of professions.

This article shall not repeal, modify or restrict any provision of the education law or the judiciary law regulating the professions referred to therein except to the extent in conflict herewith.

S 1516. Corporate mergers, consolidations and other reorganizations.

Notwithstanding any inconsistent provision of this article, a professional service corporation, pursuant to the provisions of article nine of this chapter, may be merged or consolidated with another corporation formed pursuant to the provisions of this chapter or with a corporation authorized and registered to practice the same profession pursuant to the applicable provisions of subdivision six of section seventy-two hundred nine of the education law (engineer or land surveyor) or subdivision four of section seventy-three hundred seven of the education law (architect) of article one hundred forty-five of the education law, or with a foreign corporation, or may be otherwise reorganized, provided that the corporation which survives or which is formed pursuant thereto is a professional service corporation or a foreign professional service corporation practicing the same profession or professions in this state or the state of incorporation or, if one of the original corporations is authorized to practice pursuant to the provisions of either subdivision six of section seven thousand two hundred nine or subdivision four of section seven thousand three hundred seven, a corporation authorized and registered to practice the same profession pursuant to the applicable provisions of subdivision six of section seventy-two hundred nine of the education law (engineer or land surveyor) or subdivision four of section seventy-three hundred seven of the education law (architect) of article one hundred forty-five of the education law. The restrictions on the issuance, transfer or sale of shares of a professional service corporation shall be suspended for a period not exceeding thirty days with respect to any issuance, transfer or sale of shares made pursuant to such merger, consolidation or reorganization, provided that (i) no person who would not be eligible to be a shareholder in the absence of this section shall vote the shares of or receive any distribution from such corporation; (ii) after such merger, consolidation or reorganization, any professional service corporation which survives or which is created thereby shall be subject to all of the provisions of this article, and (iii) shares thereafter only may be held by persons who are eligible to receive shares of such professional service corporation or such other corporation authorized and registered to practice the same profession pursuant to the applicable provisions of subdivision six of section seventy-two hundred nine of the education law (engineer or land surveyor) or subdivision four of section seventy-three hundred seven of the education law (architect) of article one hundred forty-five of the education law, which survives. Nothing herein contained shall be construed as permitting the practice of a profession in this state by a corporation which is not incorporated pursuant to the provisions of this article or authorized to do business in this state pursuant to the provisions of article fifteen-A of this chapter or authorized and registered to practice a profession pursuant to the applicable provisions of article one hundred forty-five of the education law. For the purposes of this section, other reorganizations shall be limited to those reorganizations defined in paragraph one of subsection (a) of section three hundred sixty-eight of the internal revenue code.

Appendix C
Corporate Forms

Form 1: Transmittal Letter to Secretary of State 125

Form 2: Application for Reservation of Name 127

Form 3: Certificate of Incorporation 129

Form 4: Certificate of Incorporation—Professional Corporation 131

Form 5: IRS Form SS-4 133

Form 6: Waiver of Notice of Organizational Meeting 137

Form 7: Minutes of Organizational Meeting 139

Form 8: Bylaws 143

Form 9: Bylaws (Professional Corporations) 149

Form 10: Banking Resolution 155

Form 11: Offer to Purchase Stock/Offer to Sell Stock 157

Form 12: Resolution to Reimburse Expenses 159

Form 13: Bill of Sale 161

Form 14: IRS Form 2553 (S corporation election) 163

FORM 15: RESOLUTION ADOPTING S CORPORATION STATUS 167

FORM 16: WAIVER OF NOTICE OF ANNUAL MEETING OF BOARD OF DIRECTORS 169

FORM 17: MINUTES OF ANNUAL MEETING OF BOARD OF DIRECTORS 171

FORM 18: WAIVER OF NOTICE OF ANNUAL MEETING OF SHAREHOLDERS 173

FORM 19: MINUTES OF ANNUAL MEETING OF SHAREHOLDERS 175

FORM 20: WAIVER OF NOTICE OF SPECIAL MEETING OF BOARD OF DIRECTORS 177

FORM 21: MINUTES OF SPECIAL MEETING OF BOARD OF DIRECTORS 179

FORM 22: WAIVER OF NOTICE OF SPECIAL MEETING OF SHAREHOLDERS 181

FORM 23: MINUTES OF SPECIAL MEETING OF SHAREHOLDERS 183

FORM 24: CERTIFICATE OF DISSOLUTION 185

FORM 25: CERTIFICATE OF AMENDMENT 187

FORM 26: OFFICER/DIRECTOR RESIGNATION 189

FORM 27: REGISTERED AGENT RESIGNATION 191

FORM 28: STOCK TRANSFER LEDGER 193

FORM 29: STOCK CERTIFICATE STUBS 195

FORM 30: STOCK CERTIFICATES 199

FORM 31: RESTATED CERTIFICATE OF INCORPORATION 209

Form 1

TRANSMITTAL LETTER

New York State
Department of State
Division of Corporations, State Records,
and Uniform Commercial Code
41 State Street
Albany, NY 12231

SUBJECT: _____
(Proposed corporate name - must include suffix)

❏ Enclosed is an original and one (1) copy of the certificate of incorporation and a check for $135 including $125 filing fee and $10 tax.

❏ Enclosed is an additional $10 for a certified copy.

FROM: _____
Name (Printed or typed)

_____
Address

_____
City, State & Zip

_____
Daytime Telephone number

Application for Reservation of Name
Under §303 of the Business Corporation Law

NYS Department of State
DIVISION OF CORPORATIONS, STATE RECORDS
and UNIFORM COMMMERCIAL CODE
41 State Street
Albany, NY 12231-0001

PLEASE TYPE OR PRINT

APPLICANT'S NAME AND ADDRESS

NAME TO BE RESERVED

RESERVATION IS INTENDED FOR (CHECK ONE)

☐ New domestic corporation

☐ Foreign corporation intending to apply for authority to do business in New York State*

☐ Proposed foreign corporation, not yet incorporated, intending to apply for authority to conduct business in New York State

☐ Change of name of an existing domestic or an authorized foreign corporation*

☐ Foreign corporation intending to apply for authority to do business in New York State whose corporate name is not available for use in New York State*

☐ Authorized foreign corporation intending to change its fictitious name under which it does business in this state*

☐ Authorized foreign corporation which has changed its corporate name in its jurisdiction, such new corporate name not being available for use in New York State*

X_____
Signature of applicant, applicant's attorney or agent
(If attorney or agent, so specify)

_____
Typed/printed name of signer

INSTRUCTIONS:
1. Upon filing this application, the name will be reserved for 60 days and a certificate of reservation will be issued.
2. The certificate of reservation must be returned with and attached to the certificate of incorporation or application for authority, amendment or with a cancellation of the reservation.
3. The name used must be the same as appears in the reservation.
4. A $20 fee payable to the Department of State must accompany this application.
5. Only names for business, transportation, cooperative and railroad corporations may be reserved under §303 of the Business Corporation Law.

*If the reservation is for an existing corporation, domestic or foreign, the corporation must be the applicant.

DOS-234 (Rev. 10/97)

New York State
Department of State
Division of Corporations, State Records and Uniform Commercial Code
Albany, NY 12231

(This form must be printed or typed in black ink)
CERTIFICATE OF INCORPORATION
OF

_____

(Insert corporate name)
Under Section 402 of the Business Corporation Law

FIRST: The name of the corporation is: _____

SECOND: This corporation is formed to engage in any lawful act or activity for which a corporation may be organized under the Business Corporation Law, provided that it is not formed to engage in any act or activity requiring the consent or approval of any state official, department, board, agency or other body.

THIRD: The county within this state, in which the office of the corporation is to be located is: _____.

FOURTH: The total number of shares which the corporation shall have authority to issue and a statement of the par value of each share or a statement that the shares are without par value are: 200 No Par Value

FIFTH: The Secretary of State is designated as agent of the corporation upon whom process against the corporation may be served. The **post office address** to which the Secretary of State shall mail a copy of any process accepted on behalf of the corporation is:

_____
_____
_____

SIXTH: *(optional)* The name and **street address in this state** of the registered agent upon whom process against the corporation may be served is:

_____
_____
_____

SEVENTH: (*optional - is this provision is used, a specific date must be stated which is not before, nor more than 90 days after the date of filing*) The date corporate existence shall begin, if other than the date of filing, is: _____

IN WITNESS WHEREOF, this certificate has been subscribed this _____ day of _____, _____, by the undersigned, who affirms that the statements made herein are true under the penalties of perjury.

X_____
(*Signature*)

_____
(*Type or print*)

_____
(*Street address*)

_____
(*City, State, Zip code*)

This form may not contain any attachments or riders
except an original receipt evidencing reservation of name.

CERTIFICATE OF INCORPORATION
OF

Under Section 402 of the Business Corporation Law

Filed by: _____
      (*Name*)

_____
(*Mailing Address*)

_____
(*City, State, Zip Code*)

New York State
Department of State
Division of Corporations, State Records and Uniform Commercial Code
Albany, NY 12231

(This form must be printed or typed in black ink)
CERTIFICATE OF INCORPORATION (PROFESSIONAL CORPORATION) OF

_____

(*Insert corporate name*)
Under Section 402 of the Business Corporation Law

FIRST: The name of the corporation is: _____

_____

SECOND: This corporation is formed to engage in any lawful act or activity for which a corporation may be organized under the Business Corporation Law, provided that it is not formed to engage in any act or activity requiring the consent or approval of any state official, department, board, agency or other body.

THIRD: The county within this state, in which the office of the corporation is to be located is: _____.

FOURTH: The total number of shares which the corporation shall have authority to issue and a statement of the par value of each share or a statement that the shares are without par value are: 200 No Par Value

FIFTH: The Secretary of State is designated as agent of the corporation upon whom process against the corporation may be served. The **post office address** to which the Secretary of State shall mail a copy of any process accepted on behalf of the corporation is:

_____

_____

SIXTH: (*optional*) The name and **street address in this state** of the registered agent upon whom process against the corporation may be served is:

_____

_____

SEVENTH: (*optional - is this provision is used, a specific date must be stated which is not before, nor more than 90 days after the date of filing*) The date corporate existence shall begin, if other than the date of filing, is: _____

EIGHTH: The profession to be practiced by this corporation is: _____.

NINTH: The names and residential addresses of all shareholders, directors and officers of the corporation are as follows:

_____
_____
_____

TENTH: Certificate of Authority for the above named individuals are annexed hereto.

IN WITNESS WHEREOF, this certificate has been subscribed this _____ day of _____, _____, by the undersigned, who affirms that the statements made herein are true under the penalties of perjury.

X_____
(*Signature*)

_____
(*Type or print*)

_____
(*Street address*)

_____
(*City, State, Zip code*)

This form may not contain any attachments or riders
except an original receipt evidencing reservation of name.

CERTIFICATE OF INCORPORATION
(PROFESSIONAL CORPORATION)
OF

Under Section 402 of the Business Corporation Law

Filed by: _____
  (*Name*)

_____
  (*Mailing Address*)

_____
  (*City, State, Zip Code*)

Form **SS-4**
(Rev. February 1998)
Department of the Treasury
Internal Revenue Service

Application for Employer Identification Number
(For use by employers, corporations, partnerships, trusts, estates, churches, government agencies, certain individuals, and others. See instructions.)
▶ Keep a copy for your records.

EIN

OMB No. 1545-0003

Please type or print clearly.

1 Name of applicant (legal name) (see instructions)	
2 Trade name of business (if different from name on line 1)	**3** Executor, trustee, "care of" name
4a Mailing address (street address) (room, apt., or suite no.)	**5a** Business address (if different from address on lines 4a and 4b)
4b City, state, and ZIP code	**5b** City, state, and ZIP code
6 County and state where principal business is located	
7 Name of principal officer, general partner, grantor, owner, or trustor—SSN or ITIN may be required (see instructions) ▶	

8a Type of entity (Check only one box.) (see instructions)
Caution: *If applicant is a limited liability company, see the instructions for line 8a.*

☐ Sole proprietor (SSN) _____
☐ Partnership   ☐ Personal service corp.
☐ REMIC   ☐ National Guard
☐ State/local government   ☐ Farmers' cooperative
☐ Church or church-controlled organization
☐ Other nonprofit organization (specify) ▶ _____
☐ Other (specify) ▶

☐ Estate (SSN of decedent) _____
☐ Plan administrator (SSN) _____
☐ Other corporation (specify) ▶ _____
☐ Trust
☐ Federal government/military
(enter GEN if applicable) _____

8b If a corporation, name the state or foreign country (if applicable) where incorporated | State | Foreign country

9 Reason for applying (Check only one box.) (see instructions)
☐ Started new business (specify type) ▶ _____
☐ Hired employees (Check the box and see line 12.)
☐ Created a pension plan (specify type) ▶
☐ Banking purpose (specify purpose) ▶ _____
☐ Changed type of organization (specify new type) ▶ _____
☐ Purchased going business
☐ Created a trust (specify type) ▶ _____
☐ Other (specify) ▶

10 Date business started or acquired (month, day, year) (see instructions) | **11** Closing month of accounting year (see instructions)

12 First date wages or annuities were paid or will be paid (month, day, year). **Note:** *If applicant is a withholding agent, enter date income will first be paid to nonresident alien. (month, day, year)* ▶

13 Highest number of employees expected in the next 12 months. **Note:** *If the applicant does not expect to have any employees during the period, enter -0-. (see instructions)* ▶ | Nonagricultural | Agricultural | Household

14 Principal activity (see instructions) ▶

15 Is the principal business activity manufacturing? . . . . ☐ Yes ☐ No
If "Yes," principal product and raw material used ▶

16 To whom are most of the products or services sold? Please check one box.   ☐ Business (wholesale)
☐ Public (retail)   ☐ Other (specify) ▶   ☐ N/A

17a Has the applicant ever applied for an employer identification number for this or any other business? . . . ☐ Yes ☐ No
Note: *If "Yes," please complete lines 17b and 17c.*

17b If you checked "Yes" on line 17a, give applicant's legal name and trade name shown on prior application, if different from line 1 or 2 above.
Legal name ▶   Trade name ▶

17c Approximate date when and city and state where the application was filed. Enter previous employer identification number if known.
Approximate date when filed (mo., day, year) | City and state where filed | Previous EIN

Under penalties of perjury, I declare that I have examined this application, and to the best of my knowledge and belief, it is true, correct, and complete. | Business telephone number (include area code)
| Fax telephone number (include area code)

Name and title (Please type or print clearly.) ▶

Signature ▶   Date ▶

Note: *Do not write below this line. For official use only.*

Please leave blank ▶	Geo.	Ind.	Class	Size	Reason for applying

For Paperwork Reduction Act Notice, see page 4.   Cat. No. 16055N   Form **SS-4** (Rev. 2-98)

Form SS-4 (Rev. 2-98)　　Page **2**

General Instructions

Section references are to the Internal Revenue Code unless otherwise noted.

Purpose of Form

Use Form SS-4 to apply for an employer identification number (EIN). An EIN is a nine-digit number (for example, 12-3456789) assigned to sole proprietors, corporations, partnerships, estates, trusts, and other entities for tax filing and reporting purposes. The information you provide on this form will establish your business tax account.

Caution: *An EIN is for use in connection with your business activities only. Do NOT use your EIN in place of your social security number (SSN).*

Who Must File

You must file this form if you have not been assigned an EIN before and:

• You pay wages to one or more employees including household employees.

• You are required to have an EIN to use on any return, statement, or other document, even if you are not an employer.

• You are a withholding agent required to withhold taxes on income, other than wages, paid to a nonresident alien (individual, corporation, partnership, etc.). A withholding agent may be an agent, broker, fiduciary, manager, tenant, or spouse, and is required to file **Form 1042**, Annual Withholding Tax Return for U.S. Source Income of Foreign Persons.

• You file **Schedule C**, Profit or Loss From Business, **Schedule C-EZ**, Net Profit From Business, or **Schedule F**, Profit or Loss From Farming, of **Form 1040**, U.S. Individual Income Tax Return, **and** have a Keogh plan or are required to file excise, employment, or alcohol, tobacco, or firearms returns.

The following must use EINs even if they do not have any employees:

• State and local agencies who serve as tax reporting agents for public assistance recipients, under Rev. Proc. 80-4, 1980-1 C.B. 581, should obtain a separate EIN for this reporting. See **Household employer** on page 3.

• Trusts, except the following:

　1. Certain grantor-owned trusts. (See the **Instructions for Form 1041**.)

　2. Individual Retirement Arrangement (IRA) trusts, unless the trust has to file **Form 990-T**, Exempt Organization Business Income Tax Return. (See the **Instructions for Form 990-T**.)

• Estates
• Partnerships
• REMICs (real estate mortgage investment conduits) (See the **Instructions for Form 1066**, U.S. Real Estate Mortgage Investment Conduit Income Tax Return.)
• Corporations
• Nonprofit organizations (churches, clubs, etc.)
• Farmers' cooperatives
• Plan administrators (A plan administrator is the person or group of persons specified as the administrator by the instrument under which the plan is operated.)

When To Apply for a New EIN

New Business. If you become the new owner of an existing business, **do not** use the EIN of the former owner. IF YOU ALREADY HAVE AN EIN, USE THAT NUMBER. If you do not have an EIN, apply for one on this form. If you become the "owner" of a corporation by acquiring its stock, use the corporation's EIN.

Changes in Organization or Ownership. If you already have an EIN, you may need to get a new one if either the organization or ownership of your business changes. If you incorporate a sole proprietorship or form a partnership, you must get a new EIN. However, **do not** apply for a new EIN if:

• You change only the name of your business,

• You elected on **Form 8832**, Entity Classification Election, to change the way the entity is taxed, or

• A partnership terminates because at least 50% of the total interests in partnership capital and profits were sold or exchanged within a 12-month period. (See Regulations section 301.6109-1(d)(2)(iii).) The EIN for the terminated partnership should continue to be used. This rule applies to terminations occurring after May 8, 1997. If the termination took place after May 8, 1996, and before May 9, 1997, a new EIN must be obtained for the new partnership unless the partnership and its partners are consistent in using the old EIN.

Note: *If you are electing to be an "S corporation," be sure you file **Form 2553**, Election by a Small Business Corporation.*

File Only One Form SS-4. File only one Form SS-4, regardless of the number of businesses operated or trade names under which a business operates. However, each corporation in an affiliated group must file a separate application.

EIN Applied for, But Not Received. If you do not have an EIN by the time a return is due, write "Applied for" and the date you applied in the space shown for the number. **Do not** show your social security number (SSN) as an EIN on returns.

If you do not have an EIN by the time a tax deposit is due, send your payment to the Internal Revenue Service Center for your filing area. (See **Where To Apply** below.) Make your check or money order payable to Internal Revenue Service and show your name (as shown on Form SS-4), address, type of tax, period covered, and date you applied for an EIN. Send an explanation with the deposit.

For more information about EINs, see **Pub. 583**, Starting a Business and Keeping Records, and **Pub. 1635**, Understanding your EIN.

How To Apply

You can apply for an EIN either by mail or by telephone. You can get an EIN immediately by calling the Tele-TIN number for the service center for your state, or you can send the completed Form SS-4 directly to the service center to receive your EIN by mail.

Application by Tele-TIN. Under the Tele-TIN program, you can receive your EIN by telephone and use it immediately to file a return or make a payment. To receive an EIN by telephone, complete Form SS-4, then call the Tele-TIN number listed for your state under **Where To Apply**. The person making the call must be authorized to sign the form. (See **Signature** on page 4.)

An IRS representative will use the information from the Form SS-4 to establish your account and assign you an EIN. Write the number you are given on the upper right corner of the form and sign and date it.

Mail or fax (facsimile) the signed SS-4 **within 24 hours** to the Tele-TIN Unit at the service center address for your state. The IRS representative will give you the fax number. The fax numbers are also listed in Pub. 1635.

Taxpayer representatives can receive their client's EIN by telephone if they first send a fax of a completed **Form 2848**, Power of Attorney and Declaration of Representative, or **Form 8821**, Tax Information Authorization, to the Tele-TIN unit. The Form 2848 or Form 8821 will be used solely to release the EIN to the representative authorized on the form.

Application by Mail. Complete Form SS-4 at least 4 to 5 weeks before you will need an EIN. Sign and date the application and mail it to the service center address for your state. You will receive your EIN in the mail in approximately 4 weeks.

Where To Apply

The Tele-TIN numbers listed below will involve a long-distance charge to callers outside of the local calling area and can be used only to apply for an EIN. THE NUMBERS MAY CHANGE WITHOUT NOTICE. Call 1-800-829-1040 to verify a number or to ask about the status of an application by mail.

If your principal business, office or agency, or legal residence in the case of an individual, is located in:	Call the Tele-TIN number shown or file with the Internal Revenue Service Center at:
Florida, Georgia, South Carolina	Attn: Entity Control Atlanta, GA 39901 770-455-2360
New Jersey, New York City and counties of Nassau, Rockland, Suffolk, and Westchester	Attn: Entity Control Holtsville, NY 00501 516-447-4955
New York (all other counties), Connecticut, Maine, Massachusetts, New Hampshire, Rhode Island, Vermont	Attn: Entity Control Andover, MA 05501 978-474-9717
Illinois, Iowa, Minnesota, Missouri, Wisconsin	Attn: Entity Control Stop 6800 2306 E. Bannister Rd. Kansas City, MO 64999 816-926-5999
Delaware, District of Columbia, Maryland, Pennsylvania, Virginia	Attn: Entity Control Philadelphia, PA 19255 215-516-6999
Indiana, Kentucky, Michigan, Ohio, West Virginia	Attn: Entity Control Cincinnati, OH 45999 606-292-5467

Form SS-4 (Rev. 2-98) Page **3**

Kansas, New Mexico, Oklahoma, Texas	Attn: Entity Control Austin, TX 73301 512-460-7843
Alaska, Arizona, California (counties of Alpine, Amador, Butte, Calaveras, Colusa, Contra Costa, Del Norte, El Dorado, Glenn, Humboldt, Lake, Lassen, Marin, Mendocino, Modoc, Napa, Nevada, Placer, Plumas, Sacramento, San Joaquin, Shasta, Sierra, Siskiyou, Solano, Sonoma, Sutter, Tehama, Trinity, Yolo, and Yuba), Colorado, Idaho, Montana, Nebraska, Nevada, North Dakota, Oregon, South Dakota, Utah, Washington, Wyoming	Attn: Entity Control Mail Stop 6271 P.O. Box 9941 Ogden, UT 84201 801-620-7645
California (all other counties), Hawaii	Attn: Entity Control Fresno, CA 93888 209-452-4010
Alabama, Arkansas, Louisiana, Mississippi, North Carolina, Tennessee	Attn: Entity Control Memphis, TN 37501 901-546-3920
If you have no legal residence, principal place of business, or principal office or agency in any state	Attn: Entity Control Philadelphia, PA 19255 215-516-6999

Specific Instructions

The instructions that follow are for those items that are not self-explanatory. Enter N/A (nonapplicable) on the lines that do not apply.

Line 1. Enter the legal name of the entity applying for the EIN exactly as it appears on the social security card, charter, or other applicable legal document.

Individuals. Enter your first name, middle initial, and last name. If you are a sole proprietor, enter your individual name, not your business name. Enter your business name on line 2. Do not use abbreviations or nicknames on line 1.

Trusts. Enter the name of the trust.

Estate of a decedent. Enter the name of the estate.

Partnerships. Enter the legal name of the partnership as it appears in the partnership agreement. **Do not** list the names of the partners on line 1. See the specific instructions for line 7.

Corporations. Enter the corporate name as it appears in the corporation charter or other legal document creating it.

Plan administrators. Enter the name of the plan administrator. A plan administrator who already has an EIN should use that number.

Line 2. Enter the trade name of the business if different from the legal name. The trade name is the "doing business as" name.

*Note: Use the full legal name on line 1 on all tax returns filed for the entity. However, if you enter a trade name on line 2 and choose to use the trade name instead of the legal name, enter the trade name on all returns you file. To prevent processing delays and errors, **always** use either the legal name only or the trade name only on all tax returns.*

Line 3. Trusts enter the name of the trustee. Estates enter the name of the executor, administrator, or other fiduciary. If the entity applying has a designated person to receive tax information, enter that person's name as the "care of" person. Print or type the first name, middle initial, and last name.

Line 7. Enter the first name, middle initial, last name, and SSN of a principal officer if the business is a corporation; of a general partner if a partnership; of the owner of a single member entity that is disregarded as an entity separate from its owner; or of a grantor, owner, or trustor if a trust. If the person in question is an alien individual with a previously assigned individual taxpayer identification number (ITIN), enter the ITIN in the space provided, instead of an SSN. You are not required to enter an SSN or ITIN if the reason you are applying for an EIN is to make an entity classification election (see Regulations section 301.7701-1 through 301.7701-3), and you are a nonresident alien with no effectively connected income from sources within the United States.

Line 8a. Check the box that best describes the type of entity applying for the EIN. If you are an alien individual with an ITIN previously assigned to you, enter the ITIN in place of a requested SSN.

Caution: *This is not an election for a tax classification of an entity. See "Limited liability company" below.*

If not specifically mentioned, check the "Other" box, enter the type of entity and the type of return that will be filed (for example, common trust fund, Form 1065). Do not enter N/A. If you are an alien individual applying for an EIN, see the **Line 7** instructions above.

Sole proprietor. Check this box if you file Schedule C, C-EZ, or F (Form 1040) and have a Keogh plan, or are required to file excise, employment, or alcohol, tobacco, or firearms returns, or are a payer of gambling winnings. Enter your SSN (or ITIN) in the space provided. If you are a nonresident alien with no effectively connected income from sources within the United States, you do not need to enter an SSN or ITIN.

REMIC. Check this box if the entity has elected to be treated as a real estate mortgage investment conduit (REMIC). See the **Instructions for Form 1066** for more information.

Other nonprofit organization. Check this box if the nonprofit organization is other than a church or church-controlled organization and specify the type of nonprofit organization (for example, an educational organization).

If the organization also seeks tax-exempt status, you must file either **Package 1023**, Application for Recognition of Exemption, or **Package 1024**, Application for Recognition of Exemption Under Section 501(a). Get **Pub. 557**, Tax Exempt Status for Your Organization, for more information.

Group exemption number (GEN). If the organization is covered by a group exemption letter, enter the four-digit GEN. (Do not confuse the GEN with the nine-digit EIN.) If you do not know the GEN, contact the parent organization. Get Pub. 557 for more information about group exemption numbers.

Withholding agent. If you are a withholding agent required to file Form 1042, check the "Other" box and enter "Withholding agent."

Personal service corporation. Check this box if the entity is a personal service corporation. An entity is a personal service corporation for a tax year only if:

- The principal activity of the entity during the testing period (prior tax year) for the tax year is the performance of personal services substantially by employee-owners, and
- The employee-owners own at least 10% of the fair market value of the outstanding stock in the entity on the last day of the testing period.

Personal services include performance of services in such fields as health, law, accounting, or consulting. For more information about personal service corporations, see the **Instructions for Form 1120**, U.S. Corporation Income Tax Return, and **Pub. 542**, Corporations.

Limited liability company (LLC). See the definition of limited liability company in the **Instructions for Form 1065**. An LLC with two or more members can be a partnership or an association taxable as a corporation. An LLC with a single owner can be an association taxable as a corporation or an entity disregarded as an entity separate from its owner. See Form 8832 for more details.

- If the entity is classified as a partnership for Federal income tax purposes, check the "partnership" box.
- If the entity is classified as a corporation for Federal income tax purposes, mark the "Other corporation" box and write "limited liability co." in the space provided.
- If the entity is disregarded as an entity separate from its owner, check the "Other" box and write in "disregarded entity" in the space provided.

Plan administrator. If the plan administrator is an individual, enter the plan administrator's SSN in the space provided.

Other corporation. This box is for any corporation other than a personal service corporation. If you check this box, enter the type of corporation (such as insurance company) in the space provided.

Household employer. If you are an individual, check the "Other" box and enter "Household employer" and your SSN. If you are a state or local agency serving as a tax reporting agent for public assistance recipients who become household employers, check the "Other" box and enter "Household employer agent." If you are a trust that qualifies as a household employer, you do not need a separate EIN for reporting tax information relating to household employees; use the EIN of the trust.

QSSS. For a qualified subchapter S subsidiary (QSSS) check the "Other" box and specify "QSSS."

Line 9. Check only **one** box. Do not enter N/A.

Started new business. Check this box if you are starting a new business that requires an EIN. If you check this box, enter the type of business being started. **Do not** apply if you already have an EIN and are only adding another place of business.

Hired employees. Check this box if the existing business is requesting an EIN because it has hired or is hiring employees and is therefore required to file employment tax returns. **Do not** apply if you already have an EIN and are only hiring employees. For information on the applicable employment taxes for family members, see **Circular E**, Employer's Tax Guide (Publication 15).

Created a pension plan. Check this box if you have created a pension plan and need this number for reporting purposes. Also, enter the type of plan created.

Note: Check this box if you are applying for a trust EIN when a new pension plan is established.

Banking purpose. Check this box if you are requesting an EIN for banking purposes only, and enter the banking purpose (for example, a bowling league for depositing dues or an investment club for dividend and interest reporting).

Changed type of organization. Check this box if the business is changing its type of organization, for example, if the business was a sole proprietorship and has been incorporated or has become a partnership. If you check this box, specify in the space provided the type of change made, for example, "from sole proprietorship to partnership."

Purchased going business. Check this box if you purchased an existing business. **Do not** use the former owner's EIN. **Do not** apply for a new EIN if you already have one. Use your own EIN.

Created a trust. Check this box if you created a trust, and enter the type of trust created. For example, indicate if the trust is a nonexempt charitable trust or a split-interest trust.

Note: *Do not check this box if you are applying for a trust EIN when a new pension plan is established. Check "Created a pension plan."*

Exception. Do **not** file this form for certain grantor-type trusts. The trustee does not need an EIN for the trust if the trustee furnishes the name and TIN of the grantor/owner and the address of the trust to all payors. See the Instructions for Form 1041 for more information.

Other (specify). Check this box if you are requesting an EIN for any reason other than those for which there are checkboxes, and enter the reason.

Line 10. If you are starting a new business, enter the starting date of the business. If the business you acquired is already operating, enter the date you acquired the business. Trusts should enter the date the trust was legally created. Estates should enter the date of death of the decedent whose name appears on line 1 or the date when the estate was legally funded.

Line 11. Enter the last month of your accounting year or tax year. An accounting or tax year is usually 12 consecutive months, either a calendar year or a fiscal year (including a period of 52 or 53 weeks). A calendar year is 12 consecutive months ending on December 31. A fiscal year is either 12 consecutive months ending on the last day of any month other than December or a 52-53 week year. For more information on accounting periods, see **Pub. 538,** Accounting Periods and Methods.

Individuals. Your tax year generally will be a calendar year.

Partnerships. Partnerships generally must adopt one of the following tax years:
- The tax year of the majority of its partners,
- The tax year common to all of its principal partners,
- The tax year that results in the least aggregate deferral of income, or
- In certain cases, some other tax year.

See the **Instructions for Form 1065,** U.S. Partnership Return of Income, for more information.

REMIC. REMICs must have a calendar year as their tax year.

Personal service corporations. A personal service corporation generally must adopt a calendar year unless:
- It can establish a business purpose for having a different tax year, or
- It elects under section 444 to have a tax year other than a calendar year.

Trusts. Generally, a trust must adopt a calendar year except for the following:
- Tax-exempt trusts,
- Charitable trusts, and
- Grantor-owned trusts.

Line 12. If the business has or will have employees, enter the date on which the business began or will begin to pay wages. If the business does not plan to have employees, enter N/A.

Withholding agent. Enter the date you began or will begin to pay income to a nonresident alien. This also applies to individuals who are required to file Form 1042 to report alimony paid to a nonresident alien.

Line 13. For a definition of agricultural labor (farmwork), see **Circular A,** Agricultural Employer's Tax Guide (Publication 51).

Line 14. Generally, enter the exact type of business being operated (for example, advertising agency, farm, food or beverage establishment, labor union, real estate agency, steam laundry, rental of coin-operated vending machine, or investment club). Also state if the business will involve the sale or distribution of alcoholic beverages.

Governmental. Enter the type of organization (state, county, school district, municipality, etc.).

Nonprofit organization (other than governmental). Enter whether organized for religious, educational, or humane purposes, and the principal activity (for example, religious organization—hospital, charitable).

Mining and quarrying. Specify the process and the principal product (for example, mining bituminous coal, contract drilling for oil, or quarrying dimension stone).

Contract construction. Specify whether general contracting or special trade contracting. Also, show the type of work normally performed (for example, general contractor for residential buildings or electrical subcontractor).

Food or beverage establishments. Specify the type of establishment and state whether you employ workers who receive tips (for example, lounge—yes).

Trade. Specify the type of sales and the principal line of goods sold (for example, wholesale dairy products, manufacturer's representative for mining machinery, or retail hardware).

Manufacturing. Specify the type of establishment operated (for example, sawmill or vegetable cannery).

Signature. The application must be signed by (a) the individual, if the applicant is an individual, (b) the president, vice president, or other principal officer, if the applicant is a corporation, (c) a responsible and duly authorized member or officer having knowledge of its affairs, if the applicant is a partnership or other unincorporated organization, or (d) the fiduciary, if the applicant is a trust or an estate.

How To Get Forms and Publications

Phone. You can order forms, instructions, and publications by phone. Just call 1-800-TAX-FORM (1-800-829-3676). You should receive your order or notification of its status within 7 to 15 workdays.

Personal computer. With your personal computer and modem, you can get the forms and information you need using:
- IRS's Internet Web Site at **www.irs.ustreas.gov**
- Telnet at **iris.irs.ustreas.gov**
- File Transfer Protocol at **ftp.irs.ustreas.gov**

You can also dial direct (by modem) to the Internal Revenue Information Services (IRIS) at 703-321-8020. IRIS is an on-line information service on FedWorld.

For small businesses, return preparers, or others who may frequently need tax forms or publications, a CD-ROM containing over 2,000 tax products (including many prior year forms) can be purchased from the Government Printing Office.

CD-ROM. To order the CD-ROM call the Superintendent of Documents at 202-512-1800 or connect to **www.access.gpo.gov/su_docs**

Privacy Act and Paperwork Reduction Act Notice. We ask for the information on this form to carry out the Internal Revenue laws of the United States. We need it to comply with section 6109 and the regulations thereunder which generally require the inclusion of an employer identification number (EIN) on certain returns, statements, or other documents filed with the Internal Revenue Service. Information on this form may be used to determine which Federal tax returns you are required to file and to provide you with related forms and publications. We disclose this form to the Social Security Administration for their use in determining compliance with applicable laws. We will be unable to issue an EIN to you unless you provide all of the requested information which applies to your entity.

You are not required to provide the information requested on a form that is subject to the Paperwork Reduction Act unless the form displays a valid OMB control number. Books or records relating to a form or its instructions must be retained as long as their contents may become material in the administration of any Internal Revenue law. Generally, tax returns and return information are confidential, as required by section 6103.

The time needed to complete and file this form will vary depending on individual circumstances. The estimated average time is:

Recordkeeping	7 min.
Learning about the law or the form	19 min.
Preparing the form	45 min.
Copying, assembling, and sending the form to the IRS . .	20 min.

If you have comments concerning the accuracy of these time estimates or suggestions for making this form simpler, we would be happy to hear from you. You can write to the Tax Forms Committee, Western Area Distribution Center, Rancho Cordova, CA 95743-0001. **Do not** send this form to this address. Instead, see **Where To Apply** on page 2.

Form 6

WAIVER OF NOTICE

OF THE ORGANIZATION MEETING

OF

_____

We, the undersigned incorporators named in the Certificate of Incorporation of the above-named corporation hereby agree and consent that the organization meeting of the corporation be held on the date and time and place stated below and hereby waive all notice of such meeting and of any adjournment thereof.

Place of meeting: _____

Date of Meeting: _____

Time of meeting: _____

Dated: _____

_____
Incorporator

_____
Incorporator

_____
Incorporator

Form 7

MINUTES OF THE ORGANIZATIONAL MEETING OF

INCORPORATORS AND DIRECTORS OF

_____

The organization meeting of the above corporation was held on _____, _____ at _____ _____ at ____ o'clock ___m.

The following persons were present:
_____   _____
_____   _____
_____   _____

The Waiver of notice of this meeting was signed by all directors and incorporators named in the Certificate of Incorporation and filed in the minute book.

The meeting was called to order by _____ an Incorporator named in the Certificate of Incorporation. _____ was nominated and elected Chairman and acted as such until relieved by the president. _____ was nominated and elected temporary secretary, and acted as such until relieved by the permanent secretary.

A copy of the Certificate of Incorporation which was filed with the Secretary of State of the State of _____ on _____, _____ was examined by the Directors and Incorporators and filed in the minute book.

The election of officers for the coming year was then held and the following were duly nominated and elected by the Board of Directors to be the officers of the corporation, to serve until such time as their successors are elected and qualified:

President: _____
Vice President: _____
Secretary: _____
Treasurer: _____

The proposed Bylaws for the corporation were then presented to the meeting and discussed. Upon motion duly made, seconded and carried, the Bylaws were adopted and added to the minute book.

❏ No corporate seal was adopted.
           OR
❏ A corporate seal for the corporation was then presented to the meeting and upon motion duly made, seconded and carried, it was adopted as the seal of the corporation. An impression thereof was then made in the margin of these minutes

The necessity of opening a bank account was then discussed and upon motion duly made, seconded and carried, the following resolution was adopted:

    RESOLVED that the corporation open bank accounts with _____ _____ and that the officers of the corporation are authorized to take such action as is necessary to open such accounts; that the bank's printed form of resolution is hereby adopted and incorporated into these minutes by reference and shall be placed in the minute book; that any ____ of the following persons shall have signature authority over the account:

_____ _____

_____ _____

_____ _____

Proposed stock certificates and stock transfer ledger were then presented to the meeting and examined. Upon motion duly made, seconded and carried the stock certificates and ledger were adopted as the certificates and transfer book to be used by the corporation. A sample stock certificate marked "VOID" and the stock transfer ledger were then added to the minute book. Upon motion duly made, seconded and carried, it was then resolved that the stock certificates, when issued, would be signed by the President and the Secretary of the corporation.

The tax status of the corporation was then discussed and it was moved, seconded and carried that the stock of the corporation be issued under §1244 of the Internal Revenue Code and that the officers of the corporation take the necessary action to:

    1.   Obtain an employer tax number by filing form SS-4,

    2.   ❏   Become an S-Corporation for tax purposes,
           ❏   Remain a C-Corporation for tax purposes,

The expenses of organizing the corporation were then discussed and it was moved, seconded and carried that the corporation pay in full from the corporate funds the expenses and reimburse any advances made by the incorporators upon proof of payment.

The Directors named in the Certificate of Incorporation then tendered their resignations, effective upon the adjournment of this meeting. Upon motion duly made, seconded and carried, the following named persons were elected as Directors of the corporation, each to hold office until the first annual meeting of shareholders, and until a successor of each shall have been elected and qualified.

_____
_____
_____

There were presented to the corporation, the following offer(s) to purchase shares of capital stock:

FROM	NO. OF SHARES	CONSIDERATION
_____	_____	_____
_____	_____	_____
_____	_____	_____
_____	_____	_____

The offers were discussed and after motion duly made, seconded and carried were approved. It was further resolved that the Board of Directors has determined that the consideration was valued at least equal to the value of the shares to be issued and that upon tender of the consideration, fully paid non-assessable shares of the corporation be issued.

There being no further business before the meeting, on motion duly made, seconded and carried, the meeting adjourned.

DATED: _____

_____
President

_____
Secretary

Form 8

BYLAWS OF

_____

A NEW YORK CORPORATION

ARTICLE I - OFFICES

The principal office of the Corporation shall be located in the City of _____ and the State of New York. The Corporation may also maintain offices at such other places as the Board of Directors may, from time to time, determine.

ARTICLE II - SHAREHOLDERS

<u>Section 1 - Annual Meetings</u>: The annual meeting of the shareholders of the Corporation shall be held each year on _____ at _____m. at the principal office of the Corporation or at such other places, within or without the State of New York, as the Board may authorize, for the purpose of electing directors, and transacting such other business as may properly come before the meeting.

<u>Section 2 - Special Meetings</u>: Special meetings of the shareholders may be called at any time by the Board, the President, or by the holders of twenty-five percent (25%) of the shares then outstanding and entitled to vote.

<u>Section 3 - Place of Meetings</u>: All meetings of shareholders shall be held at the principal office of the Corporation, or at such other places as the board shall designate in the notice of such meetings.

<u>Section 4 - Notice of Meetings</u>: Written or printed notice stating the place, day, and hour of the meeting and, in the case of a special meeting, the purpose of the meeting, shall be delivered personally or by mail not less than ten days, nor more than sixty days, before the date of the meeting. Notice shall be given to each Member of record entitled to vote at the meeting. If mailed, such notice shall be deemed to have been delivered when deposited in the United States Mail with postage paid and addressed to the Member at his address as it appears on the records of the Corporation.

<u>Section 5 - Waiver of Notice:</u> A written waiver of notice signed by a Member, whether before or after a meeting, shall be equivalent to the giving of such notice. Attendance of a Member at a meeting shall constitute a waiver of notice of such meeting, except when the Member attends for the express purpose of objecting, at the beginning of the meeting, to the transaction of any business because the meeting is not lawfully called or convened.

<u>Section 6 - Quorum</u>: Except as otherwise provided by Statute, or the Certificate of Incorporation, at all meetings of shareholders of the Corporation, the presence at the commencement of such meetings in person or by proxy of shareholders of record holding a majority of the total number of shares of the Corporation then issued and outstanding and entitled to vote, but in no event less than one-third of the shares entitled to vote at the meeting, shall constitute a quorum for the transaction of any business. If any shareholder leaves after the commencement of a meeting, this shall have no effect on the existence of a quorum, after a quorum has been established at such meeting.

Despite the absence of a quorum at any annual or special meeting of shareholders, the shareholders, by a majority of the votes cast by the holders of shares entitled to vote thereon, may adjourn the meeting. At any such adjourned meeting at which a quorum is present, any business may be transacted at the meeting as originally called as if a quorum had been present.

<u>Section 7 - Voting</u>: Except as otherwise provided by Statute or by the Certificate of Incorporation, any corporate action, other than the election of directors, to be taken by vote of the shareholders, shall be authorized by a majority of votes cast at a meeting of shareholders by the holders of shares entitled to vote thereon.

Except as otherwise provided by Statute or by the Certificate of Incorporation, at each meeting of shareholders, each holder of record of stock of the Corporation entitled to vote thereat, shall be entitled to one vote for each share of stock registered in his name on the stock transfer books of the corporation.

Each shareholder entitled to vote may do so by proxy; provided, however, that the instrument authorizing such proxy to act shall have been executed in writing by the shareholder himself. No proxy shall be valid after the expiration of eleven months from the date of its execution, unless the person executing it shall have specified therein, the length of time it is to continue in force. Such instrument shall be exhibited to the Secretary at the meeting and shall be filed with the records of the corporation.

Any resolution in writing, signed by all of the shareholders entitled to vote thereon, shall be and constitute action by such shareholders to the effect therein expressed, with the same force and effect as if the same had been duly passed by unanimous vote at a duly called meeting of shareholders and such resolution so signed shall be inserted in the Minute Book of the Corporation under its proper date.

ARTICLE III - BOARD OF DIRECTORS

Section 1 - Number, Election and Term of Office: The number of the directors of the Corporation shall be (____) This number may be increased or decreased by the amendment of these bylaws by the Board but shall in no case be less than ____ director(s). The members of the Board, who need not be shareholders, shall be elected by a majority of the votes cast at a meeting of shareholders entitled to vote in the election. Each director shall hold office until the annual meeting of the shareholders next succeeding his election, and until his successor is elected and qualified, or until his prior death, resignation or removal.

Section 2 - Vacancies: Any vacancy in the Board shall be filled for the unexpired portion of the term by a majority vote of the remaining directors, though less than a quorum, at any regular meeting or special meeting of the Board called for that purpose. Any such director so elected may be replaced by the shareholders at a regular or special meeting of shareholders.

Section 3 - Duties and Powers: The Board shall be responsible for the control and management of the affairs, property and interests of the Corporation, and may exercise all powers of the Corporation, except as limited by statute.

Section 4 - Annual Meetings: An annual meeting of the Board shall be held immediately following the annual meeting of the shareholders, at the place of such annual meeting of shareholders. The Board from time to time, may provide by resolution for the holding of other meetings of the Board, and may fix the time and place thereof.

Section 5 - Special Meetings: Special meetings of the Board shall be held whenever called by the President or by one of the directors, at such time and place as may be specified in the respective notice or waivers of notice thereof.

Section 6 - Notice and Waiver: Notice of any special meeting shall be given at least five days prior thereto by written notice delivered personally, by mail or by telegram to each Director at his address. If mailed, such notice shall be deemed to be delivered when deposited in the United States Mail with postage prepaid. If notice is given by telegram, such notice shall be deemed to be delivered when the telegram is delivered to the telegraph company.

Any Director may waive notice of any meeting, either before, at, or after such meeting, by signing a waiver of notice. The attendance of a Director at a meeting shall constitute a waiver of notice of such meeting and a waiver of any and all objections to the place of such meeting, or the manner in which it has been called or convened, except when a Director states at the beginning of the meeting any objection to the transaction of business because the meeting is not lawfully called or convened.

Section 7 - Chairman: The Board may, at its discretion, elect a Chairman. At all meetings of the Board, the Chairman of the Board, if any and if present, shall preside. If there is no Chairman, or he is absent, then the President shall preside, and in his absence, a Chairman chosen by the directors shall preside.

Section 8 - Quorum and Adjournments: At all meetings of the Board, the presence of a majority of the entire Board shall be necessary and sufficient to constitute a quorum for the transaction of business, except as otherwise provided by law, by the Certificate of Incorporation, or by these bylaws. A majority of the directors present at the time and place of any regular or special meeting, although less than a quorum, may adjourn the same from time to time without notice, until a quorum shall be present.

Section 9 - Board Action: At all meetings of the Board, each director present shall have one vote, irrespective of the number of shares of stock, if any, which he may hold. Except as otherwise provided by Statute, the action of a majority of the directors present at any meeting at which a quorum is present shall be the act of the Board. Any action authorized, in writing, by all of the Directors entitled to vote thereon and filed with the minutes of the Corporation shall be the act of the Board with the same force and effect as if the same had been passed by unanimous vote at a duly called meeting of the Board. Any action taken by the Board may be taken without a meeting if agreed to in writing by all members before or after the action is taken and if a record of such action is filed in the minute book.

Section 10 - Telephone Meetings: Directors may participate in meetings of the Board through use of a telephone if such can be arranged so that all Board members can hear all other members. The use of a telephone for participation shall constitute presence in person.

Section 11 - Resignation and Removal: Any director may resign at any time by giving written notice to another Board member, the President or the Secretary of the Corporation. Unless otherwise specified in such written notice, such resignation shall take effect upon receipt thereof by the Board or by such officer, and the acceptance of such resignation shall not be necessary to make it effective. Any director may be removed with or without cause at any time by the affirmative vote of shareholders holding of record in the aggregate at least a majority of the outstanding shares of the Corporation at a special meeting of the shareholders called for that purpose, and may be removed for cause by action of the Board.

Section 12 - Compensation: No stated salary shall be paid to directors, as such for their services, but by resolution of the Board a fixed sum and/or expenses of attendance, if any, may be allowed for attendance at each regular or special meeting of the Board. Nothing herein contained shall be construed to preclude any director from serving the Corporation in any other capacity and receiving compensation therefor.

ARTICLE IV - OFFICERS

Section 1 - Number, Qualification, Election and Term: The officers of the Corporation shall consist of a President, a Secretary, a Treasurer, and such other officers, as the Board may from time to time deem advisable. Any officer may be, but is not required to be, a director of the Corporation. The officers of the Corporation shall be elected by the Board at the regular annual meeting of the Board. Each officer shall hold office until the annual meeting of the Board next succeeding his election, and until his successor shall have been elected and qualified, or until his death, resignation or removal.

Section 2 - Resignation and Removal: Any officer may resign at any time by giving written notice of such resignation to the President or the Secretary of the Corporation or to a member of the Board. Unless otherwise specified in such written notice, such resignation shall take effect upon receipt thereof by the Board member or by such officer, and the acceptance of such resignation shall not be necessary to make it effective. Any officer may be removed, either with or without cause, and a successor elected by a majority vote of the Board at any time.

Section 3 - Vacancies: A vacancy in any office may at any time be filled for the unexpired portion of the term by a majority vote of the Board.

Section 4 - Duties of Officers: Officers of the Corporation shall, unless otherwise provided by the Board, each have such powers and duties as generally pertain to their respective offices as well as such powers and duties as may from time to time be specifically decided by the Board. The President shall be the chief executive officer of the Corporation.

Section 5 - Compensation: The officers of the Corporation shall be entitled to such compensation as the Board shall from time to time determine.

Section 6 - Delegation of Duties: In the absence or disability of any Officer of the Corporation or for any other reason deemed sufficient by the Board of Directors, the Board may delegate his powers or duties to any other Officer or to any other Director.

Section 7 - Shares of Other Corporations: Whenever the Corporation is the holder of shares of any other Corporation, any right or power of the Corporation as such shareholder (including the attendance, acting and voting at shareholders' meetings and execution of waivers, consents, proxies or other instruments) may be exercised on behalf of the Corporation by the President, any Vice President, or such other person as the Board may authorize.

ARTICLE V - COMMITTEES

The Board of Directors may, by resolution, designate an Executive Committee and one or more other committees. Such committees shall have such functions and may exercise such power of the Board of Directors as can be lawfully delegated, and to the extent provided in the resolution or resolutions creating such committee or committees. Meetings of committees may be held without notice at such time and at such place as shall from time to time be determined by the committees. The committees of the corporation shall keep regular minutes of their proceedings, and report these minutes to the Board of Directors when required.

ARTICLE VI - BOOKS, RECORDS AND REPORTS

Section 1 - Annual Report: The Corporation shall send an annual report to the Members of the Corporation not later than _____ months after the close of each fiscal year of the Corporation. Such report shall include a balance sheet as of the close of the fiscal year of the Corporation and a revenue and disbursement statement for the year ending on such closing date. Such financial statements shall be prepared from and in accordance with the books of the Corporation, and in conformity with generally accepted accounting principles applied on a consistent basis.

Section 2 - Permanent Records: The corporation shall keep current and correct records of the accounts, minutes of the meetings and proceedings and membership records of the corporation. Such records shall be kept at the registered office or the principal place of business of the corporation. Any such records shall be in written form or in a form capable of being converted into written form.

Section 3 - Inspection of Corporate Records: Any person who is a Voting Member of the Corporation shall have the right at any reasonable time, and on written demand stating the purpose thereof, to examine and make copies from the relevant books and records of accounts, minutes, and records of the Corporation. Upon the written request of any Voting Member, the Corporation shall mail to such Member a copy of the most recent balance sheet and revenue and disbursement statement.

ARTICLE VII - SHARES OF STOCK

Section 1 - Certificates: Each shareholder of the corporation shall be entitled to have a certificate representing all shares which he or she owns. The form of such certificate shall be adopted by a majority vote of the Board of Directors and shall be signed by the President and Secretary of the Corporation and sealed with the seal of the corporation if one is adopted. No certificate representing shares shall be issued until the full amount of consideration therefore has been paid.

Section 2 - Stock Ledger: The corporation shall maintain a ledger of the stock records of the Corporation. Transfers of shares of the Corporation shall be made on the stock ledger of the Corporation only at the direction of the holder of record upon surrender of the outstanding certificate(s). The Corporation shall be entitled to treat the holder of record of any share or shares as the absolute owner thereof for all purposes and, accordingly, shall not be bound to recognize any legal, equitable or other claim to, or interest in, such share or shares on the part of any other person, whether or not it shall have express or other notice thereof, except as otherwise expressly provided by law.

ARTICLE VIII - DIVIDENDS

Upon approval by the Board of Directors the corporation may pay dividends on its shares in the form of cash, property or additional shares at any time that the corporation is solvent and if such dividends would not render the corporation insolvent.

ARTICLE IX - FISCAL YEAR

The fiscal year of the Corporation shall be the period selected by the Board of Directors as the tax year of the Corporation for federal income tax purposes.

ARTICLE X - CORPORATE SEAL

The Board of Directors may adopt, use and modify a corporate seal. Failure to affix the seal to corporate documents shall not affect the validity of such document.

ARTICLE XI - AMENDMENTS

The Certificate of Incorporation may be amended by the Shareholders as provided by New York statutes. These Bylaws may be altered, amended, or replaced by the Board of Directors; provided, however, that any Bylaws or amendments thereto as adopted by the Board of Directors may be altered, amended, or repealed by vote of the Shareholders. Bylaws adopted by the Members may not be amended or repealed by the Board.

ARTICLE XII - INDEMNIFICATION

Any officer, director or employee of the Corporation shall be indemnified to the full extent allowed by the laws of the State of New York.

Certified to be the Bylaws of the corporation adopted by the Board of Directors on _____, _____.

_____
Secretary

Form 9

BYLAWS OF
_____
A NEW YORK PROFESSIONAL CORPORATION

ARTICLE I - OFFICES

The principal office of the Corporation shall be located in the City of _____ and the State of New York. The Corporation may also maintain offices at such other places as the Board of Directors may, from time to time, determine.

ARTICLE II - PURPOSES

The business purpose of the Corporation shall be to engage in all aspects of the practice of _____ and its fields of specialization. The Corporation shall render professional services only through its legally authorized officers, agents and employees.

ARTICLE III - SHAREHOLDERS

Section 1 - Qualifications: Only persons who are duly licensed and in good standing in the profession by the State of New York may be shareholders of the Corporation. Neither the Corporation nor the shareholders may transfer any shares to persons who are not duly licensed. All share certificates of the corporation shall contain a notice that the transfer is restricted by the bylaws of the Corporation. If any shareholder shall become disqualified to practice the profession, he or she shall immediately make arrangements to transfer his or her shares to a qualified person or to the Corporation and shall no longer participate in the profits of the Corporation related to the profession.

Section 2 - Annual Meetings: The annual meeting of the shareholders of the Corporation shall be held each year on_____ at _____m. at the principal office of the Corporation or at such other places, within or without the State of New York, as the Board may authorize, for the purpose of electing directors, and transacting such other business as may properly come before the meeting.

Section 3 - Special Meetings: Special meetings of the shareholders may be called at any time by the Board, the President, or by the holders of twenty-five percent (25%) of the shares then outstanding and entitled to vote.

Section 4 - Place of Meetings: All meetings of shareholders shall be held at the principal office of the Corporation, or at such other places as the Board shall designate in the notice of such meetings.

Section 5 - Notice of Meetings: Written or printed notice stating the place, day, and hour of the meeting and, in the case of a special meeting, the purpose of the meeting, shall be delivered personally or by mail not less than ten days, nor more than sixty days, before the date of the meeting. Notice shall be given to each Member of record entitled to vote at the meeting. If mailed, such notice shall be deemed to have been delivered when deposited in the United States Mail with postage paid and addressed to the Member at his address as it appears on the records of the Corporation.

Section 6 - Waiver of Notice: A written waiver of notice signed by a Member, whether before or after a meeting, shall be equivalent to the giving of such notice. Attendance of a Member at a meeting shall constitute a waiver of notice of such meeting, except when the Member attends for the express purpose of objecting, at the beginning of the meeting, to the transaction of any business because the meeting is not lawfully called or convened.

Section 7 - Quorum: Except as otherwise provided by Statute, or the by Certificate of Incorporation, at all meetings of shareholders of the Corporation, the presence at the commencement of such meetings of shareholders of record holding a majority of the total number of shares of the Corporation then issued and outstanding and entitled to vote, but in no event less than one-third of the shares entitled to vote at the meeting, shall constitute a quorum for the transaction of any business. If any shareholder leaves after the commencement of a meeting, this shall have no effect on the existence of a quorum, after a quorum has been established at such meeting.

Despite the absence of a quorum at any annual or special meeting of shareholders, the shareholders, by a majority of the votes cast by the holders of shares entitled to vote thereon, may adjourn the meeting. At any such adjourned meeting at which a quorum is present, any business may be transacted at the meeting as originally called as if a quorum had been present.

Section 8 - Voting: Except as otherwise provided by Statute or by the Certificate of Incorporation, any corporate action, other than the election of directors, to be taken by vote of the shareholders, shall be authorized by a majority of votes cast at a meeting of shareholders by the holders of shares entitled to vote thereon.

Except as otherwise provided by Statute or by the Certificate of Incorporation, at each meeting of shareholders, each holder of record of stock of the Corporation entitled to vote thereat, shall be entitled to one vote for each share of stock registered in his name on the stock transfer books of the corporation.

Any resolution in writing, signed by all of the shareholders entitled to vote thereon, shall be and constitute action by such shareholders to the effect therein expressed, with the same force and effect as if the same had been duly passed by unanimous vote at a duly called meeting of shareholders and such resolution so signed shall be inserted in the Minute Book of the Corporation under its proper date.

Section 9 - Proxies: Shareholders may not at any time vote by proxy or enter into any voting trust or other agreement vesting another person with the voting power of his stock.

ARTICLE IV - BOARD OF DIRECTORS

Section 1 Qualifications: Only persons who are duly licensed and in good standing in the profession by the State of New York may be directors of the Corporation. If any director shall become disqualified from practicing the profession, he or she shall immediately resign his or her directorship and any other employment with the Corporation.

Section 2 - Number, Election and Term of Office: The number of the directors of the Corporation shall be (____) This number may be increased or decreased by the amendment of these bylaws by the Board but shall in no case be less than one director. The members of the Board, who need not be shareholders, shall be elected by a majority of the votes cast at a meeting of shareholders entitled to vote in the election. Each director shall hold office until the annual meeting of the shareholders next succeeding his election, and until his successor is elected and qualified, or until his prior death, resignation or removal.

Section 3 - Vacancies: Any vacancy in the Board shall be filled for the unexpired portion of the term by a majority vote of the remaining directors, though less than a quorum, at any regular meeting or special meeting of the Board called for that purpose. Any such director so elected may be replaced by the shareholders at a regular or special meeting of shareholders.

Section 4 - Duties and Powers: The Board shall be responsible for the control and management of the affairs, property and interests of the Corporation, and may exercise all powers of the Corporation, except as limited by statute.

Section 5 - Annual Meetings: An annual meeting of the Board shall be held immediately following the annual meeting of the shareholders, at the place of such annual meeting of shareholders. The Board, from time to time, may provide by resolution for the holding of other meetings of the Board, and may fix the time and place thereof.

Section 6 - Special Meetings: Special meetings of the Board shall be held whenever called by the President or by one of the directors, at such time and place as may be specified in the respective notice or waivers of notice thereof.

Section 7 - Notice and Waiver: Notice of any special meeting shall be given at least five days prior thereto by written notice delivered personally, by mail or by telegram to each director at his address. If mailed, such notice shall be deemed to be delivered when deposited in the United States Mail with postage prepaid. If notice is given by telegram, such notice shall be deemed to be delivered when the telegram is delivered to the telegraph company.

Any director may waive notice of any meeting, either before, at, or after such meeting, by signing a waiver of notice. The attendance of a director at a meeting shall constitute a waiver of notice of such meeting and a waiver of any and all objections to the place of such meeting, or the manner in which it has been called or convened, except when a director states at the beginning of the meeting any objection to the transaction of business because the meeting is not lawfully called or convened.

Section 8 - Chairman: The Board may, at its discretion, elect a Chairman. At all meetings of the Board, the Chairman of the Board, if any and if present, shall preside. If there is no Chairman, or he is absent, then the President shall preside, and in his absence, a Chairman chosen by the directors shall preside.

Section 9 - Quorum and Adjournments: At all meetings of the Board, the presence of a majority of the entire Board shall be necessary and sufficient to constitute a quorum for the transaction of business, except as otherwise provided by law, by the Articles of Incorporation, or by these bylaws. A majority of the directors present at the time and place of any regular or special meeting, although less than a quorum, may adjourn the same from time to time without notice, until a quorum shall be present.

Section 10 - Board Action: At all meetings of the Board, each director present shall have one vote, irrespective of the number of shares of stock, if any, which he may hold. Except as otherwise provided by Statute, the action of a majority of the directors present at any meeting at which a quorum is present shall be the act of the Board. Any action authorized, in writing, by all of the Directors entitled to vote thereon and filed with the minutes of the Corporation shall be the act of the Board with the same force and effect as if the same had been passed by unanimous vote at a duly called meeting of the Board. Any action taken by the Board may be taken without a meeting if agreed to in writing by all members before or after the action is taken and if a record of such action is filed in the Minute Book.

Section 11 - Telephone Meetings: Directors may participate in meetings of the Board through use of a telephone if such can be arranged so that all Board members can hear all other members. The use of a telephone for participation shall constitute presence in person.

Section 12 - Resignation and Removal: Any director may resign at any time by giving written notice to another Board member, the President or the Secretary of the Corporation. Unless otherwise specified in such written notice, such resignation shall take effect upon receipt thereof by the Board or by such officer, and the acceptance of such resignation shall not be necessary to make it effective. Any director may be removed with or without cause at any time by the affirmative vote of shareholders holding of record in the aggregate at least a majority of the outstanding shares of the Corporation at a special meeting of the shareholders called for that purpose, and may be removed for cause by action of the Board.

Section 13 - Compensation: No stated salary shall be paid to directors, as such for their services, but by resolution of the Board a fixed sum and/or expenses of attendance, if any, may be allowed for attendance at each regular or special meeting of the Board. Nothing herein contained shall be construed to preclude any director from serving the Corporation in any other capacity and receiving compensation therefor.

ARTICLE V - OFFICERS

Section 1 Qualifications: Only persons who are duly licensed and in good standing in the profession by the State of New York may be officers of the Corporation. If any director shall become disqualified from practicing the profession, he or she shall immediately resign his or her directorship and any other employment with the corporation.

Section 2 - Number, Election and Term: The officers of the Corporation shall consist of a President, a Secretary, a Treasurer, and such other officers, as the Board may from time to time deem advisable. Any officer may be, but is not required to be, a director of the Corporation. Any two or more offices may be held by the same person. The officers of the Corporation shall be elected by the Board at the regular annual meeting of the Board. Each officer shall hold office until the annual meeting of the Board next succeeding his election, and until his successor shall have been elected and qualified, or until his death, resignation or removal.

Section 3 - Resignation and Removal: Any officer may resign at any time by giving written notice of such resignation to the President or the Secretary of the Corporation or to a member of the Board. Unless otherwise specified in such written notice, such resignation shall take effect upon receipt thereof by the Board member or by such officer, and the acceptance of such resignation shall not be necessary to make it effective. Any officer may be removed, either with or without cause, and a successor elected by a majority vote of the Board at any time.

Section 4 - Vacancies: A vacancy in any office may at any time be filled for the unexpired portion of the term by a majority vote of the Board.

Section 5 - Duties of Officers: The officers of the Corporation shall, unless otherwise provided by the Board, each have such powers and duties as generally pertain to their respective offices as well as such powers and duties as may from time to time be specifically decided by the Board. The President shall be the chief executive officer of the Corporation.

Section 6 - Compensation: The officers of the Corporation shall be entitled to such compensation as the Board shall from time to time determine.

Section 7 - Delegation of Duties: In the absence or disability of any Officer of the Corporation or for any other reason deemed sufficient by the Board of Directors, the Board may delegate his powers or duties to any other Officer or to any other director.

Section 8 - Shares of Other Corporations: Whenever the Corporation is the holder of shares of any other Corporation, any right or power of the Corporation as such shareholder (including the attendance, acting and voting at shareholders' meetings and execution of waivers, consents, proxies or other instruments) may be exercised on behalf of the Corporation by the President, any Vice President, or such other person as the Board may authorize.

ARTICLE VI - COMMITTEES

The Board of Directors may, by resolution, designate an Executive Committee and one or more other committees. Such committees shall have such functions and may exercise such power of the Board of Directors as can be lawfully delegated, and to the extent provided in the resolution or resolutions creating such committee or committees. Meetings of committees may be held without notice at such time and at such place as shall from time to time be determined by the committees. The committees of the corporation shall keep regular minutes of their proceedings, and report these minutes to the Board of Directors when required.

ARTICLE VII - BOOKS, RECORDS AND REPORTS

Section 1 - Annual Report: The Corporation shall send an annual report to the Members of the Corporation not later than four months after the close of each fiscal year of the Corporation. Such report shall include a balance sheet as of the close of the fiscal year of the Corporation and a revenue and disbursement statement for the year ending on such closing date. Such financial statements shall be prepared from and in accordance with the books of the Corporation, and in conformity with generally accepted accounting principles applied on a consistent basis.

Section 2 - Permanent Records: The Corporation shall keep current and correct records of the accounts, minutes of the meetings and proceedings and membership records of the Corporation. Such records shall be kept at the registered office or the principal place of business of the Corporation. Any such records shall be in written form or in a form capable of being converted into written form.

Section 3 - Inspection of Corporate Records: Any person who is a Voting Member of the Corporation shall have the right at any reasonable time, and on written demand stating the purpose thereof, to examine and make copies from the relevant books and records of accounts, minutes, and records of the Corporation. Upon the written request of any Voting Member, the Corporation shall mail to such Member a copy of the most recent balance sheet and revenue and disbursement statement.

ARTICLE VIII - SHARES OF STOCK

Section 1 - Authorized shares: The Corporation shall be authorized to issue _____ shares of stock in one class only, each with a par value of $_____.

Section 2 - Certificates: Each shareholder of the Corporation shall be entitled to have a certificate representing all shares which he or she owns. The form of such certificate shall be adopted by a majority vote of the Board of Directors and shall be signed by the President and Secretary of the Corporation and sealed with the seal of the Corporation if one is adopted. No certificate representing shares shall be issued until the full amount of consideration therefore has been paid.

Section 3 - Stock Ledger: The Corporation shall maintain a ledger of the stock records of the Corporation. Transfers of shares of the Corporation shall be made on the stock ledger of the Corporation only at the direction of the holder of record upon surrender of the outstanding certificate(s). The Corporation shall be entitled to treat the holder of record of any share or shares as the absolute owner thereof for all purposes and, accordingly, shall not be bound to recognize any legal, equitable or other claim to, or interest in, such share or shares on the part of any other person, whether or not it shall have express or other notice thereof, except as otherwise expressly provided by law.

ARTICLE IX - DIVIDENDS

Upon approval by the Board of Directors the corporation may pay dividends on its shares in the form of cash, property or additional shares at any time that the Corporation is solvent and if such dividends would not render the Corporation insolvent.

ARTICLE X - FISCAL YEAR

The fiscal year of the Corporation shall be the period selected by the Board of Directors as the tax year of the Corporation for federal income tax purposes.

ARTICLE XI - CORPORATE SEAL

The Board of Directors may adopt, use and modify a corporate seal. Failure to affix the seal to corporate documents shall not affect the validity of such document.

ARTICLE XII - AMENDMENTS

The Certificate of Incorporation may be amended by the shareholders as provided by Florida statutes. These bylaws may be altered, amended, or replaced by the Board of Directors; provided, however, that any bylaws or amendments thereto as adopted by the Board of Directors may be altered, amended, or repealed by vote of the shareholders. Bylaws adopted by the Members may not be amended or repealed by the Board.

ARTICLE XIII - INDEMNIFICATION

Any officer, director or employee of the Corporation shall be indemnified to the full extent allowed by the laws of the State of New York.

Certified to be the bylaws of the corporation adopted by the Board of Directors on _____, _____.

_____
Secretary

Form 10

Banking Resolution of

_____

The undersigned, being the corporate secretary of the above corporation, hereby certifies that on the _____ day of _____, _____ the Board of Directors of the corporation adopted the following resolution:

RESOLVED that the corporation open bank accounts with _____ _____ and that the officers of the corporation are authorized to take such action as is necessary to open such accounts; that the bank's printed form of resolution is hereby adopted and incorporated into these minutes by reference and shall be placed in the minute book; that any ____ of the following persons shall have signature authority over the account:

_____   _____

_____   _____

and that said resolution has not been modified or rescinded.

Date: _____

_____
Corporate Secretary

Form 11

Offer to Purchase Stock

Date: _____

To the Board of Directors of

_____

    The undersigned, hereby offers to purchase _____ shares of the _____ stock of your corporation at a total purchase price of _____.

Very truly yours,

_____

- -

Offer to Sell Stock
Pursuant to Sec. 1244 I.R.C.

Date: _____

To: _____

Dear

    The corporation hereby offers to sell to you _____ shares of its common stock at a price of $_____ per share. These shares are issued pursuant to Section 1244 of the Internal Revenue Code,

    Your signature below shall constitute an acceptance of our offer as of the date it is received by the corporation.

Very truly yours,

_____

By:_____

Accepted:

_____

Resolution to Reimburse Expenses
of
_____
a New York Corporation

RESOLVED that the corporation shall reimburse the following parties for the organizational expenses of the organizers of this corporation and that the corporation shall amortize these expenses as allowed by IRS regulations.

Name	Expense	Amount
_____	_____	$_____
_____	_____	$_____
_____	_____	$_____
_____	_____	$_____
_____	_____	$_____

Date:_____

_____

_____

_____

_____

Bill of Sale

The undersigned, in consideration of the issuance of _____ shares of common stock of _____, a New York corporation, hereby grants, bargains, sells, transfers and delivers unto said corporation the following goods and chattels:

To have and to hold the same forever.

And the undersigned, their heirs, successors and administrators, covenant and warrant that they are the lawful owners of the said goods and chattels and that they are free from all encumbrances. That the undersigned have the right to sell this property and that they will warrant and defend the sale of said property against the lawful claims and demands of all persons. IN WITNESS whereof the undersigned have executed this Bill of Sale this ____ day of _____, _____.

_____

_____

_____

Instructions for Form 2553
(Revised September 1997)
Election by a Small Business Corporation

Department of the Treasury
Internal Revenue Service

Section references are to the Internal Revenue Code unless otherwise noted.

General Instructions

Purpose.— To elect to be an S corporation, a corporation must file Form 2553. The election permits the income of the S corporation to be taxed to the shareholders of the corporation rather than to the corporation itself, except as noted below under **Taxes an S Corporation May Owe.**

Who May Elect.— A corporation may elect to be an S corporation only if it meets all of the following tests:

1. It is a domestic corporation.

2. It has no more than 75 shareholders. A husband and wife (and their estates) are treated as one shareholder for this requirement. All other persons are treated as separate shareholders.

3. Its only shareholders are individuals, estates, certain trusts described in section 1361(c)(2)(A), or, for tax years beginning after 1997, exempt organizations described in section 401(a) or 501(c)(3). Trustees of trusts that want to make the election under section 1361(e)(3) to be an electing small business trust should see Notice 97-12, 1997-3 I.R.B. 11.

Note: *See the instructions for Part III regarding qualified subchapter S trusts.*

4. It has no nonresident alien shareholders.

5. It has only one class of stock (disregarding differences in voting rights). Generally, a corporation is treated as having only one class of stock if all outstanding shares of the corporation's stock confer identical rights to distribution and liquidation proceeds. See Regulations section 1.1361-1(l) for more details.

6. It is not one of the following ineligible corporations:

   a. A bank or thrift institution that uses the reserve method of accounting for bad debts under section 585;

   b. An insurance company subject to tax under the rules of subchapter L of the Code;

   c. A corporation that has elected to be treated as a possessions corporation under section 936; or

   d. A domestic international sales corporation (DISC) or former DISC.

7. It has a permitted tax year as required by section 1378 or makes a section 444 election to have a tax year other than a permitted tax year. Section 1378 defines a permitted tax year as a tax year ending December 31, or any other tax year for which the corporation establishes a business purpose to the satisfaction of the IRS. See Part II for details on requesting a fiscal tax year based on a business purpose or on making a section 444 election.

8. Each shareholder consents as explained in the instructions for column K.

See sections 1361, 1362, and 1378 for additional information on the above tests.

An election can be made by a parent S corporation to treat the assets, liabilities, and items of income, deduction, and credit of an eligible wholly-owned subsidiary as those of the parent. For details, see Notice 97-4, 1997-2 I.R.B. 24.

Taxes an S Corporation May Owe.— An S corporation may owe income tax in the following instances:

1. If, at the end of any tax year, the corporation had accumulated earnings and profits, and its passive investment income under section 1362(d)(3) is more than 25% of its gross receipts, the corporation may owe tax on its excess net passive income.

2. A corporation with net recognized built-in gain (as defined in section 1374(d)(2)) may owe tax on its built-in gains.

3. A corporation that claimed investment credit before its first year as an S corporation will be liable for any investment credit recapture tax.

4. A corporation that used the LIFO inventory method for the year immediately preceding its first year as an S corporation may owe an additional tax due to LIFO recapture.

For more details on these taxes, see the Instructions for Form 1120S.

Where To File.— File this election with the Internal Revenue Service Center listed below.

If the corporation's principal business, office, or agency is located in	Use the following Internal Revenue Service Center address
New Jersey, New York (New York City and counties of Nassau, Rockland, Suffolk, and Westchester)	Holtsville, NY 00501
New York (all other counties), Connecticut, Maine, Massachusetts, New Hampshire, Rhode Island, Vermont	Andover, MA 05501
Florida, Georgia, South Carolina	Atlanta, GA 39901
Indiana, Kentucky, Michigan, Ohio, West Virginia	Cincinnati, OH 45999
Kansas, New Mexico, Oklahoma, Texas	Austin, TX 73301
Alaska, Arizona, California (counties of Alpine, Amador, Butte, Calaveras, Colusa, Contra Costa, Del Norte, El Dorado, Glenn, Humboldt, Lake, Lassen, Marin, Mendocino, Modoc, Napa, Nevada, Placer, Plumas, Sacramento, San Joaquin, Shasta, Sierra, Siskiyou, Solano, Sonoma, Sutter, Tehama, Trinity, Yolo, and Yuba), Colorado, Idaho, Montana, Nebraska, Nevada, North Dakota, Oregon, South Dakota, Utah, Washington, Wyoming	Ogden, UT 84201
California (all other counties), Hawaii	Fresno, CA 93888
Illinois, Iowa, Minnesota, Missouri, Wisconsin	Kansas City, MO 64999
Alabama, Arkansas, Louisiana, Mississippi, North Carolina, Tennessee	Memphis, TN 37501
Delaware, District of Columbia, Maryland, Pennsylvania, Virginia	Philadelphia, PA 19255

When To Make the Election.— Complete and file Form 2553 **(a)** at any time before the 16th day of the 3rd month of the tax year, if filed during the tax year the election is to take effect, or **(b)** at any time during the preceding tax year. An election made no later than 2 months and 15 days after the beginning of a tax year that is less than 2½ months long is treated as timely made for that tax year. An election made after the 15th day of the 3rd month but before the end of the tax year is effective for the next year. For example, if a calendar tax year corporation makes the election in April 1998, it is effective for the corporation's 1999 calendar tax year.

However, an election made after the due date will be accepted as timely filed if the corporation can show that the failure to file on time was due to reasonable cause. To request relief for a late election, the corporation generally must request a private letter ruling and pay a user fee in accordance with Rev. Proc. 97-1, 1997-1 I.R.B. 11 (or its successor). But if the election is filed within 6 months of its due date and the original due date for filing the corporation's initial Form 1120S has not passed, the ruling and user fee requirements do not apply. To request relief in this case, write "FILED PURSUANT TO REV. PROC. 97-40" at the top of page 1 of Form 2553, attach a statement explaining the reason for failing to file the election on time, and file Form 2553 as otherwise instructed. See Rev. Proc. 97-40, 1997-33 I.R.B. 50, for more details.

See Regulations section 1.1362-6(b)(3)(iii) for how to obtain relief for an inadvertent invalid election if the corporation filed a timely election, but one or more shareholders did not file a timely consent.

Acceptance or Nonacceptance of Election.— The service center will notify the corporation if its election is accepted and when it will take effect. The corporation will also be notified if its election is not accepted. The corporation should generally receive a determination on its election within 60 days after it has filed Form 2553. If box Q1 in Part II is checked on page 2, the corporation will receive a ruling letter from the IRS in Washington, DC, that either approves or denies the selected tax year. When box Q1 is checked, it will generally take an additional 90 days for the Form 2553 to be accepted.

Do not file Form 1120S for any tax year before the year the election takes effect. If the corporation is now required to file **Form 1120**, U.S. Corporation Income Tax Return, or any other applicable tax return, continue filing it until the election takes effect.

Care should be exercised to ensure that the IRS receives the election. If the corporation is not notified of acceptance or nonacceptance of its election within 3 months of date of filing (date mailed), or within 6 months if box Q1 is checked, take follow-up action by corresponding with the service center where the corporation filed the election. If the IRS questions whether Form 2553 was filed, an acceptable proof of filing is **(a)** certified or registered mail receipt (timely filed) from the U.S. Postal Service or its equivalent from a designated private delivery service (see Notice 97-26, 1997-17 I.R.B. 6); **(b)** Form 2553 with accepted stamp; **(c)** Form 2553 with stamped IRS received date; or **(d)** IRS letter stating that Form 2553 has been accepted.

End of Election.— Once the election is made, it stays in effect until it is terminated. If the election is terminated in a tax year beginning after 1996, the corporation (or a successor corporation) can make another election on Form 2553 only with IRS consent for any tax year before the 5th tax year after the first tax year in which the termination took effect. See Regulations section 1.1362-5 for more details.

Cat. No. 49978N

Specific Instructions

Part I

Note: *All corporations must complete Part I.*

Name and Address of Corporation.— Enter the true corporate name as stated in the corporate charter or other legal document creating it. If the corporation's mailing address is the same as someone else's, such as a shareholder's, enter "c/o" and this person's name following the name of the corporation. Include the suite, room, or other unit number after the street address. If the Post Office does not deliver to the street address and the corporation has a P.O. box, show the box number instead of the street address. If the corporation changed its name or address after applying for its employer identification number, be sure to check the box in item G of Part I.

Item A. Employer Identification Number (EIN).— If the corporation has applied for an EIN but has not received it, enter "applied for." If the corporation does not have an EIN, it should apply for one on **Form SS-4**, Application for Employer Identification Number. You can order Form SS-4 by calling 1-800-TAX-FORM (1-800-829-3676).

Item D. Effective Date of Election.— Enter the beginning effective date (month, day, year) of the tax year requested for the S corporation. Generally, this will be the beginning date of the tax year for which the ending effective date is required to be shown in item I, Part I. For a new corporation (first year the corporation exists) it will generally be the date required to be shown in item H, Part I. The tax year of a new corporation starts on the date that it has shareholders, acquires assets, or begins doing business, whichever happens first. If the effective date for item D for a newly formed corporation is later than the date in item H, the corporation should file Form 1120 or Form 1120-A for the tax period between these dates.

Column K. Shareholders' Consent Statement.— Each shareholder who owns (or is deemed to own) stock at the time the election is made must consent to the election. If the election is made during the corporation's tax year for which it first takes effect, any person who held stock at any time during the part of that year that occurs before the election is made, must consent to the election, even though the person may have sold or transferred his or her stock before the election is made.

An election made during the first 2½ months of the tax year is effective for the following tax year if any person who held stock in the corporation during the part of the tax year before the election was made, and who did not hold stock at the time the election was made, did not consent to the election.

Each shareholder consents by signing and dating in column K or signing and dating a separate consent statement described below. The following special rules apply in determining who must sign the consent statement.

- If a husband and wife have a community interest in the stock or in the income from it, both must consent.
- Each tenant in common, joint tenant, and tenant by the entirety must consent.
- A minor's consent is made by the minor, legal representative of the minor, or a natural or adoptive parent of the minor if no legal representative has been appointed.
- The consent of an estate is made by the executor or administrator.
- The consent of an electing small business trust is made by the trustee.
- If the stock is owned by a trust (other than an electing small business trust), the deemed owner of the trust must consent. See section 1361(c)(2) for details regarding trusts that are permitted to be shareholders and rules for determining who is the deemed owner.

*Continuation sheet or separate consent statement.—*If you need a continuation sheet or use a separate consent statement, attach it to Form 2553. The separate consent statement must contain the name, address, and EIN of the corporation and the shareholder information requested in columns J through N of Part I. If you want, you may combine all the shareholders' consents in one statement.

Column L.— Enter the number of shares of stock each shareholder owns and the dates the stock was acquired. If the election is made during the corporation's tax year for which it first takes effect, do not list the shares of stock for those shareholders who sold or transferred all of their stock before the election was made. However, these shareholders must still consent to the election for it to be effective for the tax year.

Column M.— Enter the social security number of each shareholder who is an individual. Enter the EIN of each shareholder that is an estate, a qualified trust, or an exempt organization.

Column N.— Enter the month and day that each shareholder's tax year ends. If a shareholder is changing his or her tax year, enter the tax year the shareholder is changing to, and attach an explanation indicating the present tax year and the basis for the change (e.g., automatic revenue procedure or letter ruling request).

Signature.— Form 2553 must be signed by the president, treasurer, assistant treasurer, chief accounting officer, or other corporate officer (such as tax officer) authorized to sign.

Part II

Complete Part II if you selected a tax year ending on any date other than December 31 (other than a 52-53-week tax year ending with reference to the month of December).

Box P1.— Attach a statement showing separately for each month the amount of gross receipts for the most recent 47 months as required by section 4.03(3) of Rev. Proc. 87-32, 1987-2 C.B. 396. A corporation that does not have a 47-month period of gross receipts cannot establish a natural business year under section 4.01(1).

Box Q1.— For examples of an acceptable business purpose for requesting a fiscal tax year, see Rev. Rul. 87-57, 1987-2 C.B. 117.

In addition to a statement showing the business purpose for the requested fiscal year, you must attach the other information necessary to meet the ruling request requirements of Rev. Proc. 97-1 (or its successor). Also attach a statement that shows separately the amount of gross receipts from sales or services (and inventory costs, if applicable) for each of the 36 months preceding the effective date of the election to be an S corporation. If the corporation has been in existence for fewer than 36 months, submit figures for the period of existence.

If you check box Q1, you will be charged a $250 user fee (subject to change). Do not pay the fee when filing Form 2553. The service center will send Form 2553 to the IRS in Washington, DC, who, in turn, will notify the corporation that the fee is due.

Box Q2.— If the corporation makes a back-up section 444 election for which it is qualified, then the election will take effect in the event the business purpose request is not approved. In some cases, the tax year requested under the back-up section 444 election may be different than the tax year requested under business purpose. See **Form 8716**, Election To Have a Tax Year Other Than a Required Tax Year, for details on making a back-up section 444 election.

Boxes Q2 and R2.— If the corporation is not qualified to make the section 444 election after making the item Q2 back-up section 444 election or indicating its intention to make the election in item R1, and therefore it later files a calendar year return, it should write "Section 444 Election Not Made" in the top left corner of the first calendar year Form 1120S it files.

Part III

Certain qualified subchapter S trusts (QSSTs) may make the QSST election required by section 1361(d)(2) in Part III. Part III may be used to make the QSST election only if corporate stock has been transferred to the trust on or before the date on which the corporation makes its election to be an S corporation. However, a statement can be used instead of Part III to make the election.

Note: *Use Part III only if you make the election in Part I (i.e., Form 2553 cannot be filed with only Part III completed).*

The deemed owner of the QSST must also consent to the S corporation election in column K, page 1, of Form 2553. See section 1361(c)(2).

Paperwork Reduction Act Notice.— We ask for the information on this form to carry out the Internal Revenue laws of the United States. You are required to give us the information. We need it to ensure that you are complying with these laws and to allow us to figure and collect the right amount of tax.

You are not required to provide the information requested on a form that is subject to the Paperwork Reduction Act unless the form displays a valid OMB control number. Books or records relating to a form or its instructions must be retained as long as their contents may become material in the administration of any Internal Revenue law. Generally, tax returns and return information are confidential, as required by section 6103.

The time needed to complete and file this form will depend on individual circumstances. The estimated average time is:

Recordkeeping .... 6 hr., 28 min.

Learning about the law or the form .... 3 hr., 41 min.

Preparing, copying, assembling, and sending the form to the IRS .... 3 hr., 56 min.

If you have comments concerning the accuracy of these time estimates or suggestions for making this form simpler, we would be happy to hear from you. You can write to the Tax Forms Committee, Western Area Distribution Center, Rancho Cordova, CA 95743-0001. **DO NOT** send the form to this address. Instead, see **Where To File** on page 1.

Form 2553
(Rev. September 1997)
Department of the Treasury
Internal Revenue Service

Election by a Small Business Corporation
(Under section 1362 of the Internal Revenue Code)
▶ For Paperwork Reduction Act Notice, see page 2 of instructions.
▶ See separate instructions.

OMB No. 1545-0146

Notes:
1. This election to be an S corporation can be accepted only if all the tests are met under **Who May Elect** on page 1 of the instructions; all signatures in Parts I and III are originals (no photocopies); and the exact name and address of the corporation and other required form information are provided.
2. Do not file **Form 1120S**, U.S. Income Tax Return for an S Corporation, for any tax year before the year the election takes effect.
3. If the corporation was in existence before the effective date of this election, see **Taxes an S Corporation May Owe** on page 1 of the instructions.

Part I — Election Information

Please Type or Print

Name of corporation (see instructions)

Number, street, and room or suite no. (If a P.O. box, see instructions.)

City or town, state, and ZIP code

A Employer identification number

B Date incorporated

C State of incorporation

D Election is to be effective for tax year beginning (month, day, year) ▶ / /

E Name and title of officer or legal representative who the IRS may call for more information

F Telephone number of officer or legal representative
( )

G If the corporation changed its name or address after applying for the EIN shown in **A** above, check this box ▶ ☐

H If this election takes effect for the first tax year the corporation exists, enter month, day, and year of the **earliest** of the following: (1) date the corporation first had shareholders, (2) date the corporation first had assets, or (3) date the corporation began doing business ▶ / /

I Selected tax year: Annual return will be filed for tax year ending (month and day) ▶ ....
If the tax year ends on any date other than December 31, except for an automatic 52-53-week tax year ending with reference to the month of December, you **must** complete Part II on the back. If the date you enter is the ending date of an automatic 52-53-week tax year, write "52-53-week year" to the right of the date. See Temporary Regulations section 1.441-2T(e)(3).

J Name and address of each shareholder; shareholder's spouse having a community property interest in the corporation's stock; and each tenant in common, joint tenant, and tenant by the entirety. (A husband and wife (and their estates) are counted as one shareholder in determining the number of shareholders without regard to the manner in which the stock is owned.)	K Shareholders' Consent Statement. Under penalties of perjury, we declare that we consent to the election of the above-named corporation to be an S corporation under section 1362(a) and that we have examined this consent statement, including accompanying schedules and statements, and to the best of our knowledge and belief, it is true, correct, and complete. We understand our consent is binding and may not be withdrawn after the corporation has made a valid election. (Shareholders sign and date below.)		L Stock owned		M Social security number or employer identification number (see instructions)	N Shareholder's tax year ends (month and day)
	Signature	Date	Number of shares	Dates acquired		

Under penalties of perjury, I declare that I have examined this election, including accompanying schedules and statements, and to the best of my knowledge and belief, it is true, correct, and complete.

Signature of officer ▶   Title ▶   Date ▶

See Parts II and III on back.

Cat. No. 18629R

Form **2553** (Rev. 9-97)

Form 2553 (Rev. 9-97) Page **2**

Part II Selection of Fiscal Tax Year (All corporations using this part must complete item O and item P, Q, or R.)

O Check the applicable box to indicate whether the corporation is:
   1. ☐ A new corporation adopting the tax year entered in item I, Part I.
   2. ☐ An existing corporation retaining the tax year entered in item I, Part I.
   3. ☐ An existing corporation changing to the tax year entered in item I, Part I.

P Complete item P if the corporation is using the expeditious approval provisions of Rev. Proc. 87-32, 1987-2 C.B. 396, to request **(1)** a natural business year (as defined in section 4.01(1) of Rev. Proc. 87-32) or **(2)** a year that satisfies the ownership tax year test in section 4.01(2) of Rev. Proc. 87-32. Check the applicable box below to indicate the representation statement the corporation is making as required under section 4 of Rev. Proc. 87-32.

   1. Natural Business Year ▶ ☐ I represent that the corporation is retaining or changing to a tax year that coincides with its natural business year as defined in section 4.01(1) of Rev. Proc. 87-32 and as verified by its satisfaction of the requirements of section 4.02(1) of Rev. Proc. 87-32. In addition, if the corporation is changing to a natural business year as defined in section 4.01(1), I further represent that such tax year results in less deferral of income to the owners than the corporation's present tax year. I also represent that the corporation is not described in section 3.01(2) of Rev. Proc. 87-32. (See instructions for additional information that must be attached.)

   2. Ownership Tax Year ▶ ☐ I represent that shareholders holding more than half of the shares of the stock (as of the first day of the tax year to which the request relates) of the corporation have the same tax year or are concurrently changing to the tax year that the corporation adopts, retains, or changes to per item I, Part I. I also represent that the corporation is not described in section 3.01(2) of Rev. Proc. 87-32.

Note: If you do not use item P and the corporation wants a fiscal tax year, complete either item Q or R below. Item Q is used to request a fiscal tax year based on a business purpose and to make a back-up section 444 election. Item R is used to make a regular section 444 election.

Q Business Purpose—To request a fiscal tax year based on a business purpose, you must check box Q1 and pay a user fee. See instructions for details. You may also check box Q2 and/or box Q3.

   1. Check here ▶ ☐ if the fiscal year entered in item I, Part I, is requested under the provisions of section 6.03 of Rev. Proc. 87-32. Attach to Form 2553 a statement showing the business purpose for the requested fiscal year. See instructions for additional information that must be attached.

   2. Check here ▶ ☐ to show that the corporation intends to make a back-up section 444 election in the event the corporation's business purpose request is not approved by the IRS. (See instructions for more information.)

   3. Check here ▶ ☐ to show that the corporation agrees to adopt or change to a tax year ending December 31 if necessary for the IRS to accept this election for S corporation status in the event (1) the corporation's business purpose request is not approved and the corporation makes a back-up section 444 election, but is ultimately not qualified to make a section 444 election, or (2) the corporation's business purpose request is not approved and the corporation did not make a back-up section 444 election.

R Section 444 Election—To make a section 444 election, you must check box R1 and you may also check box R2.

   1. Check here ▶ ☐ to show the corporation will make, if qualified, a section 444 election to have the fiscal tax year shown in item I, Part I. To make the election, you must complete **Form 8716**, Election To Have a Tax Year Other Than a Required Tax Year, and either attach it to Form 2553 or file it separately.

   2. Check here ▶ ☐ to show that the corporation agrees to adopt or change to a tax year ending December 31 if necessary for the IRS to accept this election for S corporation status in the event the corporation is ultimately not qualified to make a section 444 election.

Part III Qualified Subchapter S Trust (QSST) Election Under Section 1361(d)(2)*

Income beneficiary's name and address	Social security number
Trust's name and address	Employer identification number

Date on which stock of the corporation was transferred to the trust (month, day, year) . . . . ▶ / /

In order for the trust named above to be a QSST and thus a qualifying shareholder of the S corporation for which this Form 2553 is filed, I hereby make the election under section 1361(d)(2). Under penalties of perjury, I certify that the trust meets the definitional requirements of section 1361(d)(3) and that all other information provided in Part III is true, correct, and complete.

_____ _____
Signature of income beneficiary or signature and title of legal representative or other qualified person making the election   Date

*Use Part III to make the QSST election only if stock of the corporation has been transferred to the trust on or before the date on which the corporation makes its election to be an S corporation. The QSST election must be made and filed separately if stock of the corporation is transferred to the trust after the date on which the corporation makes the S election.

Printed on recycled paper   *U.S. Government Printing Office: 1997 - 432-190/60239

Form 15

Banking Resolution of

_____
a New York Corporation

The undersigned, being the corporate secretary of the above corporation, hereby certifies that on the _____ day of _____, _____ the Board of Directors of the corporation adopted the following resolution:

> RESOLVED that the corporation elects "S-Corporation" status for tax purposes under the Internal Revenue Code and that the officers of the corporation are directed to file IRS Form 2553 and to take any further action necessary for the corporation to qualify for S-Corporation status.

and that said resolution has not been modified or rescinded.

Date: _____

_____
Corporate Secretary

Shareholders' Consent

The undersigned shareholders being all of the shareholders of the above corporation, a _____ corporation hereby consent to the election of the corporation to obtain S-corporation status

Name and Address of Shareholder	Shares Owned	Date Acquired
_____	_____	_____
_____	_____	_____
_____	_____	_____

Date:_____

_____
Signature of Shareholder

_____
Signature of Shareholder

_____
Signature of Shareholder

_____
Signature of Shareholder

Form 16

WAIVER OF NOTICE OF THE ANNUAL MEETING OF THE BOARD OF DIRECTORS OF

_____

The undersigned, being all the Directors of the Corporation, hereby agree and consent that an annual meeting of the Board of Directors of the Corporation be held on the ____ day of _____, _____ at ___ o'clock __m at _____ _____ and do hereby waive all notice whatsoever of such meeting and of any adjournment or adjournments thereof.

We do further agree and consent that any and all lawful business may be transacted at such meeting or at any adjournment or adjournments thereof as may be deemed advisable by the Directors present. Any business transacted at such meeting or at any adjournment or adjournments thereof shall be as valid and legal as if such meeting or adjourned meeting were held after notice.

Date: _____

_____
Director

_____
Director

_____
Director

_____
Director

Form 17

MINUTES OF THE ANNUAL MEETING OF
THE BOARD OF DIRECTORS OF

_____

The annual meeting of the Board of Directors of the Corporation was held on the date and at the time and place set forth in the written waiver of notice signed by the directors, and attached to the minutes of this meeting.

The following were present, being all the directors of the Corporation:

_____   _____

_____   _____

The meeting was called to order and it was moved, seconded and unanimously carried that _____ act as Chairman and that _____ act as Secretary.

The minutes of the last meeting of the Board of Directors which was held on _____, _____ were read and approved by the Board.

Upon motion duly made, seconded and carried, the following were elected officers for the following year and until their successors are elected and qualify:

President:
Vice President:
Secretary
Treasurer:

There being no further business to come before the meeting, upon motion duly made, seconded and unanimously carried, it was adjourned.

_____
Secretary

Directors:

_____

_____

_____

171

Form 18

WAIVER OF NOTICE OF THE ANNUAL MEETING OF THE SHAREHOLDERS OF

_____

  The undersigned, being all the shareholders of the Corporation, hereby agree and consent that an annual meeting of the shareholders of the Corporation be held on the ____ day of _____, _____ at ____ o'clock ____m at _____ _____ and do hereby waive all notice whatsoever of such meeting and of any adjournment or adjournments thereof.

  We do further agree and consent that any and all lawful business may be transacted at such meeting or at any adjournment or adjournments thereof. Any business transacted at such meeting or at any adjournment or adjournments thereof shall be as valid and legal as if such meeting or adjourned meeting were held after notice.

Date: _____

_____
Shareholder

_____
Shareholder

_____
Shareholder

_____
Shareholder

Form 19

MINUTES OF THE ANNUAL MEETING OF SHAREHOLDERS OF

_____

The annual meeting of Shareholders of the Corporation was held on the date and at the time and place set forth in the written waiver of notice signed by the shareholders, and attached to the minutes of this meeting.

There were present the following shareholders:

Shareholder	No. of Shares
_____	_____
_____	_____
_____	_____
_____	_____

The meeting was called to order and it was moved, seconded and unanimously carried that _____ act as Chairman and that _____ act as Secretary.

A roll call was taken and the Chairman noted that all of the outstanding shares of the Corporation were represented in person or by proxy. Any proxies were attached to these minutes.

The minutes of the last meeting of the shareholders which was held on _____, _____ were read and approved by the shareholders.

Upon motion duly made, seconded and carried, the following were elected directors for the following year:

_____   _____
_____   _____

There being no further business to come before the meeting, upon motion duly made, seconded and unanimously carried, it was adjourned.

_____
Secretary

Shareholders:

_____

_____

_____

Form 20

WAIVER OF NOTICE OF SPECIAL MEETING OF THE BOARD OF DIRECTORS OF

_____

The undersigned, being all the Directors of the Corporation, hereby agree and consent that a special meeting of the Board of Directors of the Corporation be held on the ____ day of _____, _____ at ___ o'clock __m at _____ _____ and do hereby waive all notice whatsoever of such meeting and of any adjournment or adjournments thereof.

The purpose of the meeting is:

We do further agree and consent that any and all lawful business may be transacted at such meeting or at any adjournment or adjournments thereof as may be deemed advisable by the Directors present. Any business transacted at such meeting or at any adjournment or adjournments thereof shall be as valid and legal as if such meeting or adjourned meeting were held after notice.

Date: _____

_____
Director

_____
Director

_____
Director

_____
Director

Form 21

MINUTES OF SPECIAL MEETING OF
THE BOARD OF DIRECTORS OF

_____

A special meeting of the Board of Directors of the Corporation was held on the date and at the time and place set forth in the written waiver of notice signed by the directors, and attached to the minutes of this meeting.

The following were present, being all the directors of the Corporation:

_____   _____
_____   _____

The meeting was called to order and it was moved, seconded and unanimously carried that _____ act as Chairman and that _____ act as Secretary.

The minutes of the last meeting of the Board of Directors which was held on _____, _____ were read and approved by the Board.

Upon motion duly made, seconded and carried, the following resolution was adopted:

There being no further business to come before the meeting, upon motion duly made, seconded and unanimously carried, it was adjourned.

_____
Secretary

Directors:

_____

_____

_____

Form 22

WAIVER OF NOTICE OF SPECIAL MEETING OF THE SHAREHOLDERS OF

_____

The undersigned, being all the shareholders of the Corporation, hereby agree and consent that a special meeting of the shareholders of the Corporation be held on the ____ day of _____, _____ at ___ o'clock __m at _____ _____ and do hereby waive all notice whatsoever of such meeting and of any adjournment or adjournments thereof.

The purpose of the meeting is

We do further agree and consent that any and all lawful business may be transacted at such meeting or at any adjournment or adjournments thereof. Any business transacted at such meeting or at any adjournment or adjournments thereof shall be as valid and legal as if such meeting or adjourned meeting were held after notice.

Date: _____

_____
Shareholder

_____
Shareholder

_____
Shareholder

_____
Shareholder

Form 23

MINUTES OF SPECIAL MEETING OF SHAREHOLDERS OF

_____

A special meeting of Shareholders of the Corporation was held on the date and at the time and place set forth in the written waiver of notice signed by the shareholders, and attached to the minutes of this meeting.

There were present the following shareholders:

Shareholder	No. of Shares
_____	_____
_____	_____
_____	_____
_____	_____

The meeting was called to order and it was moved, seconded and unanimously carried that _____ act as Chairman and that _____ act as Secretary.

A roll call was taken and the Chairman noted that all of the outstanding shares of the Corporation were represented in person or by proxy. Any proxies were attached to these minutes.

The minutes of the last meeting of the shareholders which was held on _____, _____ were read and approved by the shareholders.

Upon motion duly made, seconded and carried, the following resolution was adopted:

There being no further business to come before the meeting, upon motion duly made, seconded and unanimously carried, it was adjourned.

_____
Secretary

Shareholders:

_____

_____

_____

Form 24

CERTIFICATE OF DISSOLUTION

of

_____

UNDER SECTION 1003 OF THE BUSINESS CORPORATION LAW

WE, THE UNDERSIGNED, _____ and _____, being respectively the _____ and the _____ of _____, Corporation hereby certify:

FIRST: The name of the corporation is _____.

SECOND: The Certificate of Incorporation was filed with the Department of State on _____.

THIRD: The name and address of each of its officers and directors is:

_____

_____

_____

FOURTH: That this corporation elects to dissolve.

FIFTH: Dissolution was authorized by: _____

_____

IN WITNESS WHEREOF, we have signed this certificate on _____ (date) and we affirm the statements contained therein are true under penalties of perjury.

_____

_____

Form 25

CERTIFICATE OF AMENDMENT
OF THE CERTIFICATE OF INCORPORATION
OF

_____

Under Section 805 of the Business Corporation Law

We, the undersigned, _____, Chief Executive Officer, and _____, Secretary, of _____, a corporation organized and existing under the Business Corporation Law of the State of New York, do hereby certify as follows:

1. The name of the Corporation is _____

2. The Certificate of Incorporation of the Corporation was filed with the Department of State on _____.

3. The Certificate of Incorporation of the Corporation, as heretofore amended, is hereby further amended to: _____
_____

4. The following provisions are modified as follows: _____
_____

5. The foregoing amendments to the Certificate of Incorporation of the Corporation have been duly authorized by: _____
_____

IN WITNESS WHEREOF, the undersigned have signed this Certificate and affirm under the penalties of perjury that the statements made herein are true this _____ day of _____, _____.

_____
Chief Executive Officer

_____
Secretary

Form 26

OFFICER / DIRECTOR RESIGNATION

I, _____, hereby resign as _____
(Title)

of _____,
(Name of Corporation)

a corporation organized under the laws of the State of _____

and affirm that the corporation has been notified in writing of the resignation.

_____
(Signature of resigning officer/director)

Form 27

CERTIFICATE OF RESIGNATION OF REGISTERED AGENT OF

_____

UNDER SECTION 305 OF THE BUSINESS CORPORATION LAW

Pursuant to the provisions of NYBCL 305, the undersigned, _____
_____, (registered agent),

Hereby resigns as Registered Agent for, _____
(corporation), a corporation formed in New York State.

Said corporation filed its certificate of incorporation in New York on _____
_____ (date).

I hereby affirm that a copy of this certificate of resignation has been served upon said corporation by registered mail at the Post Office address on file in the Department of State specified for mailing of process. If such address is the address of the above resigning agent, then the copy was sent to the office of the corporation in the jurisdiction of its formation or incorporation.

_____
signature of resigning agent

If signing on behalf of an entity:

_____
typed or printed name

_____
capacity

Stock Ledger

Form 28

Certificates Issued						Transfer of Shares				
Cert. No.	No. of Shares	Date of Acquisition	Shareholder Name and Address	From Whom Transferred	Amount Paid	Date of Transfer	To Whom Transferred	Cert. No. Surrendered	No. of Shares Transferred	Cert. No.

Form 30

Certificate No. _____	☐ Original issue	☐ Transferred from: _____	Received Cert. No. _____
No. of shares _____	Documentary stamp tax paid:	_____	No. of shares _____
Dated _____	$ _____	Date: _____	New certificates issued:
Issued to:	(Attach stamps to this stub.)	Original No. of Shares	Cert. No. No. of Shares
_____		Original No. Shares Transferred	_____ _____
_____		Cert. No.	_____ _____
_____		_____ _____ _____	

Certificate No. _____	☐ Original issue	☐ Transferred from: _____	Received Cert. No. _____
No. of shares _____	Documentary stamp tax paid:	_____	No. of shares _____
Dated _____	$ _____	Date: _____	New certificates issued:
Issued to:	(Attach stamps to this stub.)	Original No. of Shares	Cert. No. No. of Shares
_____		Original No. Shares Transferred	_____ _____
_____		Cert. No.	_____ _____
_____		_____ _____ _____	

Certificate No. _____	☐ Original issue	☐ Transferred from: _____	Received Cert. No. _____
No. of shares _____	Documentary stamp tax paid:	_____	No. of shares _____
Dated _____	$ _____	Date: _____	New certificates issued:
Issued to:	(Attach stamps to this stub.)	Original No. of Shares	Cert. No. No. of Shares
_____		Original No. Shares Transferred	_____ _____
_____		Cert. No.	_____ _____
_____		_____ _____ _____	

Certificate No. _____	☐ Original issue	☐ Transferred from: _____	Received Cert. No. _____
No. of shares _____	Documentary stamp tax paid:	_____	No. of shares _____
Dated _____	$ _____	Date: _____	New certificates issued:
Issued to: _____	(Attach stamps to this stub.)	Original No. Shares No. of Shares Transferred	Cert. No. No. of Shares
_____		Cert. No. _____ _____ _____	_____ _____
_____			_____ _____

Certificate No. _____	☐ Original issue	☐ Transferred from: _____	Received Cert. No. _____
No. of shares _____	Documentary stamp tax paid:	_____	No. of shares _____
Dated _____	$ _____	Date: _____	New certificates issued:
Issued to: _____	(Attach stamps to this stub.)	Original No. Shares No. of Shares Transferred	Cert. No. No. of Shares
_____		Cert. No. _____ _____ _____	_____ _____
_____			_____ _____

Certificate No. _____	☐ Original issue	☐ Transferred from: _____	Received Cert. No. _____
No. of shares _____	Documentary stamp tax paid:	_____	No. of shares _____
Dated _____	$ _____	Date: _____	New certificates issued:
Issued to: _____	(Attach stamps to this stub.)	Original No. Shares No. of Shares Transferred	Cert. No. No. of Shares
_____		Cert. No. _____ _____ _____	_____ _____
_____			_____ _____

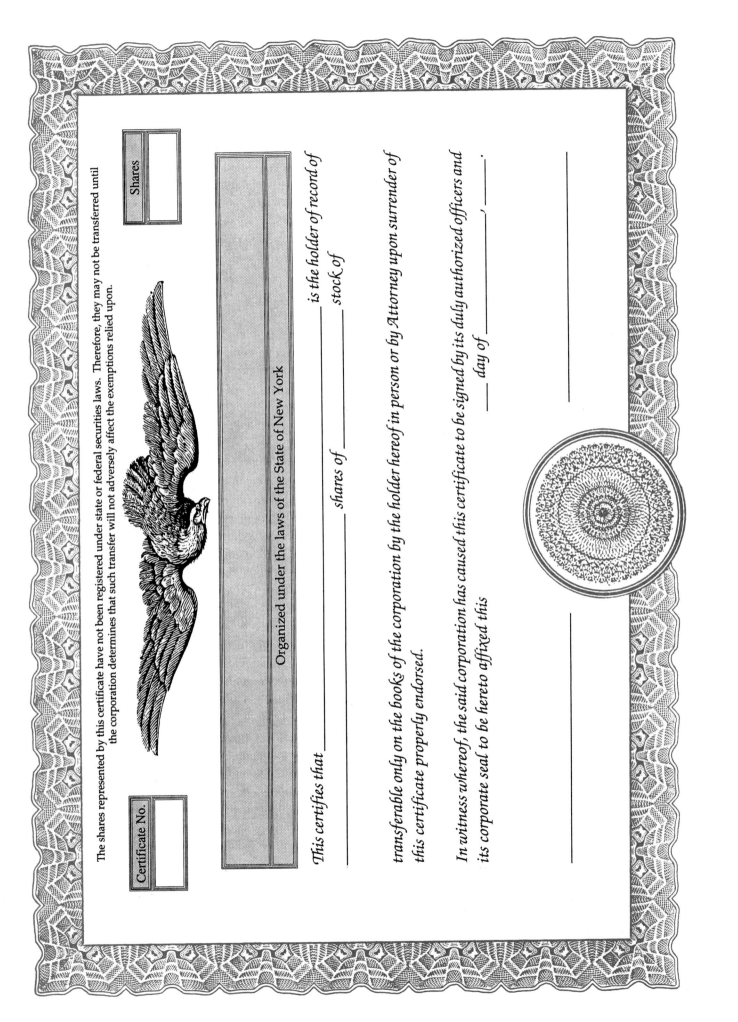

For value received, ____ hereby sell, assign and transfer unto _____
_____,
_____ *shares represented by this certificate and do hereby irrevocably constitute and appoint* _____ *attorney to transfer the said shares on the books of the corporation with full power of substitution in the premises.*

Dated _____

_____

Witness:

_____

Certificate No. _____   Shares _____

The shares represented by this certificate have not been registered under state or federal securities laws. Therefore, they may not be transferred until the corporation determines that such transfer will not adversely affect the exemptions relied upon.

Organized under the laws of the State of New York

This certifies that _____ is the holder of record of _____ shares of _____ stock of _____ transferable only on the books of the corporation by the holder hereof in person or by Attorney upon surrender of this certificate properly endorsed.

In witness whereof, the said corporation has caused this certificate to be signed by its duly authorized officers and its corporate seal to be hereto affixed this _____ day of _____, _____.

_____

For value received, _____ hereby sell, assign and transfer unto _____
_____,
_____ *shares represented by this certificate and do hereby irrevocably constitute and appoint* _____ *attorney to transfer the said shares on the books of the corporation with full power of substitution in the premises.*

Dated _____

_____

Witness:

_____

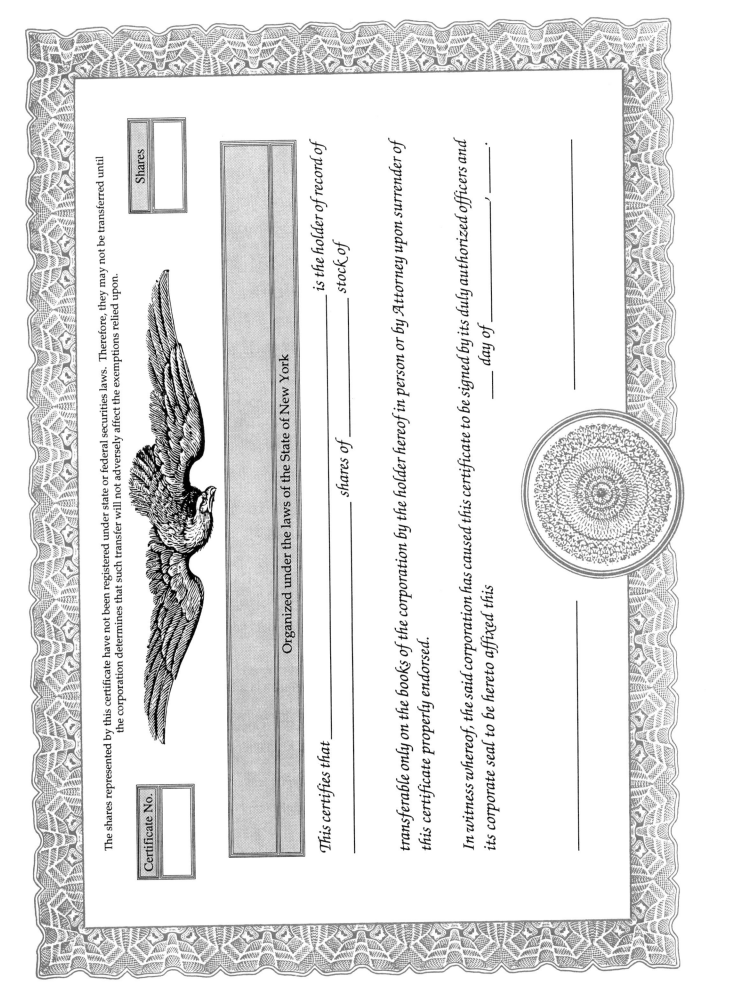

For value received, _____ hereby sell, assign and transfer unto _____
_____,
_____ shares represented by this certificate and do hereby irrevocably constitute and appoint _____ attorney to transfer the said shares on the books of the corporation with full power of substitution in the premises.

Dated _____

_____

Witness:

_____

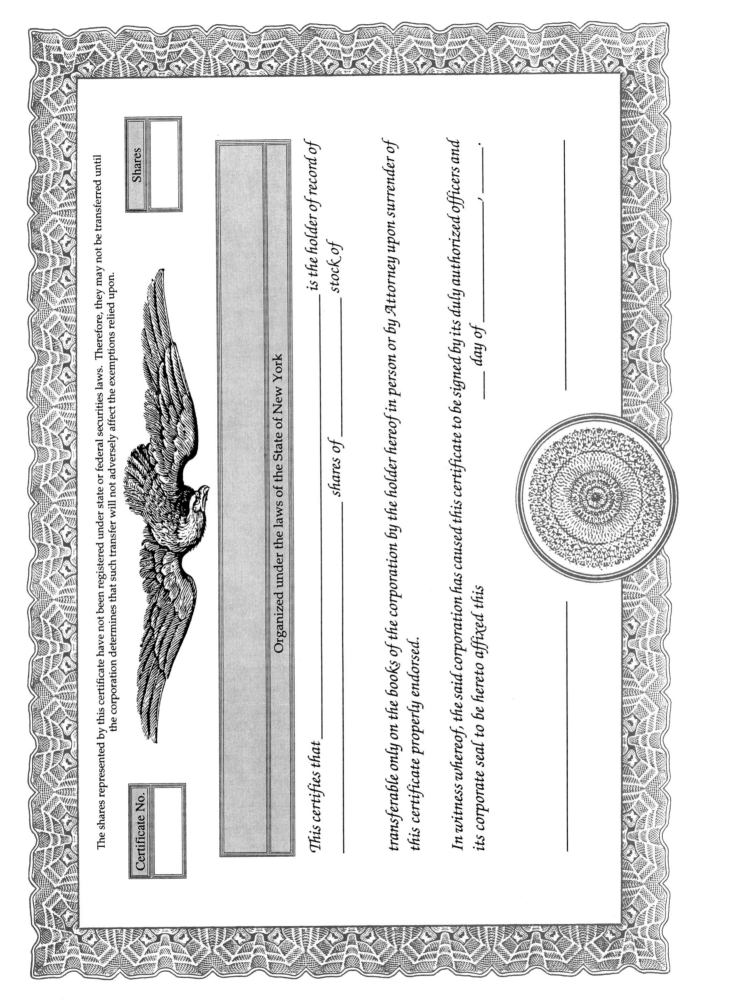

For value received, _____ hereby sell, assign and transfer unto _____
_____,
_____ shares represented by this certificate and do hereby irrevocably constitute and appoint _____ attorney to transfer the said shares on the books of the corporation with full power of substitution in the premises.

Dated _____

_____

Witness:

_____

The shares represented by this certificate have not been registered under state or federal securities laws. Therefore, they may not be transferred until the corporation determines that such transfer will not adversely affect the exemptions relied upon.

Certificate No. _____

Shares _____

Organized under the laws of the State of New York

This certifies that _____ is the holder of record of _____ shares of _____ stock of _____ transferable only on the books of the corporation by the holder hereof in person or by Attorney upon surrender of this certificate properly endorsed.

In witness whereof, the said corporation has caused this certificate to be signed by its duly authorized officers and its corporate seal to be hereto affixed this _____ day of _____, _____.

For value received, ____ *hereby sell, assign and transfer unto* _____, _____ *shares represented by this certificate and do hereby irrevocably constitute and appoint* _____ *attorney to transfer the said shares on the books of the corporation with full power of substitution in the premises.*

Dated _____

_____

Witness:

_____

Form 31

RESTATED
CERTIFICATE OF INCORPORATION
OF

_____

Under Section 807 of the Business Corporation Law

FIRST: The name of the Corporation is _____.

SECOND: The Certificate of Incorporation of the Corporation was filed with the Department of State on _____.

THIRD: The Certificate of Incorporation of the Corporation is hereby amended to effect amendments or changes authorized by the Business Corporation Law as follows:

FOURTH: The text of the Certificate of Incorporation of the Corporation, as heretofore amended and as hereby amended, is hereby restated to read in its entirety as follows:

1. The name of the Corporation is _____.

2. The purpose of the Corporation is to:

3. The office of the Corporation is to be located:

4. _____

_____

_____ [*insert new provision*]

5. The Secretary of State is designated as the agent of the Corporation upon whom process against it may be served. The post office address to which the Secretary of State shall mail a copy of any process against the Corporation served upon him is : _____

_____

FIFTH: This Restated Certificate and the amendments contained herein were authorized by:
_____

IN WITNESS WHEREOF, the undersigned sole shareholder of the Corporation, _____ made and subscribed this Certificate this _____ day of _____, _____.

INDEX

A

advantages of incorporating, 9
amending a corporation, 57
annual report, 13

B

bank accounts, 37
bankruptcy, 61
bi-annual reports, 55
board of directors, 6, 53
bylaws, 7, 29, 58

C

c corporation, 16
certificate of incorporation, 7, 24, 57
checking accounts, 14, 37
checklist, 64
continuous existence, 10
corporate kits, 32
corporate seal, 33
corporate supplies, 32
credit rating, 13

D

Delaware corporation, 15
dissolution, 59

E

estate planning, 12
examination of records, 50
expenses, 13

F

federal securities exemptions, 43
forbidden names, 23
foreign corporation, 15
form 2553, 31
form DTS-17, 31
form SS-4, 31

H

home businesses, 40

I

internet stock sales, 45
intrastate offering exemption, 44
involuntary dissolution, 60

L

ledger, 30
licenses, 39
limited liability, 9

M

minute book, 36
minutes, 30, 49

N

name check, 21
name reservation, 23
Nevada corporation, 15
New York securities laws, 44

New York securities registration, 47
not-for-profit corporations, 19

O

offers to purchase, 33
officers, 6
organizational meeting, 35
organizational paperwork, 29

P

payment for shares, 46
person, 5
private placement exemption, 43
professional corporation, 18, 27

R

raising capital, 12
record keeping, 12. 13, 49
registered agent, 6
resolutions, 30
restoration of a dissolved corporation, 61
running a corporation, 49

S

s corporation, 16
securities laws, 41
selling stock, 41

shareholder meetings, 51
shareholder, 6
shareholder agreement, 28
small offering exemption, 44
statutes, 65
stock certificates, 33

T

tax forms, 31
tax on shares, 34
tax returns, 13
trademark search, 22
trademarks, 23
trading property for shares, 46
trading services for shares, 46
transfer of ownership, 11
transferability, 11

V

voluntary dissolution, 59

W

waiver of meeting, 30
waiver of notice, 30

Y

yellow pages, 21

Your #1 Source for Real World Legal Information...

SPHINX® PUBLISHING
A Division of Sourcebooks, Inc.®

- Written by lawyers
- Simple English explanation of the law
- Forms and instructions included

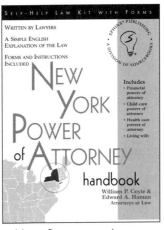

HOW TO START A BUSINESS IN NEW YORK

An essential legal guide to starting a business, including the important New York forms you need. This book explains the New York laws you need to know, including tax and labor laws.

176 pages; $16.95;
ISBN 1-57071-185-2

HOW TO WIN IN SMALL CLAIMS COURT IN NEW YORK

File and defend your own case with critical information about filing your case, settling your case and collecting judgment.

160 pages; $14.95;
ISBN 1-57071-187-9

NEW YORK POWER OF ATTORNEY HANDBOOK

Helpful New York forms with instructions are included. Sections cover powers of attorney for child care, health care and real estate.

144 pages; $12.95;
ISBN 1-57071-188-7

See the following order form for books written specifically for California, Florida, Georgia, Illinois, Massachusetts, Michigan, Minnesota, New York, North Carolina, Pennsylvania, and Texas! *Coming soon—Ohio and New Jersey!*

What our customers say about our books:

"It couldn't be more clear for the lay person." —R.D.

"I want you to know I really appreciate your book. It has saved me a lot of time and money." —L.T.

"Your real estate contracts book has saved me nearly $12,000.00 in closing costs over the past year." —A.B.

"...many of the legal questions that I have had over the years were answered clearly and concisely through your plain English interpretation of the law." —C.E.H.

"If there weren't people out there like you I'd be lost. You have the best books of this type out there." —S.B.

"...your forms and directions are easy to follow." —C.V.M.

*Sphinx Publishing's Legal Survival Guides
are directly available from the Sourcebooks, Inc., or from your local bookstores.
For credit card orders call 1–800–43–BRIGHT, write P.O. Box 372, Naperville, IL 60566,
or fax 630-961-2168*

SPHINX® PUBLISHING'S NATIONAL TITLES
Valid in All 50 States

LEGAL SURVIVAL IN BUSINESS

How to Form a Limited Liability Company	$19.95
How to Form Your Own Corporation (2E)	$19.95
How to Form Your Own Partnership	$19.95
How to Register Your Own Copyright (2E)	$19.95
How to Register Your Own Trademark (3E)	$19.95
Most Valuable Business Legal Forms You'll Ever Need (2E)	$19.95
Most Valuable Corporate Forms You'll Ever Need (2E)	$24.95
Software Law (with diskette)	$29.95

LEGAL SURVIVAL IN COURT

Crime Victim's Guide to Justice	$19.95
Debtors' Rights (3E)	$12.95
Defend Yourself against Criminal Charges	$19.95
Grandparents' Rights (2E)	$19.95
Help Your Lawyer Win Your Case (2E)	$12.95
Jurors' Rights (2E)	$9.95
Legal Malpractice and Other Claims against Your Lawyer (2E)	$18.95
Legal Research Made Easy (2E)	$14.95
Simple Ways to Protect Yourself from Lawsuits	$24.95
Victims' Rights	$12.95
Winning Your Personal Injury Claim	$19.95

LEGAL SURVIVAL IN REAL ESTATE

How to Buy a Condominium or Townhome	$16.95
How to Negotiate Real Estate Contracts (3E)	$16.95
How to Negotiate Real Estate Leases (3E)	$16.95
Successful Real Estate Brokerage Management	$19.95

LEGAL SURVIVAL IN PERSONAL AFFAIRS

Your Right to Child Custody, Visitation and Support	$19.95
The Nanny and Domestic Help Legal Kit	$19.95
How to File Your Own Bankruptcy (4E)	$19.95
How to File Your Own Divorce (3E)	$19.95
How to Make Your Own Will	$12.95
How to Write Your Own Living Will	$9.95
How to Write Your Own Premarital Agreement (2E)	$19.95
How to Win Your Unemployment Compensation Claim	$19.95
Living Trusts and Simple Ways to Avoid Probate (2E)	$19.95
Neighbor v. Neighbor (2E)	$12.95
The Power of Attorney Handbook (3E)	$19.95
Simple Ways to Protect Yourself from Lawsuits	$24.95
Social Security Benefits Handbook (2E)	$14.95
Unmarried Parents' Rights	$19.95
U.S.A. Immigration Guide (3E)	$19.95
Guia de Inmigracion a Estados Unidos (2E)	$19.95

Legal Survival Guides are directly available from Sourcebooks, Inc., or from your local bookstores.

For credit card orders call 1–800–43–BRIGHT, write P.O. Box 372, Naperville, IL 60566, or fax 630-961-2168

SPHINX® PUBLISHING ORDER FORM

BILL TO:		SHIP TO:	
Phone #	Terms	F.O.B. Chicago, IL	Ship Date

Charge my: ☐ VISA ☐ MasterCard ☐ American Express

☐ Money Order or Personal Check

Credit Card Number   Expiration Date

Qty	ISBN	Title	Retail	Ext.
		SPHINX PUBLISHING NATIONAL TITLES		
	1-57071-166-6	Crime Victim's Guide to Justice	$19.95	
	1-57071-342-1	Debtors' Rights (3E)	$12.95	
	1-57071-162-3	Defend Yourself against Criminal Charges	$19.95	
	1-57248-082-3	Grandparents' Rights (2E)	$19.95	
	1-57248-087-4	Guia de Inmigracion a Estados Unidos (2E)	$19.95	
	1-57248-103-X	Help Your Lawyer Win Your Case (2E)	$12.95	
	1-57071-164-X	How to Buy a Condominium or Townhome	$16.95	
	1-57071-223-9	How to File Your Own Bankruptcy (4E)	$19.95	
	1-57071-224-7	How to File Your Own Divorce (3E)	$19.95	
	1-57248-083-1	How to Form a Limited Liability Company	$19.95	
	1-57248-099-8	How to Form a Nonprofit Corporation	$24.95	
	1-57071-227-1	How to Form Your Own Corporation (2E)	$19.95	
	1-57071-343-X	How to Form Your Own Partnership	$19.95	
	1-57071-228-X	How to Make Your Own Will	$12.95	
	1-57071-331-6	How to Negotiate Real Estate Contracts (3E)	$16.95	
	1-57071-332-4	How to Negotiate Real Estate Leases (3E)	$16.95	
	1-57071-225-5	How to Register Your Own Copyright (2E)	$19.95	
	1-57248-104-8	How to Register Your Own Trademark (3E)	$19.95	
	1-57071-349-9	How to Win Your Unemployment Compensation Claim	$19.95	
	1-57071-167-4	How to Write Your Own Living Will	$9.95	
	1-57071-344-8	How to Write Your Own Premarital Agreement (2E)	$19.95	
	1-57071-333-2	Jurors' Rights (2E)	$9.95	
	1-57248-032-7	Legal Malpractice and Other Claims against...	$18.95	
	1-57071-400-2	Legal Research Made Easy (2E)	$14.95	
	1-57071-336-7	Living Trusts and Simple Ways to Avoid Probate (2E)	$19.95	
	1-57071-345-6	Most Valuable Bus. Legal Forms You'll Ever Need (2E)	$19.95	
	1-57071-346-4	Most Valuable Corporate Forms You'll Ever Need (2E)	$24.95	
	1-57248-089-0	Neighbor v. Neighbor (2E)	$12.95	
	1-57071-348-0	The Power of Attorney Handbook (3E)	$19.95	

Qty	ISBN	Title	Retail	Ext.
	1-57248-020-3	Simple Ways to Protect Yourself from Lawsuits	$24.95	
	1-57071-337-5	Social Security Benefits Handbook (2E)	$14.95	
	1-57071-163-1	Software Law (w/diskette)	$29.95	
	0-913825-86-7	Successful Real Estate Brokerage Mgmt.	$19.95	
	1-57248-098-X	The Nanny and Domestic Help Legal Kit	$19.95	
	1-57071-399-5	Unmarried Parents' Rights	$19.95	
	1-57071-354-5	U.S.A. Immigration Guide (3E)	$19.95	
	0-913825-82-4	Victims' Rights	$12.95	
	1-57071-165-8	Winning Your Personal Injury Claim	$19.95	
	1-57248-097-1	Your Right to Child Custody, Visitation and Support	$19.95	
		CALIFORNIA TITLES		
	1-57071-360-X	CA Power of Attorney Handbook	$12.95	
	1-57071-355-3	How to File for Divorce in CA	$19.95	
	1-57071-356-1	How to Make a CA Will	$12.95	
	1-57071-408-8	How to Probate an Estate in CA	$19.95	
	1-57071-357-X	How to Start a Business in CA	$16.95	
	1-57071-358-8	How to Win in Small Claims Court in CA	$14.95	
	1-57071-359-6	Landlords' Rights and Duties in CA	$19.95	
		NEW YORK TITLES		
	1-57071-184-4	How to File for Divorce in NY	$19.95	
		FLORIDA TITLES		
	1-57071-363-4	Florida Power of Attorney Handbook (2E)	$12.95	
	1-57248-093-9	How to File for Divorce in FL (6E)	$21.95	
	1-57248-086-6	How to Form a Limited Liability Co. in FL	$19.95	
	1-57071-401-0	How to Form a Partnership in FL	$19.95	
	1-57071-380-4	How to Form a Corporation in FL (4E)	$19.95	
	1-57071-361-8	How to Make a FL Will (5E)	$12.95	
	1-57248-088-2	How to Modify Your FL Divorce Judgment (4E)	$22.95	
		Form Continued on Following Page	**SUBTOTAL**	

To order, call Sourcebooks at 1-800-43-BRIGHT or FAX (630)961-2168 (Bookstores, libraries, wholesalers—please call for discount)

SPHINX® PUBLISHING ORDER FORM

Qty	ISBN	Title	Retail	Ext.
	_____	**FLORIDA TITLES (CONT'D)**		
_____	1-57071-364-2	How to Probate an Estate in FL (3E)	$24.95	_____
_____	1-57248-081-5	How to Start a Business in FL (5E)	$16.95	_____
_____	1-57071-362-6	How to Win in Small Claims Court in FL (6E)	$14.95	_____
_____	1-57071-335-9	Landlords' Rights and Duties in FL (7E)	$19.95	_____
_____	1-57071-334-0	Land Trusts in FL (5E)	$24.95	_____
_____	0-913825-73-5	Women's Legal Rights in FL	$19.95	_____
		GEORGIA TITLES		
_____	1-57071-376-6	How to File for Divorce in GA (3E)	$19.95	_____
_____	1-57248-075-0	How to Make a GA Will (3E)	$12.95	_____
_____	1-57248-076-9	How to Start a Business in Georgia (3E)	$16.95	_____
		ILLINOIS TITLES		
_____	1-57071-405-3	How to File for Divorce in IL (2E)	$19.95	_____
_____	1-57071-415-0	How to Make an IL Will (2E)	$12.95	_____
_____	1-57071-416-9	How to Start a Business in IL (2E)	$16.95	_____
_____	1-57248-078-5	Landlords' Rights & Duties in IL	$19.95	_____
		MASSACHUSETTS TITLES		
_____	1-57071-329-4	How to File for Divorce in MA (2E)	$19.95	_____
_____	1-57248-108-0	How to Make a MA Will (2E)	$12.95	_____
_____	1-57248-109-9	How to Probate an Estate in MA (2E)	$19.95	_____
_____	1-57248-106-4	How to Start a Business in MA (2E)	$16.95	_____
_____	1-57248-107-2	Landlords' Rights and Duties in MA (2E)	$19.95	_____
		MICHIGAN TITLES		
_____	1-57071-409-6	How to File for Divorce in MI (2E)	$19.95	_____
_____	1-57248-077-7	How to Make a MI Will (2E)	$12.95	_____
_____	1-57071-407-X	How to Start a Business in MI (2E)	$16.95	_____
		MINNESOTA TITLES		
_____	1-57248-039-4	How to File for Divorce in MN	$19.95	_____
_____	1-57248-040-8	How to Form a Simple Corporation in MN	$19.95	_____
_____	1-57248-037-8	How to Make a MN Will	$9.95	_____
_____	1-57248-038-6	How to Start a Business in MN	$16.95	_____
		NEVADA TITLES		
_____	1-57248-101-3	How to Form a Corporation in NV	$19.95	_____
		NEW YORK TITLES		
_____	1-57071-184-4	How to File for Divorce in NY	$19.95	_____

Qty	ISBN	Title	Retail	Ext.
_____	1-57248-105-6	How to Form a Corporation in NY	$19.95	_____
_____	1-57248-095-5	How to Make a NY Will (2E)	$12.95	_____
_____	1-57071-185-2	How to Start a Business in NY	$16.95	_____
_____	1-57071-187-9	How to Win in Small Claims Court in NY	$14.95	_____
_____	1-57071-186-0	Landlords' Rights and Duties in NY	$19.95	_____
_____	1-57071-188-7	New York Power of Attorney Handbook	$19.95	_____
		NORTH CAROLINA TITLES		
_____	1-57071-326-X	How to File for Divorce in NC (2E)	$19.95	_____
_____	1-57071-327-8	How to Make a NC Will (2E)	$12.95	_____
_____	1-57248-096-3	How to Start a Business in NC (2E)	$16.95	_____
_____	1-57248-091-2	Landlords' Rights & Duties in NC	$19.95	_____
		OHIO TITLES		
_____	1-57248-102-1	How to File for Divorce in OH	$19.95	_____
		PENNSYLVANIA TITLES		
_____	1-57071-177-1	How to File for Divorce in PA	$19.95	_____
_____	1-57248-094-7	How to Make a PA Will (2E)	$12.95	_____
_____	1-57248-112-9	How to Start a Business in PA (2E)	$16.95	_____
_____	1-57071-179-8	Landlords' Rights and Duties in PA	$19.95	_____
		TEXAS TITLES		
_____	1-57071-330-8	How to File for Divorce in TX (2E)	$19.95	_____
_____	1-57248-009-2	How to Form a Simple Corporation in TX	$19.95	_____
_____	1-57071-417-7	How to Make a TX Will (2E)	$12.95	_____
_____	1-57071-418-5	How to Probate an Estate in TX (2E)	$19.95	_____
_____	1-57071-365-0	How to Start a Business in TX (2E)	$16.95	_____
_____	1-57248-111-0	How to Win in Small Claims Court in TX (2E)	$14.95	_____
_____	1-57248-110-2	Landlords' Rights and Duties in TX (2E)	$19.95	_____

SUBTOTAL THIS PAGE _____

SUBTOTAL PREVIOUS PAGE _____

Illinois residents add 6.75% sales tax
Florida residents add 6% state sales tax plus applicable discretionary surtax

Shipping— $4.00 for 1st book, $1.00 each additional _____

TOTAL _____